EDUCATION, DOMINANCE AND IDENT1. .

COMPARATIVE AND INTERNATIONAL EDUCATION:
A Diversity of Voices

Volume 20

Scope

Comparative and International Education: A Diversity of Voices aims to provide a comprehensive range of titles, making available to readers work from across the comparative and international education research community. Authors will represent as broad a range of voices as possible, from geographic, cultural and ideological standpoints. The editors are making a conscious effort to disseminate the work of newer scholars as well as that of well-established writers.

The series includes authored books and edited works focusing upon current issues and controversies in a field that is undergoing changes as profound as the geopolitical and economic forces that are reshaping our worlds.

The series aims to provide books which present new work, in which the range of methodologies associated with comparative education and inter-national education are both exemplified and opened up for debate. As the series develops, it is intended that new writers from settings and locations not frequently part of the English language discourse will find a place in the list.

THE WORLD COUNCIL OF COMPARATIVE EDUCATION SOCIETIES

The WCCES is an international organization of comparative education societies worldwide and is an NGO in consultative partnership with UNESCO. The WCCES was created in 1970 to advance the field of comparative education. Members usually meet every three years for a World Congress in which scholars, researchers, and administrators interact with colleagues and counterparts from around the globe on international issues of education.

The WCCES also promotes research in various countries. Foci include theory and methods in comparative education, gender discourses in education, teacher education, education for peace and justice, education in post-conflict countries, language of instruction issues, Education for All. Such topics are usually represented in thematic groups organized for the World Congresses.

Besides organizing the World Congresses, the WCCES has a section in *CERCular*, the newsletter of the Comparative Education Research Centre at the University of Hong Kong, to keep individual societies and their members abreast of activities around the world. The WCCES comprehensive web site is http://www.wcces.com.

As a result of these efforts under the auspices of the global organization, WCCES and its member societies have become better organized and identified in terms of research and other scholarly activities. They are also more effective in viewing problems and applying skills from different perspectives, and in disseminating information. A major objective is advancement of education for international understanding in the interests of peace, intercultural cooperation, observance of human rights and mutual respect among peoples.

The WCCES Series Post-Istanbul, Volume 1

Series Editors:

Suzanne Majhanovich and Allan Pitman

The WCCES Series was established to provide for the broader dissemination of discourses between scholars in its member societies. Representing as it does Societies and their members from all continents, the organization provides a special forum for the discussion of issues of interest and concern among comparativists and those working in international education.

The first series of volumes was produced from the proceedings of the World Council of Comparative Education Societies XIII World Congress, which met in Sarajevo, Bosnia and Herzegovina, 3-7 September, 2007 with the theme of *Living Together: Education and Intercultural Dialogue.* The series included the following titles:

Volume 1: Tatto, M. & Mincu, M. (Eds.), *Reforming Teaching and Learning*
Volume 2: Geo JaJa, M. A. & Majhanovich, S. (Eds.), *Education, Language and Economics: Growing National and Global Dilemmas*
Volume 3: Pampanini, G., Adly, F., & Napier, D. (Eds.), *Interculturalism, Society and Education*
Volume 4: Masemann, V., Majhanovich, S., Truong, N., & Janigan, K. (Eds.), *A Tribute to David N. Wilson. Clamoring for a Better World.*

The second series of volumes has been developed from the proceedings of the World Council of Comparative Education Societies XIV World Congress, which met in Istanbul, Turkey, 14-18 June, 2010 with the theme of *Bordering, Re-Bordering and new Possibilities in Education and Society.* This series includes the following titles, with further volumes under preparation:

Volume 1: Napier, D. B. & Majhanovich, S. (Eds.) *Education, Dominance and Identity*
Volume 2: Holmarsdottir, H. B. & Biseth, H. (Eds.), *Education and Human Rights*
Volume 3: Ginsburg, M. (Ed.), *Preparation, Practice & and Politics of Teachers*

Education, Dominance and Identity

Edited by

Diane B. Napier
University of Georgia, Athens, USA

and

Suzanne Majhanovich
The University of Western Ontario, London, Canada

SENSE PUBLISHERS
ROTTERDAM / BOSTON / TAIPEI

A C.I.P. record for this book is available from the Library of Congress.

ISBN 978-94-6209-123-8 (paperback)
ISBN 978-94-6209-124-5 (hardback)
ISBN 978-94-6209-125-2 (e-book)

Published by: Sense Publishers,
P.O. Box 21858, 3001 AW Rotterdam, The Netherlands
https://www.sensepublishers.com/

Printed on acid-free paper

TABLE OF CONTENTS

ACKNOWLEDGMENTS

The editors would like to express their appreciation to many people for their roles in bringing this volume to completion. The chapters in this collection each originated as paper presentations at the XIV World Congress of Comparative Education Societies held in Istanbul, Turkey on June 14-18, 2010 hosted by the World Council of Comparative Education Societies and by the local organizers TÜKED (Turkish Comparative Education Society) and Boğaziçi University. We would like to thank all parties involved in the XIV World Congress, and in particular the Congress Convenor, Professor Fatma Gök, and the other members of the Local Organizing Committee, Meral Apak and Soner Şimşek, for their assistance to us in reconnecting with presenters to develop their papers into essays for the volume.

We would like to thank all of the contributors to this volume for their dedication and scholarly passion. They each worked closely with us to refine and articulate in depth their respective contributions. They enabled us to bring together a variety of theoretical, methodological and conceptual perspectives in cases that offer rich insights into the complex issues underlying the volume theme of *Education, Dominance and Identity* as well as the broader Congress Theme of *Bordering, Re-Bordering and New Possibilities in Education and Society*. We believe that these contributions offer the scholarly field of comparative and international education new and significant insights from cases in several world regions. Collectively, the questions that the chapter authors raise, and the studies and perspectives they report, enrich our understanding of the importance of doing systematic research, of respecting local contextual factors and minority voices, and of recognizing trends, events, and influences that impact education and societies worldwide.

We owe a debt of gratitude to the manuscript reviewers who offered careful critique and constructive feedback to the chapter authors and to us: Jason Brown, Ashley Carr, Dawn Fyn, Daniel Gakunga, Joanna Greer, Kelly McFaden, Allyson Larkin, John Napier, Mary Michael Pontzer, and Aniko Varpalotai. We are particularly grateful to the main editors and their staff at Sense Publishers, Michel Lokhorst and Peter de Liefde, who took responsibility for the book production process. Finally, as lead editor of this volume, I would like to express my appreciation to Allan Pitman and Suzanne Majhanovich (my co-editor on this volume) who are the senior editors for the volume series emanating from the World Congresses: I appreciated the opportunity to work with you on this volume in the series.

DIANE B. NAPIER & SUZANNE MAJHANOVICH

INTRODUCTION: GLOBAL ISSUES: REGIONAL, NATIONAL AND LOCAL CULTURE CASE STUDIES

The twelve chapters in this volume are organized into five loosely geographic sections, each reflecting particular ways in which local, group, and indigenous identities have been affected by a dominant discourse. The chapters show how education can act as an agent to support or undermine identity, how languages (including dominant and sub-dominant languages) and the language of instruction in schools are at the centre of challenges to hegemony and domination in many societal and cultural environments. In those contexts, minority or dominated groups – and teachers and parents of children in schools – struggle for recognition, or education in their own language, for acceptance within larger society, or for recognition of the validity of their responses to reform initiatives and policies that address a wider agenda but that often fail to take into account key factors such as perceptions and subaltern status.

Collectively, the chapters illustrate a variety of methodological approaches and theoretical perspectives. They illustrate an array of universal and global issues in the field of comparative and international education research. However, each of the cases has its own unique character, conceptualized and presented as research findings and as personal reflections based on the authors' experiential knowledge, and focused on research in particular social, cultural and political contexts. The universal issues related to the triad of *education, dominance and identity* that underlie the papers in this collection include – but are not limited to – the use of education as an instrument of domination employed in policies at national- and lower levels within countries, and also across entire colonial empires; and the use of education as a vehicle for transformation and empowerment in independence struggles, post-colonial development, and minority rights movements within societies. Among foundational theoretical underpinnings of the works in this volume are Freire's (1970) notions of *emancipatory pedagogy* and *banking education*; Bourdieu's (1986) concept of *cultural capital* manifested in educational practices, language usage and expectations for status and success; Foucault's (1988) notion of *belief systems* that gain momentum and power when facets of the belief system become accepted as common knowledge; and aspects of *globalization theory* focusing on the general features of globalization, including an emerging global education system of global reform priorities, standards, and practices, (see for instance Zajda & Rust, 2009; and Baker & Wiseman, 2005). Another dimension illustrated in several chapters of the volume pertains to

D.B. Napier & S. Majhanovich (eds.), Education, Dominance and Identity, 1–7.

universal linguistic rights, linked to issues of metropolitan language dominance – particularly the hegemony of English – the struggle for recognition of sub-dominant languages, and the rights of minority/indigenous language speakers and language-dominance issues regarding language use in schools (see Skuttnab-Kangas & Philippson, 1995; Brook Napier, 2011). In addition, applying the work of Arnove & Torres (2007) the cases in these chapters can be viewed as illustrations of the "*dialectic of the global and the local*" or the manner in which universal, global issues manifest themselves in particular local contexts or within particular groups. The cases also conform to the principles contained within *global culture theory* wherein a global culture of schooling plays out within societies at various levels of implementation, in which resistance to imposed educational and language-related mandates results in creolization (mediation or modification) or even outright rejection of the reform mandates (see Anderson-Levitt, 2003, for the full conceptualization and cases illustrating). Some of the chapters in this volume are powerful illustrations of such processes that run counter to the dominant discourse and to the prevailing patterns of one-size-fits-all education.

The chapters in this volume were originally presented as papers in the XIV World Congress of Comparative Education Societies held in June 2010 in Istanbul, Turkey under the Congress theme of *Borders, Bordering and New Possibilities for Education*. Addressing this broad theme of the Congress as well as three of the Congress sub-themes (TG 3: *Education, Conflict and Transitions within and between Societies; TG 7: Identity, Space and Diversity in Education; TG 11: Education, Politics of Dominance, the Suppressed and Disappearing* Languages) the chapters reveal ways in which borders and barriers are transcended through struggles for identity, empowerment, and equal access in education. Furthermore, there are many comparative insights in many of the pairings or groupings of the chapters: they illustrate issues across countries or on different levels; most of them offer valuable historical context for the research and situations under examination, leading to a more thorough understanding of contemporary challenges and dilemmas.

INDIGENOUS IDENTITY AND DEVELOPMENT

The first section *focusing on* indigenous identity and development includes two cases from North America. In *Decolonizing Indigenous Education in Canada*, KP Binda and Mel Lall outline policy changes demanded by Canadian aboriginal authorities to undo the damage inflicted upon generations of indigenous people through the government and church controlled residential school system that focused on systematic eradication of aboriginal identity, language and culture, while forcibly assimilating them to the European way. Through a decentralization process that has allowed Aboriginal communities to take charge of their own education systems and to reintroduce elements of their languages and culture, restorative justice is sought. Progress has been slow but as the National Chief of the Assembly of First Nations has proclaimed, in order to realize the necessary changes, reconciliation of 'rights', fiscal responsibility, sustainability, a relevant education system, public support and partnerships must be put into effect.

In the second chapter, *Discovering the Past, Uncovering Diversity: The Reclamation of Indigenous Identity through a Community Education Project*, Lesley Graybeal presents a practical example of identity recovery in a Southeastern American State by the Occaneechi Band of the Saponi Nation. Members of the band felt an acute need to learn about their ancestors as official discourse seemed to imply that their group was extinct or had been totally assimilated into the majority population. The Occaneechi Homeland Preservation Project included the establishment of a museum and cultural centre in their ancestral region to educate their own people as well as their non-aboriginal neighbours about their history and life styles. Through this particular representation (the museum) the indigenous group has been able to redefine their space and recreate authentic identities and structures.

INTEGRATION AND DOMINATION OF ETHNIC MINORITY GROUPS

The next section deals with the integration and domination of ethnic minority groups, in four case studies from Europe. In the first paper, *Critical Analysis of School Integration of Roma Children in Nyíregyháza, Hungary*, Eva Földesi examines the issue of integrating Roma children into a majority school in a rural area of Hungary. The benefits and challenges of the integration program are discussed. Whereas educating Roma children separate from the majority in a ghetto school may allow them to retain connection to their language and culture, integration, although met with fear and mistrust on both sides may, as the author argues, lead to a de-ethnicized discourse and more benevolent relations between Roma and non-Roma. No final decision has been made whether to continue the experiment in integration of the Roma children. As Földesi reports, the educational authority is currently debating the possibility of re-opening the segregated Roma-only school. Földesi, however, sees merit in the integrated model.

In their chapter entitled *Social Equity versus Cultural Identity: Government Policies and Roma Education in East Central Europe* Katalin Forray and Tamas Kozma address Roma education in a broader context than in the previous paper by reporting on nine countries/regions in East-Central Europe with regard to the education for the Roma population according to one of two policies, the first designed to promote and protect the Roma culture and heritage, and the second intended to promote socio-economic equality. The second policy views the Roma as socially handicapped and tries to provide them with skills that will enable them to participate in the majority society and economy. The authors contend that choice of one or the other policy is connected to political ideologies, and that the prevalence of the second policy since the dissolution of the Soviet Bloc in the early 90s is related to influence from EU countries. They query whether the EU countries may be imposing their Western perspectives on the realities of the Roma minority in Eastern Europe.

3

The third paper in this section *Children's Home Languages in Early Childhood Education Systems: Handicap or Asset? A Comparative Study of Parents' and Teachers' Attitudes* by Nathalie Thomauske considers the issue of integration of minority children in France and Germany. Despite research stressing the importance of competence in the mother tongue for future school success, popular wisdom in both France and German promotes learning the national languages even if it means that children will never master their mother tongue. Both minority parents and child care workers interviewed in the study believe that it is key for minority children to learn French or German as early as possible mainly in order to succeed at school and integrate into their new country.

The fourth paper, *Constructing Spanish Discourses of Language Hegemony in Spain* by Renée de Palma and Cathryn Teasley is concerned with the relative importance accorded to the various regional official languages of Spain. The authors focus on the status of Catalá (Catalan), Euskera (Basque) and Galego (Galician) in relationship to Castilian which has come to be viewed as the dominant language of Spain. De Palma and Teasley argue that Castilian has assumed a hegemonic position thanks to neo-liberal discourses of educational choice, flexibility and competition in the marketplace. They juxtapose the favoured position of Castilian in Spain vis-à-vis other local languages with the situation in the US where English enjoys clear dominance while Spanish spoken by a sizable population has been denied status. Their study outlines the efforts of minority groups in Spain to preserve their local language and identity with varying degrees of success.

LANGUAGE, EDUCATION, LANGUAGE OF INSTRUCTION AND IDENTITY

In post-colonial states, the language of instruction is a major issue. The third section in this volume focuses on issues of language, education, language of instruction and identity. Cases from Africa and Africa/Asia illustrate the complexities of language choice, specifically in the language of instruction (or LoI) in schools. The research reported in these chapters details the domination of powerful European languages in educational contexts and the specifics of just how use of mother tongue versus a non-native language can be a powerful determinant of success or failure for students.

Zehlia Babaci-Wilhite, in *A Study of Escalating Debates on the Use of a Global or Local Language in Education*, focuses on language issues in Tanzania and Malaysia. She notes the tendency in previously colonized countries to use powerful European languages such as English, French or Portuguese as the Language of Instruction (LoI) in schooling. Since independence, many former colonies promoted local languages to replace a dominant European language as the LoI. However, pressures of globalization and internationalization have persuaded many educational authorities to continue the use of the colonial language for schooling, especially at the secondary and tertiary levels. Babaci-Whilhite uses the examples of Tanzania and Malaysia to illustrate the language debates. Malaysia after gaining independence had opted for Bahasa Malaysia as the LoI, but in the 90s reversed that policy with regard to instruction in Mathematics and Science which were henceforth to be taught beginning in elementary school in English. However, public opposition as well as disappointing results on international tests convinced authorities to return to Bahasa-Malaysia as the LoI for all subjects.

In Tanzania, which had adopted Kiswahili as its official language after independence, English as LoI has proven more difficult to dislodge. Although children receive primary education in their native tongue, plans to replace English as the language of instruction in higher grades have never been implemented. As in the Thomauske article in the previous section, parents seem to prefer education in a dominant language like English. Language continues to be a tool of neo-colonialism.

In their chapter entitled *Voices from the Classroom: Teacher and Learner Perceptions on the Use of the Learners' Home Language in the Teaching of School Mathematics and Science* Monde Mbekwa and Vuyokazi Nomlomo provide a companion piece to the previous paper, this time focusing on LoI policies in South Africa. Under the new democratic government installed in South Africa in 1994, nine African languages in addition to English and Afrikaans were recognized as official languages and work began to develop curriculum in the African languages. Mbekwa and Nomlomo's study considers the perceptions of teachers and students in grade 4 classes in the Western Cape regarding the use of isiKhosa as the LoI for Mathematics and Science. Teachers and students were generally very positive, even proud, to be using a home language in instruction. However, pedagogical, linguistic and structural challenges were noted. Dialectical variations, lack of scientific terminology in isiKhosa and lack of resources were cited as challenges. While the teachers confirm that students learn better and more easily when taught in their mother tongue, the challenges are formidable. This is especially the case for classes in the higher grades. As seems to be the case everywhere in our globalized world, parents and even teachers seem to be convinced that education, particularly higher education should be offered in a "universal" language such as English, as knowledge of English is seen as the key to admission to the world economy.

TEACHER IDENTITY, REFORM, DOMINATION AND TRANSFORMATION

In the next section that highlights issues of teacher identity, reform, and domination/transformation, the papers focus on the effect of government policies on teacher identity and attitudes. In the first case, *Reform Environment and Teacher Identity in Chile*, Beatrice Avalos and Danae de los Rios report on a massive study in Chile to ascertain how recent policy reforms affected teachers' working lives and how they navigated between demands of the reforms and their own notions of their identity as teachers. Avalos and de los Rios carried out a very comprehensive study in which the quantitative part involved over 1800 teachers from all areas of Chile, at all school levels in public, subsidized private and private schools. They investigated such areas as motivation and commitment, work demands and satisfaction, self-efficacy, and teachers in the public eye, considering those factors to be major components of teacher identity. Based on survey results, they then developed case studies with eleven elementary and secondary teachers from their survey population. They conclude that teacher identity is connected to broad education aims and that policy makers when developing policies aimed at change and reform need to take into consideration the wider sense of teacher identity or risk facing resistance to reform by the very actors charged with carrying it out.

In *Researching an Initiative on Peaceful Coexistence in Greek-Cypriot Schools: A Mixed-Methods Study on Teachers' Perceptions and Emotions*, Michalinos Zembylas, Constadina Charalambous, Panayiota Charalambous and Panayiota Kendeou explore perceptions and emotions of Greek Cypriot teachers toward a government initiative to develop a culture of peaceful co-existence between Greek-Cypriots and Turkish Cypriots. Given the history of the area and past conflicts, it is not surprising that teachers were leery of the policy. To gain understanding of the teachers' standpoints, the authors carried out a mixed-methods study involving both quantitative and qualitative methods. With some similarities to findings in the previous study in Chile, their study shows, that in order for reform initiatives in politicized contexts to have any chance of successful implementation, policy makers must recognize emotional aspects of those expected to adopt the policy.

IDENTITY, DOMINATION AND REVOLUTION

The final part of this volume focuses on identity, domination and revolution in two papers from the Middle East and North African region that deal with the way in which the political context impacts on education and the identity of the populace. Nagwa Megahed and Stephen Lack in *Women's Rights and Gender-Educational Inequality in Egypt and Tunisia: From Colonialism to Contemporary Revolution* provide a timely study on recent political upheaval in Egypt and Tunisia in the context of gender policies. By reviewing the situation in the two countries in the colonial period and since independence, they show the influence of the colonial legacy on gender-related education, current gender practices in social spheres and women's participation in pre-university and higher education. They highlight conservative versus liberal ideologies in both countries as concerns gender-related reform policies. They close with the question of how and what kind of democracy will be achieved in the new order and what the political developments will mean for gender equity and women's education.

The final paper by Amir Sabzavar Qahfarkhi, Abbas Madandar Arani and Lida Kakia, *The Impact of Educational Systems on Political Violence in the Middle East Region* confronts the issue of how young people are being inculcated into violence. The authors contend that although families, political parties and mass media, government and education systems play a role in this undesirable indoctrination, it is not at all clear the extent to which each factor plays a role in encouraging violent behavior. The authors examine the place of formal and informal education arguing that for the most part, parents in the Middle East region just seek an education for their children that will lead to skills necessary for participating in the modern global world; if they cannot procure places for their children in government schools, they will turn to informal education possibilities that may provide agendas beyond basic education. The authors also note the role comparative education can play in understanding the complex messages that the various forms of education are delivering, and they endeavour to point out stereotypical thinking about Islam, education, and culture in the Middle East region. This chapter offers readers a set of emic reflections from the authors' own lived experience in Iran, and from their interpretations of the historic shifts across the wider region and developments in education recorded in the literature.

In all, the papers in this volume provide cases from around the world that deal with identity construction in the face of the dominant discourses that globalization and internationalization have forged. The articles reflect different ways in which minority and disadvantaged groups engage in the struggle to affirm their identity—through the adaptation of, or resistance to policies affecting identity and/or reflecting power and dominance of majority groups to analyses of reaction to policies affecting identity, or, in the case of the final two papers, taking recourse in violent upheavals to address tyranny and inequality.

REFERENCES

Anderson-Levitt, K. M. (Ed.). (2003). *Local meanings, global schooling: Anthropology and world culture theory.* New York: Palgrave McMillan.

Arnove, R. F., & Torres, C. A. (Eds.). (2007). *Comparative education: The dialectic of the global and the local.* New York: Rowman & Littlefield.

Baker, D. P., & Wiseman, A. W. (Eds.). (2005). *Global trends in educational policy.* International perspectives on education and society, Volume 6. Amsterdam: Elsevier Science.

Brook Napier, D. (2011). Critical issues in language and education planning in twenty first century in South Africa. *US-China Education Review* B 1 (2011) pp. 58-76. David Publishing.

Foucault, M. (1988). Power, moral values, and the intellectual. An interview with Michel Foucault by Michael Bess. *History of the Present, 4,* 1-2.

Freire, P. (1970, Reprinted in 1993). *Pedagogy of the oppressed.* London: Penguin Books.

Skutnabb-Kangas, T., & Phillipson, R. (1995). *Linguistic human rights, overcoming linguistic discrimination.* New York: Walter de Gruyther.

Zajda, J., & Rust, V. (Eds.). (2009). *Globalisation, policy, and comparative research: Discourses of globalisation.* Volume 5. Dordrecht: Springer.

Diane Brook Napier
University of Georgia, USA

Suzanne Majhanovich
Western University, Canada

PART I

INDIGENOUS IDENTITY AND DEVELOPMENT

K. P. BINDA & MEL LALL

DECOLONIZING INDIGENOUS EDUCATION IN CANADA

INTRODUCTION, METHODOLOGY AND CONCEPTUAL FRAMEWORK

Like so many minority groups around the world the Aboriginal population in Canadian society occupies the lowest rungs of the socioeconomic and political ladder, notwithstanding the fact that Canada is rated by the United Nations as one of the best countries in the world in which to live. In the case of the Aboriginal population, the record is not a proud one but rather one that demands change. The Federal government recognized this dilemma and is adopting policies that devolve more control to the Aboriginal population. The Aboriginal peoples themselves view the changes as a decolonizing process. In this chapter the term Aboriginal peoples refer to the indigenous population for whom the Federal government has a legal and fiduciary responsibility. It should be noted that there are other indigenous groups such as the Inuit, Metis and non-status First Nations that are outside the scope of this study.

The chapter's focus is on changes to a developed, centralized controlled system of education and its impacts upon First Nations communities living on reserves. Reserves are enclaves set aside as part of the treaty making process between the Crown (Federal Government) and the First Nations communities. Using the conceptual framework of devolution and decolonization, the paper reviews the changes taking place in Aboriginal education. The description of the changes outlined in this paper involved the analysis of a variety of documents, position papers, published and unpublished papers by various researchers and organizations, conferences and personal observations while working in the field over a period of thirty-five years. As well, both authors have been participant observers in a variety of settings at the local, national and international levels. The narrative in this chapter follows a conversational pattern and viewpoints as analyzed from the documents and personal experiences.

In a context where community values are pitted against the competitiveness characteristic of the western world, such changes, as noted above, include increased community participation, increased level of political control, development of new education systems, new and relevant curricula, culturally appropriate instructional and measurement methods focusing on Aboriginal perspectives, increased attendance, participation and graduation rates. These developments are taking place in communities that are not homogenous. They vary in size, culture (language, beliefs and traditions), tribal groupings, location and

D.B. Napier & S. Majhanovich (eds.), Education, Dominance and Identity, 11–27.

socio-economic conditions. These variations add to the complexity of the context in which changes are to take place. Notwithstanding these differences, the common goal is the improvement of community wellbeing through holistic processes.

Community control, in the context of Aboriginal education discussed in this chapter, is an ecological process; it is sort of a symbiosis that recognizes the interdependence of the home, the school and community. It is a holistic enterprise. In this sense the symbiotic linkage and shift in the political framework from a centralized to a decentralized system can have a positive impact on educational development that is more related, not only to economic health, but as well, to cultural, personal and social developments. Aboriginal peoples view this change process of devolution within a larger framework of decolonization. Wesley (1993). Etzioni (1993) and Sergiovanni (1994) viewed this sense of community from a moral and ecological perspective. The decolonizing process, as visioned by Chief Ernest Wesley (1993) is the cornerstone for 'rebuilding self-determination and community wellness'.

For First Nations, community control of education is a "visioning process" for "seeing" and "influencing" their own futures and for leading the change process so necessary if socio-economic progress is to be accomplished. This visioning process is not the sacred "vision quest" practiced in traditional Aboriginal communities but rather it is a form of collaborative planning put into action. It includes going "beyond narrow educational goals" and "looks toward a collective future with hope" (Manitoba Education, Citizenship and Youth, 2007). It is an empowering, encompassing framework that gives structure, pattern and meaning to the process and fabric of change. It incorporates the values, hopes and dreams of the community. This structural change process is the very essence of decolonizing their colonial heritage. In an address to his fellow First Nations Chiefs at their General Assembly meeting in Calgary in 1993, Chief Wesley of the Wesley First Nations Band near Calgary, Alberta, stated that their renewed "education is the very essence of decolonization" (p. 10) and that "the overall goal of decolonization is to build a proud people who hold healthy values and beliefs ... a people who have hope, and who are self-sufficient in their livelihoods" (p. 6).

This inculcative function of First Nations traditional education, so brutally suppressed by Canadian colonial policy, is extremely valuable since no human society can continue to exist if it fails to maintain a system by which its common values and beliefs are transferred from one generation to the next. This theoretical framework, found expression in the various position papers (so-called Red Papers) put forward by the First Nations over the last few decades. Pre-eminent among these papers was *Indian Control of Indian Education* (1972).

The principles of community control have been advocated in the United Nations Universal Declaration of Human Rights (1948), which states that parents have a right to choose the kind of education that shall be given to their children. The U.N. Working Group on Indigenous Populations stated that:

> Indigenous populations should enjoy the right to structure, conduct and control their own educational system with complete autonomy, so that

education could be a way of developing indigenous culture and traditions ....
(Morse, 1991, p. 762)

The concept of decentralized control was described by McGinn and Street (1986)
"as a process of transferring or 'devolving' power and authority from large to small
units of governance" (p. 471). They also viewed the centralization –
decentralization process as a dyadic relation where the locus of power of
individuals, groups or organizations vis-à-vis the state can be described and located
in a continuum. In a centralized political system most authority and power are held
at the centre; in a decentralized system, power and authority are devolved or
shifted to the local level such as the community or individual school (Brown,
1994).

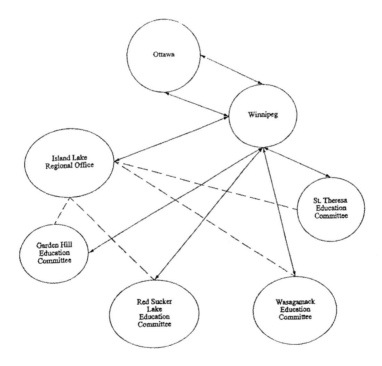

Figure 1. Centralized structure. Source: Binda and Calliou (2001, p. 41)

Figure 1 illustrates the centralized process as it operated from the central
government in Ottawa down to the community schools in one of the regions of
Manitoba. The figure shows direct interaction between Ottawa and the regional
provincial office in Winnipeg, Manitoba. Communication between the First
Nations Bands and the federal government takes place through the Winnipeg
office. Inter-tribal band communications and cooperation also take place within the

region as shown by the broken lines. The regional office is now closed but inter-band activities are now carried on informally.

Figure 2 conceptualizes the devolution process that reflects a paradigm shift which incorporates a decolonization philosophy whereby education is viewed as emanating from the wisdom of community elders who provide guidance and suggestions in all aspects of education development, particularly in the area of culturally appropriate curricula.

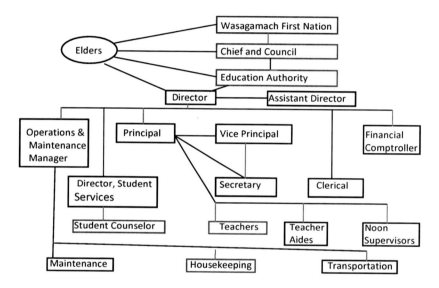

Figure 2. Wasagamach education authority organizational chart. Source: Wasagamach Education Authority, Wasagamach First Nation, MB

Decentralization as a process is energized by two main factors, socio-political and administrative (Chapman, 1973; Walker, 1972). McGinn (1996) and Putnam (1993) stressed the importance of political factors such as political equality and civic engagement. Kaufman (1969) noted that the demand for decentralization results from social and political unrest, certainly, conditions that are identifiable in Aboriginal communities and discussed further on in this chapter. The administrative argument for decentralization focuses upon the improvement of efficiency and system effectiveness, factors sorely lacking in Aboriginal communities (Binda, 2001, 1998, 1995). This presumes that the central bureaucracy operated inefficiently, ostensibly through poor central planning. In fact, numerous reports of the Auditor General of Canada have criticized several federal government departments for their shortcomings in the administration of Aboriginal education. Correspondence theory suggests that increased devolution and local participation would resolve the two thorny problems identified above –

both political and administrative. Certainly the inequitable state of affairs in the Aboriginal communities supported the argument for decentralized community control. This argument for more local control through the principle of sovereign self-government is even more vociferous today as is evident in the print, radio and television media.

HISTORICAL PERSPECTIVE

Traditional Education

Aboriginal education in Canada may be divided into various periods with well – demarcated and identifiable characteristics. Dickason (2002) described the many developments such as industrial schools, compulsory school attendance, residential schools and local control schools, which took place in the post-European period. The traditional period prior to European contact with the Indigenous people of Canada, espoused a functional system of education rooted in oral tradition with observation and practical application being the main techniques for teaching and learning (Leavitt, 1991). Kirkness (1992) pointed out that in the pre-European contact period "Indians had evolved their own forms of education. It was an education in which the community and the natural environment were the classroom, and the land was seen as the mother of people" (p. 5). The lessons to be learned in that environment were to master the skills needed for daily survival and failure to master such skills often had exacting penalties.

The oral tradition and Native ways of knowing and interacting espoused an education philosophy that viewed Mother Earth as the supreme teacher and giver of life and law. "Central to that teaching was the belief in the sacred, the Great Spirit" (Kirkness, 1992, p. 5). Through several modes of teaching, such as storytelling, emphasis was placed on developing the whole person with reference to such values as humility, kindness, courage, honesty and respect. Traditional education was not a formal process as exists today but had a direct link to a way of life. Kirkness aptly described this link in this way:

Learning was for living – for survival. Boys and girls were taught at an early age to observe and to utilize, to cope with and respect, their environment. Independence and self-reliance were valued concepts within the culture. Through observation and practice, young children learned the art of hunting, trapping, fishing, food gathering and preparation, child rearing, farming and building shelters. They learned whatever livelihood their particular environment offered, through experiential learning. (1992, p. 6)

This system of education sustained the Aboriginal communities for thousands of years until the arrival of the Europeans, and the imposition of a colonialist system of schooling that was initiated with the passing of the Indian Act (1876).

Colonial Period

The colonial period under British administration was an era of hegemonic imposition and institutionalization, particularly with the establishment of Indian Reservations and the signing of Treaties with the nomadic bands. The treaties allowed a legal framework of control and responsibility to be developed. As the churches were already operating in the territory, their assistance was sought in formally setting up and operating schools in Native (First Nations) communities. The churches were willing to comply as they could now shift the cost of Christianizing the Aboriginal people to the Federal government. Over the next century various institutional arrangements for educating Native children were tried, ranging from local day schools to area or regional residential schools. The residential schools have been described as the most horrible institutions encountered by Natives and perhaps represented the darkest chapter in their association with Euro-Canadians. Some Native scholars now believe that the system advocated cultural genocide (Bear Nicholas, 2001; Binda & Calliou, 2001; Mercredi, 1998; Chrisjohn & Young, 1997).

In the residential school system which began in the 1880s and continued until 1996, young children were taken away from their homes legally through an amendment to the Indian Act, and sometimes forcibly, and placed in these schools far away from their families in order to assimilate and enculturate them as Euro-Canadians. The last federally operated residential school in Canada closed in the province of Saskatchewan in 1996 (Alberta Education, 2005). The damage from this system as identified in numerous reports, (Aboriginal Healing Foundation (AHF), 2009; Canadian Council on Learning (CCL), 2007: Royal Commission on Aboriginal Peoples (RCAP), 1996; Assembly of First Nations (AFN) 1994), included loss of language, grade retardation, high dropout rates, rampant physical, sexual and emotional abuse, alienation and intergenerational communication breakdown. As of July 2009 the Indian Residential Schools Truth and Reconciliation Commission (TRC), established by the federal government in 2006, is in the process over a five year period of preparing a history of the policies and practices of the residential system including a report with recommendations to the Government of Canada. Interim reports with evidence given by residence school survivors across Canada are being published by the Truth and Reconciliation Commission (TRC) and the Aboriginal Healing Foundation (AHF) (2009). These hearings give evidence to the horrible treatments and subsequent dysfunctional effects that continue today as a result of the residential school system.

The symbiotic linkages of colonial politics and education in support of prevailing ideologies, socio-economic and political order, have had dysfunctional effects on First Nations. The psychological harm of alien curricula in an alien education system that devalued the Indigenous culture has proven to be persistent and problematic not only for the First Nations but also for all of Canadian society in this postmodern age. It is believed by numerous Aboriginal researchers that this external centralized control of Aboriginal affairs has been the cause of serious underdevelopment, dualisms and inequalities in Aboriginal communities.

The Aboriginal population constitutes a small minority, approximately 3.8% of Canada's total population. This population has increased by 45% since 1996 compared to an 8% increase in the non-Aboriginal population (Canadian Council of Learning, 2009). Figures shown in Table 1 would indicate that most Aboriginal people live off-reserve and in rural areas. However those living off-reserve are concentrated in larger urban centres or Census Metropolitan Areas (Table 2). Large concentrations are found in the western provinces in Canada where they make up over 15% of the total provincial inhabitants (Table 1). In the northern Territories more than half of the population is Aboriginal. Notwithstanding their minority status, the Aboriginals are severely disadvantaged in all spheres of life in Canada.

Table 1. *Aboriginal population by province, 2006.*
Source: Statistics Canada: 2006 Census Statistics

Province	Aboriginal population	On-Reserve	Urban	Rural
Newfoundland & Labrador	23,455	1,435	8,920	13,095
Prince Edward Island	1,730	400	740	590
Nova Scotia	24,175	7,980	7,400	8,790
New Brunswick	17,650	7,005	4,500	6,095
Quebec	108,425	33,180	45,005	29,620
Ontario	242,495	47,515	150,570	44,410
Manitoba	175,395	56,765	87,780	30,855
Saskatchewan	141,890	49,015	66,520	26,355
Alberta	188,365	41,275	114,535	32,560
British Columbia	196,075	51,055	117,070	27,945
Yukon	7,580	1,970	3,585	2,025
North West Territories	20,635	10,260	7,310	3,060
Nunavut	24,915	0	9,490	15,425
CANADA	1,172,790	308,490	623,470	240,825

Table 2: *Population by Aboriginal ancestry* for selected CMAs, 2006.*
Source: Statistics Canada, 2006 Census Statistics

CMA's	Population
Montreal	17,865
Toronto	26,575
Winnipeg	68,385
Regina	17,105
Saskatoon	21,535
Calgary	26,575
Edmonton	52,100
Vancouver	40,310

* persons who have declared such ancestry

The inequalities facing First Nations are obvious in the examination of several socio-economic indicators such as child welfare, juvenile delinquents, death rates, incarcerations, suicide rates and hospital admissions as well as employment and income. Education data reveal that the vast majority of Native students withdraw from school before Grade 9, the cut-off point for literacy. The low level of completion of high school in the Aboriginal population is demonstrated by the fact that in 2006, 40 percent of those in the 20-24 age group did not complete high school compared to 13 percent in the non-Aboriginal population. The rates for non-completion were much higher for those living on reserve (61%) and in remote northern Inuit communities (68%), (Canadian Council on Learning, 2009).

A World Health Organization report in 1999 "painted a grim picture of the situation of Native peoples in Canada ... who continue to occupy a very marginal position in the overall political, economic, social and cultural institutions of the country ..." (Schlein, 1999, p. 12). Recent news headlines (November/December, 2011) keep pointing out the problems related to education, housing, water quality, child and family services and land claim agreements. These problem areas were also identified in the Auditor General's Report of June 2011(Government of Canada).

SEARCH FOR EQUALITY AND JUSTICE THROUGH DEVOLUTION

It was this type of inequality and social injustice that led to the Aboriginal demand for *Indian Control of Indian Education* (Assembly of First Nations, 1972) as advocated by the Aboriginal population. Concerns about equality, justice and fairness have confronted mankind for thousands of years and continue to be a topic for discussion. In his treatise on distributive justice, John Rawls (1971) discussed the focal role education plays in allowing each individual "to enjoy the culture of his society and to take part in its affairs, and in this way to provide each individual a secure sense of his own worth" (p. 101). Chief Ernest Wesley in his address to the Assembly of First Nations (1993) emphasized the role that education can play in improving life conditions. The World Bank and The Canadian International Development Agency (CIDA) have consistently pointed to this relationship between education and socio-economic development.

The movement for Indian Control became a watershed in the history of education policy making. It was part of a political firestorm that began in 1969 when the federal government's White Paper proposed abolishing the Indian Act and integrating the Indians into the larger Canadian society. The Native organizations would have none of it and argued emphatically in their position papers on questions of equality and social justice. They emphasized that without community control by First Nations themselves, no education system can be truly successful, if those most directly concerned have no input into the system. After all, the principle of equality is a long-standing and very important part of the Canadian tradition. Why, then deny that right to the First Nations?

While the political firestorm was still raging, the Federal government, looking for a way out of its dilemma, accepted the policy papers on local control in 1973 and began to vacate the education field turning over control to the Aboriginal Bands across Canada, band by band. This process of decentralization or community control was being implemented across the country but not without difficulty. First Nations complained that the federal conception of community control is limited, restrictive, and did not reflect their notion of local control which subsumes "political equality" as a major characteristic of the "civic society" (McGinn, 1996). The Aboriginal population complained that the Federal government in many instances simply turned over the schools without any training or preparation of local authorities. This was not unlike the withdrawal of some European powers from their African colonies in the 1960s. A First Nations education director in Ontario compared the handover of power in his region to that of a driver and passenger in a car. The driver suddenly collapses and the passenger, who has never driven in his life but only saw people driving, is left with steering the vehicle. This metaphor perhaps accounts for the management problems now encountered in many First Nations schools.

However, MacPherson (1991), a jurist appointed by the Federal government to examine such complaints, commented in his report "that at least some success flows from the education policies put in place and pursued by the Federal government in recent years" (p.3). Some of that success can be measured by the increased number of schools under Band jurisdiction and where more appropriate culturally sensitive curricula are being implemented. From our own observations these improvements are indeed taking place. In 1976, Indian Bands controlled less than 5% of the student enrolment; the federal schools had 42%, and the provincial schools had 53% of the status students. Currently the Native Bands control all their status student enrollment .

Since the advent of local control, progress in First Nations education has been made in a number of areas: in the development of new systems of schooling, in the devolution process itself, in management, finance, staffing, instruction and curriculum, and in community participation at the local level. The latter has played a significant role in determining the structure and government of systems that have been put in place. For example, some communities have established local school boards or education authorities to manage their school system, while others have entered into agreements with public school boards with the goal of enhancing efficiencies by providing their students with access to a full range of instructional resources.

A process of decolonization includes cultural rejuvenation and renewal through holistic education and an inclusive system which promotes community values.. As Kumar (2009) noted, "the decolonization process serves as a redemptive ideological strategy to the colonization of Aboriginal education" (p. 49). In this context, as Chief Atleo noted, education is seen not as a "tool of oppression" (the past), but as a "tool of freedom and liberty" (the present), (Canadian Federation for the Humanities and Social Sciences, Congress, 2011).

FIRST NATIONS EDUCATION SYSTEMS

Band- and Tribal Council-operated schools are rather complex systems. These schools are becoming the major institutions in the decolonizing process and the education of on-reserve First Nations students. Various models of band-operated schools are developing on the basis of geography, regional interest or community wishes. The rationale for the variations is simple. Aboriginal control of education is a relatively new phenomenon for First Nations who do not have the experience of participation in the Euro-Canadian system and are, therefore, developing various systems that suit their individual and cultural needs. Whatever model is developed, the system operates at the pleasure of the Chief and Council and owes responsibility to them, firstly, as the government of the community, and ultimately to the Federal government. Regardless, parents and community members are committed and involved in developing culturally appropriate educational systems that benefit their children (CCL, 2009).

In some cases on-reserve schools are controlled directly by the Band council, with the Chief exerting almost despotic power, and a propensity for poor management particularly where requisite management training and skills may be lacking. In November 2011 the Federal government revoked the local management of a First Nations band placing it under federal control through a system referred to as "third party management". Under this process the government appoints a manager from the private sector to manage the Band's financial affairs until solvency is restored. In this case the *Globe and Mail*, a national newspaper in Canada, reported on December 15, 2011, that the Prime Minister "has bluntly accused the Band of mismanagement". The issue of mismanagement often results from endemic problems within the communities, problems that the federal government failed to correct--poor infrastructure, high unemployment, poorly trained personnel, among others. The band co-manager, who returned to his position after a period of absence, commented that the mismanagement was not the result of people "pocketing money", but resulted from Band officials taking too many trips outside of the community, hiring "too many staff' – young and inexperienced, "occupying positions, even when they were not capable of doing the job" (*The Globe and Mail*, December 15, 2011).

In most communities, schools are run conscientiously and diligently by elected or nominated community members, somewhat analogous to a board of education as exists in the public provincial system; others are operated as incorporated bodies; yet others, send their children to provincial schools under special arrangements with the local provincial school boards. In the latter systems, particularly in smaller communities (Fig.3), some form of trustee representation in the provincial school board is provided by special arrangement with these Boards, but the powers of these trustees are limited and so is their degree of control. However in one particular northern reserve where this model is in place some changes have taken place; a governing system has been arranged with a school division with strong management input from the local school board in such areas as the hiring of administrators and teaching staff, as well as in policy development. As Nicol

(2006) pointed out, this type of development can act as a change agent in the devolution process.

It should be noted that Aboriginal school systems are actively engaged in developing programs that are holistic and culturally appropriate. However, limited funding by the Federal government, whose fiduciary responsibility is to finance these schools, sometimes lead to financial deficits which the Federal government often interprets as mismanagement, notwithstanding the fact that Band operated schools have less per capita funding when compared with the mainstream education systems. As well, the infrastructure of band-operated schools have been found to be substandard in many cases, and overcrowded, thus necessitating repairs not allocated in current budgets. This was certainly the case in the Band that was recently placed under third party management (as reported in *The Globe and Mail*, December 15, 2011).

In addition to K-12 schools at the community level, First Nations are developing regional systems for the delivery of higher-level services that the community schools cannot individually provide. Various systems are now in place across the country. These regional organizations are helping to provide the services formerly carried out by the Federal government. For example, in Manitoba, the Manitoba First Nations Education Resource Centre (MFNERC), with qualified staff, performs such a function.

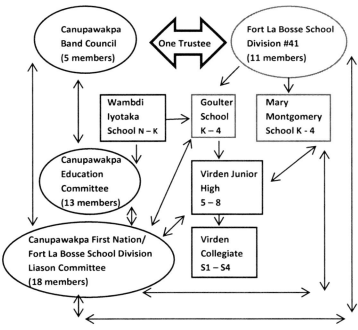

Figure 3. The Fort La Bosse School Division #41 and Canupawakpa Dakota First National partnership. Source: Fort La Bosse School Division: MB

In two Prairie provinces, Saskatchewan (First Nations University) and Manitoba (University College of the North), post-secondary programs focusing heavily on Aboriginal issues have been established. Since the 1970s Teacher Education Programs (TEPs) have been developed with a focus on the training of Aboriginal teachers and these are now being morphed into universities and colleges in other western provinces. In Manitoba an access mandate program for First Nations post-secondary students was transferred from one southern institution to a northern institution (Government of Manitoba, June 2011). The Brandon University Northern Teacher Education Program (BUNTEP) mandate was transferred, along with its budget, to the University College of the North, effective July 1, 2012. Recently steps have been initiated for the lateral transfer of course credit between institutions as per an agreement that was worked out between university presidents in concert with the province of Manitoba.

CURRICULUM, INSTRUCTION AND RESOURCES

The provincial curriculum in use in First Nations schools has been and continues to be a major problem as these do not adequately reflect *Aboriginal perspectives*. However, new curricula that are being developed in all the provinces now strongly emphasize Aboriginal issues. In First Nations schools Aboriginal history and language as well as new instructional and assessment strategies, more reflective of Aboriginal ways of learning, are emphasized and encouraged. These newer instructional strategies are being implemented by graduates of community based teacher education programs. Recently, the western provinces have issued many guidelines and documents with Aboriginal perspectives that guide instruction in all schools in those provinces. In 2008 the Government of Manitoba mandated that all teachers graduating from its teacher training programs in its universities, must have at least one course in "Aboriginal Perspectives". The authors of this chapter have acted in different capacities in the development of such a mandatory course at their post secondary institution.

The need for a philosophical basis in the development of conceptual models to address educational needs has been emphasized by First Nations educators. In attempting to integrate the traditional with the contemporary, the traditional medicine wheel (see Figure 4) is one of the models utilized in developing conceptual frameworks by many tribal councils. The medicine wheel model identifies the four quadrants of physical, intellectual, emotional and spiritual against which background, current educational developments are taking place. Similarly, holistic lifelong learning models have been developed in partnership with the Canadian Council on Learning for First Nations, Inuit and Metis people and which emphasize the importance of values, cultural traditions and ways of knowing (CCL, 2009; 2007). With respect to the First Nations model the CCL report states that this model

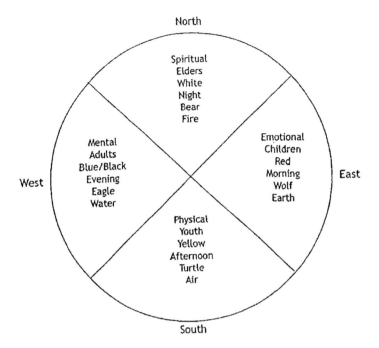

Figure 4. Medicine wheel. Source: Integrating Aboriginal Perspectives into Curriculum (2003, p.10) (MB Education)

... is premised on the understanding that the First nation learner dwells in a World of continual reformation, where interactive cycles, rather than disconnected events, occur. In this world, nothing is simply a cause or an effect, but is instead the expression of the interconnectedness of life. These relationships are circular, rather than linear, holistic and cumulative, instead of compartmentalized. The mode of learning for First Nations people reflects and honours this awareness. (2007, p. 19)

The First Nations Holistic Lifelong Learning Model is represented by a stylistic design of a living tree which depicts learning as a lifelong integrated process. The tree *roots* represent the various sources of knowledge; the tree *rings* represent the students 'learning cycle'; the *branches* represent 'personal development' and the *leaves* represent community well-being (CCL, 2007, p. 18). A full description of this model can be found on the CCL website (http://www.ccl-cca.ca). As advocated by Chief Wesley and other Aboriginals, these holistic models inform and define the decolonization process.

In this holistic approach, all factors are presumed to be intricately woven and purport to be congruent with Aboriginal philosophies and epistemologies. In a discussion on postmodernism, Doll (1989) pointed out that this type of

> postmodern curriculum will accept the student's ability to organize, construct and structure, and will emphasize this ability as a focal point in the curriculum. The development of this organizational ability is as much a key to postmodern curriculum as passive receptivity or shaping is to the modern curriculum. (p. 250)

For the majority of First Nations however, modified provincial curricula, with specific learning outcomes (SLOs) and authentic assessment protocols, are used with the rationale that First Nations students will have to live and work in the larger Canadian society and so must be prepared for future gainful employment. Similar to education changes and developments in Canada for Aboriginal Peoples, the State of Alaska (1995) in cooperation with the Alaska Native Knowledge Network, developed and adopted the Cultural Standards for Alaska Students, as part of the *Alaska Content Standards*. These standards represent what Alaskans want students *to know* and *be able to do* as a result of their schooling experience. These curricula developments are being utilized by many First Nations communities in Canada in developing their culturally appropriate content material. The introduction of Aboriginal content helps provide some balance in enhancing Aboriginal perspectives and culture, thus correcting the incongruities of the past.

Prior to these new developments, First Nations complained bitterly that devolution merely meant *delegated authority*. The new arrangements provide for increased local authority and flexibility to manage and implement programs, hire staff as needed and move funds between programs without hindrance from government officials. From a positive perspective, new decentralized funding arrangements can be regarded as a policy for self-determination, a long sought goal by First Nations. However, as Chief Atleo indicated, there is a need for sustainable funding and a fiscal guarantee to provide educational opportunities for Aboriginal children at a level commensurate to that of the mainstream society in Canada. Currently there is a substantial gap in funding of Aboriginal students under the jurisdiction of Native Bands vis-à-vis the funding levels for students in mainstream provincial jurisdictions.

CONCLUSION

In assuming the responsibility for the administration of their education system, as opposed to having it under the control of the Federal government through the Department of Indian Affairs, the First Nations communities through local control took a major step forward in bringing together traditional and contemporary values in education with the dual aims of decentralization and decolonization. In this context a partnership evolved between the community, and the various governments and institutions committed to providing for the educational needs of the First Nations. Further proof of this is manifested in the recent Joint Action Plan which was announced by the Federal Minister of Aboriginal Affairs and Northern Development and the National Chief of the Assembly of First Nations which identified "four shared priority areas for action: education; accountability, transparency, capacity and good governance; economic development; and negotiation and implementation" (*Grassroots News*, June 14/2011, p.11). With regards to education, the Action Plan calls for a " joint engagement process to make recommendations on a framework to strengthen and improve the delivery of K-12 education to First Nation children living on reserve" (Grassroots News, June 14/2011, p.11)

In February 2012 several reports highlighted the need for immediate action to bridge the gap that exists in the education of Aboriginal children. A National Panel appointed by the Federal Aboriginal Affairs Minister and the First Nations National Chief identified serious gaps in First Nations education systems when compared to public systems of education. The Panel recommended that immediate action be taken including increased funding to match that of non-reserve schools (*Winnipeg Free Press*, February 9, 2012, p. A9). In the province of Ontario (*The Toronto Star*, February 15, 2012), the Drummond Report on cost cutting measures for the province also recommended increased funding for aboriginal education in order to rectify the inadequate schooling of Aboriginal students. The Truth and Reconciliation Commission in its recently released Interim Report (2012, p. 7) recommended that all Canadian schools place an emphasis on creating public awareness and understanding of the history of residential schools; the TRC also called for increased funding to facilitate this venture. On February 27, 2012 the Canadian House of Commons gave all party support (non binding) for an Opposition motion for equal funding for First Nations education (*Toronto Sun*, February 27, 2012).

The devolution/decolonization element of change is one of the most important factors acting as a catalyst in the development of a responsive system of education for community development and wellbeing. Positive aspects of the devolution process are increasingly evident today. For example in Manitoba and Saskatchewan, the provincial governments have signed "*reversed tuition agreements*" with some Aboriginal bands whereby non-Aboriginal students, living in the general area, are enrolled in the Aboriginal schools, with the provinces paying the associated education costs for these students. In Peguis, Manitoba, the First Nations School has consistently performed at or above the provincial average in the standardized provincial examinations. Such good case studies from this and other community schools in other provinces in western Canada, prove that Aboriginal-run schools can match their mainstream counterparts.

Community leaders have therefore recognized the importance and relevance of education in the devolution towards self-government, and in the realization of a better social and economic future for First Nations communities. The objective of the First Nations is increased attendance, participation, graduation and support for expanding the school system, as well as modifying the curriculum to reflect the local environment, and promoting post-secondary education. Through these initiatives the personnel needed in education, health, social services and economic development can be realized and can be achieved from within the communities themselves. In this way the decentralization and indigenization of education, qua decolonization, in First Nations communities will not only provide benefits for them but also for a better Canada.

REFERENCES

Aboriginal Healing Foundation. (2009). *Response, responsibility and renewal: Canada's truth and reconciliation journey*. Ottawa: Author.

Alberta Education. (2005). *Our words, our ways: Teaching First Nations, Metis and Inuit learners*. Edmonton, Alberta: Department of Education.

Assembly of First Nations. (1994). *Breaking the silence: An interpretative study of residential school impact and healing*. Ottawa: Author.

Assembly of First Nations. (1972). *Indian control of Indian education*. Ottawa: Author.

Atleo, S. (2011). Can we afford to miss out? Congress 2011, Fredericton, May.

Bear Nicholas, A. (2001). The great white bird – Canada's colonial mission. In K. P. Binda & S. Calliou (Eds.), *Aboriginal education in Canada: A study in decolonization*. Mississauga: Ontario, Canadian Educator's Press.

Binda, K. P. (1994). A constructivist strategy for improving student achievement in the community-based education program – BUNTEP. In K. P. Binda (Ed.), *Critical issues in First Nations education*. Brandon, MB: Brandon University.

Binda, K. P. (1995). Perceptions of local control in a First Nations tribal community. *McGill Journal of Education, 30*(2), 199-209.

Binda, K. P. (1998). Financing Aboriginal education. In Y. L. Jack Lam (Ed.), *Education finance: Current Canadian issues*. Calgary: Detselig.

Binda, K. P. (2001). Decentralization and the development of Aboriginal education systems. In K. P. Binda & S. Calliou (Eds.), *Aboriginal education in Canada: A study in decolonization*. Mississauga, Ontario: Canadian Educator's Press.

Binda, K. P., & Calliou, S. (Eds.). (2001). *Aboriginal education in Canada: A study in decolonization*. Mississauga, Ontario: Canadian Educator's Press.

Brown, D. J. (1994). Decentralization in educational governance and management. In *International Encyclopedia of Education* (pp. 1407-1411).

Canadian Council on Learning. (2009). *The state of Aboriginal learning in Canada: A holistic approach to measuring success*. Ottawa: Author.

Canadian Council on Learning. (2007). *Redefining how success is measured in First Nations, Inuit and Metis learning*. Report on Learning in Canada 2007. Ottawa: Author.

Canadian Federation for the Humanities and Social Sciences, Congress 2011. Frederiction, N.B., May 28– June 1.

Chapman, R. (1973). Decentralization: Another perspective. *Comparative Education, 9*(3), 127-134.

Chrisjohn, R. & Young, S. L. (1997). *The circle game*. Penticton, B.C.: Theytus Books.

Dickason, O. P. (2002). *Canada's First Nations: A history of founding peoples from earliest times* (3rd ed.). Toronto: Oxford University Press.

Doll, W. E. Jr. (1989). Foundations for a postmodern curriculum. *Journal of Curriculum Studies, 31*(3), 243-253.

Etzioni, A. (1993). *The spirit of community rights responsibilities and the communitarion agenda*. New York: Crown Publishers.

Government of Canada. (2011). Auditor General's Report, June 2011 Status Report, Ottawa.

Government of Manitoba. (2011). *Memorandum of understanding*. Winnipeg.

Grassroots News. (2011). INAC: Minister Duncan and AFN National Chief Atleo Announce Joint Action Plan, June 14, 2011, p. 11.

Kaufman, H. (1969). Administrative decentralization and political power. *Public Administration Review, 29*, 3-14.

Kirkness, V. J. (1992). *First Nations and schools: Triumphs and struggles.* Toronto: Canadian Education Association.

Kumar, M. P. (2009). Aboriginal education in Canada: A postcolonial analysis. *AlterNative: An International Journal of Indigenous Peoples, 5*(1), 42-57.

Leavitt, R. M. (1991). Language and culture content in native education. *The Canadian Modern Language Review, 47*(2), 266-279.

MacPherson, J. C. (1991). *MacPherson report on tradition and education.* Ottawa: DIAND.

Manitoba Education, Citizenship and Youth. (2007). Canada in the contemporary world: A foundation for implementation (social studies). Winnipeg: Government of Manitoba.

McGinn, N. F. (1996). Education, decentralization, and globalization: A challenge for comparative education. *Comparative Education Review, 40*(4), 341-357.

McGinn, N., & Street, S. (1986). Educational decentralization: Weak state or strong state? *Comparative Education Review, 30*(4), 471-490.

Mercredi, O. (1998, May). Restoring indigenous knowledge and history in Canada. Paper presented at the 26th Annual conference of the Canadian Society for the Study of Education. Ottawa, Ontario.

Morse, W. B. (1991). *Aboriginal peoples and the law.* Ottawa: Carlton University Press.

Nicol, D. G. (2006). *An historical and theoretical study of the Brandon University Northern Teacher Education Project: From infancy through maturity – 1974 to 1990.* Unpublished Doctoral Thesis, University of Vancouver: Vancouver University.

Putnam, R. D. (1993). *Making democracy work: Civic traditions in modern Italy.* Princeton, NJ: Princeton University Press.

Rawls, J. (1971). *A theory of justice.* Cambridge, MA: Harvard University Press.

Royal Commission on Aboriginal Peoples. (1996). *Report of the Royal Commission on Aboriginal Peoples.* Ottawa: Queens Printer.

Schlein, L. (1999). Canada's indigenous peoples face health crisis. *Brandon Sun,* November 27, p. 12.

Sergiovanni, T. J. (1994). *Building community schools.* San Francisco: Jossey Bass.

State of Alaska. (1995). Alaska content standards. Juneau: State of Alaska: Department of Education and Early Development (www.eed.state.ak.us/contentstandards/).

Statistics Canada. (2006). *Aboriginal identity population, by province and territory, 2006 Census.* Ottawa: Author.

The Globe and Mail (2011). Toronto: December 15.

The Toronto Star (2012). Drummond Report: First Nations education 'urgently needs improvement'. February 15.

Toronto Sun (2012). Aboriginal education motion receives full support in House. February 27. Toronto Truth and Reconciliation Commission of Canada (2012) Interim Report. Winnipeg, Manitoba.

United Nations. (1948). UN Document A/811. New York: UN.

Walker, W. G. (1972). *Centralization and decentralization: An international viewpoint or an American dilemma.* Eugene, OR: Centre for the Advanced Study of Educational Administration.

Wesley, Ernest (Chief). (1993). Wesley decolonization project (Rebuilding self-determination: Community wellness). Address to the Assembly of First Nations, XIV Annual General Assembly. Calgary, Alberta.

Winnipeg Free Press. (2012). National panel urges action on First Nations education. February 9, A9. Winnipeg, Manitoba.

K. P. Binda & Mel Lall
Faculty of Education
Brandon University
Brandon, Manitoba

LESLEY GRAYBEAL

DISCOVERING THE PAST, UNCOVERING DIVERSITY

*The Reclamation of Indigenous Identity through a
Community Education Project*

INTRODUCTION

Museums and heritage parks serve as significant sources of nonformal education, for everyone from children and teachers attending field trip visits to adult hobbyists to tourists of all ages. Many new types of museums also offer alternative visions of history, ethnic identity, and cultural knowledge, whether through consultation with Indigenous communities or complete tribal control. While the heritage of the museum as an institution is Western and colonial (Bennett, 1995; Dubin, 1999), neighborhood museums, ethnic museums, tribal museums, and many other local forms of the museum have both adopted the institution as a preservation and education tool and adapted it to local needs. Indigenous people have been active in protesting museum representations for many decades – whether calling for a new museum, as Alcatraz Island protestors from several tribes did in the 1970s when they suggested the island be turned into an American Indian cultural center, or opposing existing museum exhibits, as Cree protestors opposed to Shell Oil sponsorship of an exhibit at the Winter Olympics did in 1988 (Cooper, 1997). Many groups have used the recovery of Indigenous artifacts from mainstream museums to validate their history and sovereignty, and over 200 tribal museums exist today to continue the work of crafting museum representations that are controlled by Indigenous peoples (Cooper, 1997; Hoxie & Nelson, 2007; Silva, 2004).

Many museum scholars have examined the ways that these new museums offer visitors an alternative educational experience, but few have explored the significance that planning and execution of preservation and education initiatives hold for local communities themselves. The objective of this study was to gain an in-depth understanding of the experience of a specific group of American Indian tribal members using community educational programming to gain recognition and representation of Indigenous heritage and identity within contemporary political, legal, and educational structures.

Because many mainstream museum representations of Indigenous peoples have been contested by tribes and activists in the United States, Canada, Australia, and elsewhere, I anticipated that tribal members in my study would view educational programming as an important way to counteract stereotypes. Furthermore, because the participants in my study gained state recognition only very recently in 2002, and because the tribe's home is in the Southeastern United States where American

D.B. Napier & S. Majhanovich (eds.), Education, Dominance and Identity, 29–46.

Indian people became subject to complex racial politics and a society divided into an explicit Black-and-White binary, I anticipated that my participants would view educating their local community about the continued existence and cultural distinctness of American Indian people in the South as closely linked to the revitalization of their own individual and group identities outside of Black-and-White racial constructs. Although the scope of this study was quite localized, another objective was to contribute to a broader understanding of the educational uses of museums and heritage projects by underrepresented groups globally. As my findings reflected, local groups may create opportunities for broader regional, national, and even global social participation through community heritage revitalization and recognition.

The findings discussed here were drawn from a study that addressed the following questions (Graybeal, 2011): 1) how educational outreach and heritage preservation initiatives encouraged visitors to ask relevant questions about their community, 2) how tribal members perceived the heritage preservation project as it related to personal and group identity and the representation of that identity to others, 3) how a grassroots approach influenced the structure, representation, and significance of place of the project, 4) what types of knowledge and power were constructed, exercised, and transferred in the heritage project, and 5) how the preservation project differed from traditional museums in the physical, temporal, and ontological boundaries applied to its representations. This chapter examines a selection of thematic issues from the study: the importance of heritage revitalization for reconstructing Indigenous identity, the use of historical knowledge to increase the visibility of contemporary Indigenous people, and the use of community education to revise historically binary race constructs in the American South. As exhibited in the literature and explored through in-depth case study, community education programs constructed within the framework of local museums and heritage projects are sites not only for representing uncovered understandings of culture and identity within a community, but also for revising existing knowledge and identity constructs on a regional, national, and global scale.

THEORETICAL FRAMWORK: MUSEUMS IN POSTCOLONIAL CONTEXTS

Examinations of museums and heritage projects today belong to a brief but rich theoretical tradition in which many scholars agree that every museum exhibition, regardless of the subject it displays or the goals it espouses, inevitably draws on the ideologies, cultural assumptions, and resources of whoever is in charge of the exhibit (Lavine & Karp, 1991). Yet these taken-for-granted critical positions on museums and their displays mainly arose in the 1970s with theorists such as Wittlin (1970/2004) and Cameron (1971/2004), who compellingly addressed the need for museums to shift from being temples of knowledge to social forums. In formulating my study, I worked from the assumption that Bennett (1995) and Ames (1992) share that mainstream Western museums largely appropriated, objectified, classified, and interpreted the cultures of non-White peoples – and often the people themselves. Thus, the objects museums display are much more than illustrative examples from antiquity – they are pawns in a culture war (Buntix & Karp, 2006; Loukaitou-Sideris & Grodach, 2004; Stocking, 1985). In this war of position, Indigenous people look for ways to assert their sovereignty and identity in a modern world that persists in defining Indigenous cultures as heritage and historical only (Clifford, 1988). While the practices of traditional Western museums have made the use of the museum institution by Indigenous peoples a complex issue (Cooper, 1997), nevertheless new museums work to disrupt and subvert the power imbalances inherited within the institutional form using a diversity of new iterations of the museum (Clifford, 1997). If the museum is a site for the exercise of power (Bernstein, 1992; Davis, 1999; Dubin, 1999; Leask & Fyall, 2006; Peltomaki, 1999), then power imbalances in the museum can also be reshaped to promote cross-cultural understanding of differences that have been historically racialized (Bennett, 2006; Buntix & Karp 2006).

While the study was informed by a range of critical and poststructural perspectives from museum studies (Bennett, 2006; Buntix & Karp, 2006; Duncan, 1991; Lavine & Karp, 1991; Leask & Fyall, 2006; Loukiaitou-Sideris & Grodach, 2004), my examination of museums as nonformal educators also incorporated the language and assumptions of post-colonial studies (Cooper, 1997; French, 1994; Hirschfelder & Kreipe de Montaño, 1993; Monroe & Echo-Hawk, 2004; Rectanus, 2002), and the methodological approaches of Indigenous methodologists (Tuhiwai Smith, 1999). While not addressed explicitly in this chapter, Foucault's power/knowledge framework as employed by several key museum scholars in exploring authority and authenticity in museum displays and performances was also a notable component of the study (Heumann Gurian, 2004; Kirschenblatt-Gimblett, 1991; Luke, 2002; Weil, 2004, 1990/2004). I hoped to make a theoretical contribution to the mosaic of understanding about how museums have come to represent the "overlapping engagements, contradictory intentions, multiple mediations, and critical reformulations" of people's lives and experiences (Kratz & Rassool, 2006, p. 347).

METHODOLOGY: EXPLORING PERSONAL EXPERIENCES

The data discussed in this chapter were drawn from a qualitative single-case study (Glesne, 2006; Payne & Payne, 2004; Yin, 2009), utilizing ethnographic methods of data collection and inductive, comparative processes of analysis (Glesne, 2006; Patton, 2002; Payne & Payne, 2004; Vogt, 2002). The mode of inquiry I used also drew widely from assumptions promoted by Indigenous methodologists (Tuhiwai Smith, 1999) regarding respect for Indigenous research subjects, concern for Indigenous interests and needs, and the integral role of reciprocity in an effort to avoid the over-research of Indigenous people and appropriation of Indigenous Knowledges. Data sources consisted primarily of semi-structured in-depth interviews with tribal organization members involved in the heritage project being studied, unobtrusive and participant observations of events in the tribal office and visits by school groups and community members to the project site, and analysis of existing documents, photographs, and educational materials. These sources have been bolstered by a broad review of the museum studies literature, including a range of theoretical perspectives and single- and multiple-case studies of other museums and heritage projects.

The subject of the study was the Homeland Preservation Project, a historical reconstruction and community education project begun by the Occaneechi Band of the Saponi Nation in Alamance County, North Carolina in 2004. The tribal organization consisted of about 700 members residing primarily in Alamance and Orange Counties in the piedmont region of North Carolina. The organization was founded as the Eno-Occaneechi Indian Association in 1984, but the group changed its name to the Occaneechi Band of the Saponi Nation in 1995 to reflect intertribal ties forged in the late 1600s (Hazel & Dunmore, 1995). The earliest recorded contact between the Occaneechi and European settlers occurred in 1670 and was documented by German physician John Lederer (Ross, 1999). At that time, the Occaneechi inhabited an advantageous position on an island on the Roanoke River near present-day Clarksville, Virginia. The Occaneechi lost this position after Bacon's Rebellion in 1676; survivors of the battle relocated to the banks of the Eno River near present-day Hillsborough North Carolina. The archaeological remains of this village, referred to in historical records as Occaneechi Town, were dated from 1680 to 1710 (Ward & Davis, 1999). This town, which was excavated in the 1980s, was used as the model for part of the Homeland Preservation Project, but it did not mark the end of the tribe's migration and dispersal (Dickens, Ward, & Davis, 1987; Ethridge, 2010; Oakley, 2005; Ward & Davis, 1999).

The Occaneechi left Occaneechi Town to relocate to a trading fort, Fort Christanna, Virginia, established by the Commonwealth of Virginia for the Occaneechi and several other small tribes. After the fort closed in 1717, many of the Occaneechi continued to live in the area. Beginning around the 1720s, the Occaneechi began to abandon the Tutelo-Saponi language for English and to adopt European names. Since reorganization, tribal members have made an ongoing effort to recover this language using linguistic and historical research (Interview transcripts, February 4, 2010; February 19, 2010; April 25, 2010). Christopher Oakley (2005) described the Occaneechi and other small, isolated American Indian communities in North Carolina during this time period as being "acculturated but not assimilated" (p. 15). Their reservation land in Virginia was sold to settlers in 1730, after which the tribe began to disperse and migrate once again. Some moved west to Ohio and Indiana, others went north to join loyalist factions of the Saponi during the Revolutionary War, and others returned to North Carolina (Hazel & Dunmore, 1995; Ross, 1999). Those who returned to North Carolina settled about 15 miles from the previous Occaneechi Town. By 1830, a community made up of the ancestors of present-day tribal members had solidified in the area of Alamance Country where the Homeland Preservation Project was constructed (Ross, 1999). While the tribe's present-day membership includes people who have moved throughout the United States and who have pursued a wide variety of occupations, the local community remained predominantly agricultural and the Homeland

Preservation Project was designed to preserve the tribe's agricultural traditions from the 1700s to the 1900s.

The Homeland Preservation Project consists of several reconstructions on a 25-acre piece of farmland purchased by the tribe. The plot of farmland itself was sharecropped by older generations of one family of tribal members, giving the term "homeland" both a collective and familial meaning. The reconstructions completed at the time of the study included a replica of Occaneechi Town, a reconstructed 1880s farm, and a reconstructed 1930s farm (Observation field notes, October 8, 2009; October 9, 2009). The site also had orchards with heirloom apple trees and other produce indigenous to the area. Finally, the site is the location for the tribe's annual powwow, and as such, includes a designated site for powwow grounds and an outdoor pavilion (Observation field notes, October 8, 2009; October 9, 2009). In 2011, the tribal office was relocated to the site. The tribe's website publicized future plans for the site that included a multi-purpose building with office space, a formal museum, and classrooms – among other uses for the structure – and educational nature trails (Occaneechi Band of the Saponi Nation, n.d.b). The largest reoccurring event on the site aside from the annual powwow is the School Days: a two day event in the fall during which area school children take field trips to the site and the tribe sets up stations to showcase archaeology, Native American history, pre-contact Indigenous lifeways (means of fulfilling the basic needs of everyday life), the Tutelo-Saponi language, storytelling, dance, and the traditional agricultural practices of the local area using the on-site reconstructions and resources brought by presenters from within and outside the tribe (Observation field notes, October 8, 2009; October 9, 2009).

FINDINGS: INDIGENOUS IDENTITY ON DISPLAY

The Homeland Preservation Project was first and foremost a place-based site for preservation and education through the use of historic reconstructions and demonstrations. Through the use of this place-based initiative, a group of Indigenous people not only reclaimed tribal ownership of historic homeland property, but also created opportunities for reclaiming Indigenous identities within the community. Through the use of this educational space, the Occaneechi people also created opportunities to exercise power over self-representations, perceptions of Indigenous people among non-Indigenous community members, recognition and legitimation, and their image as Indigenous people. The political borders defined by colonial governments presented challenges for the Occaneechi and other small tribes in achieving recognition; colonial American politics required the tribes to relocate multiple times, while contemporary requirements for recognition require tribes to document sustained settlement in a particular geographic location. The Homeland Preservation Project has also served the Occaneechi people as a platform for redefining the borders of their own social and political participation to encompass multiple layers of community from local to international.

Change and Persistence in Indigenous Identity

When the site for the Homeland Preservation Project was purchased, it was the first tribally-owned land that the Occaneechi people had held in over 200 years. As such, this site was a significant place for Occaneechi tribal members, who regarded the site as not only a place to educate visitors about the history of the Occaneechi, but also a place to ground their own experiences, interact with other Indigenous people, and participate in Occaneechi cultural practices. The site visibly and tangibly indicated the tribe's existence, serving a significant role in supporting the identities of tribal members whose parents and grandparents hid their Indigenous heritage to blend into a biracial South. Prior to reorganization in the 1980s, many Occaneechi families were identified as "colored" or African American for several generations in order to fit into the biracial social structure and avoid specific types of legal disenfranchisement following the Indian Removal Act of 1830 that relocated federally-recognized tribes west. As one Occaneechi tribal member described,

> [Andrew Jackson said], 'The Indians have been removed to Indian territory.' By the stroke of a pen, a whole nation of people were wiped out. So, you weren't Indian – you were mulatto, you were colored, you were an issue, you were yellow, you were red – everything but Indigenous. And so that's what happened. (Interview transcript, March 30, 2010)

The fact that American Indian people had to hide their Indigenous identities in order to survive in the South had a major impact on the way that Occaneechi people talked about their history through the Homeland Preservation Project. Occaneechi participants emphasized the importance of their ancestors adapting to survive in the American South, and the Homeland Preservation Project traced this adaptation from the contact-era village to the contemporary lives of the tribal members who volunteered their time to educate visitors. By presenting the reconstructed Occaneechi village along with the recovered cabin that was the childhood home of an Occaneechi family, the Homeland Preservation Project reflected and legitimated adaptation and change in Indigenous life. As one tribal staff member explained,

> Times change and the lifeways change, and in 1930 just because you were plowing tobacco with a mule didn't mean you weren't Indian, it just means that the lifeways change. We want people to understand that Indian people are still here, it's just things are different than they were 300 years ago. (Interview transcript, December 1, 2009)

He went on to explain, "Indian culture did not freeze in 1680 – it continued to change and evolve" (Interview transcript, December 1, 2009). The tribal members who participated in educating visitors used the site to illustrate that Indigenous people have remained in the local community for centuries. Another staff member explained the change as ongoing: "the Homeland Preservation Project is not just a place to preserve history, but continue the making of history" (Interview transcript,

March 24, 2010). While the site was presented as a historic reconstruction for visitors, it was also a contemporary homeland, where the Occaneechi held their annual powwow each June as a homecoming event for the tribe's core families to get together in addition to a cultural performance for tribal members and the public (Interview transcript, February 4, 2010). The many functions of the site went hand in hand, and the tribe's future visions for the site reflected the holistic importance of the Homeland Preservation Project space. The final plan for the Homeland Preservation Project included a multi-use building to house the administrative offices, an auditorium and meeting space, a museum exhibit space, classrooms, and even a shelter for severe weather emergencies (Interview transcripts, December 10, 2009; February 19, 2010; March 24, 2010).

Heritage Project as Alternative Representational Space

By creating their own educational space, the Occaneechi people were able to control their self-representations and visitors' perceptions of them. Occaneechi preservation initiatives also strove to recover the hidden histories of Indigenous people in the American South. Tribal members repeatedly asserted that correcting what they perceived to be an inaccurate or simply incomplete history was a major goal for the Homeland Preservation Project (Interview transcript, January 22, 2010; January 25, 2010; January 29, 2010; March 30, 2010). The tribal constitution identified the pursuit of an "honest history" as a central goal of the tribal organization, and tribal members voiced similar beliefs that "there's more to history than what's taught in the history books" (Occaneechi Band of the Saponi Nation, n.d.a, "Preamble"; Interview transcript, January 29, 2010). Many tribal members felt that although local area children learned a little bit in school about local Indigenous populations, they remained for the most part unaware of the small tribes that historically resided in North Carolina and the present-day pockets of Indigenous people in the state (Interview transcripts, January 22, 2010; January 25, 2010; April 25, 2010). Instead, students get the bulk of their knowledge about Indigenous people in North Carolina from the Eastern Band of the Cherokee Nation, the state's only federally-recognized tribe. The history is also deeply personal, however, and many tribal members saw uncovering their ancestral heritage as crucial to making progress in the future (Interview transcripts, January 25, 2010; January 29, 2010; February 4, 2010; February 19, 2010; March 24, 2010; April 25, 2010). As one tribal member explained, the purpose of recovering and preserving historical knowledge was "so that our youth don't have to dig around like we had to dig around to get information about ourselves and our ancestors" (Interview transcript, January 25, 2010).

Tribal members noted that overall, non-Indigenous people also tended to learn very little about Indigenous people in the United States from mainstream textbooks and museums. As one tribal member stated, "So many times you go to a museum and the sum total about Indians is cases of arrowheads" (Interview transcript, December 10, 2009). Some tribal members felt that mainstream representations whitewashed the painful history of Indigenous people by avoiding direct mention of colonization, racism, or "policies that were directly aimed at Indian people," and by ignoring the contemporary realities of Indigenous people that were shaped by this history (Interview transcript, April 25, 2010). One tribal member voiced concern that the material available to non-Indigenous people about Indigenous peoples was more likely to support "the notion that the people that this came from are extinct" than to foster a sense of respect for living cultures (Interview transcript, February 19, 2010). As another tribal member commented, even those museum and textbook representations that he felt were intended to offer a positive portrayal of Indigenous cultures seemed to say, "Look at the beadwork, look at the tools that people made, look how beautiful their culture was – and I do mean *was*" (Interview transcript, April 25, 2010). As this tribal member went on to explain,

> To make something look like it's just a historical object, that it's not part of someone's reality, that's detrimental really. Because if you see everything that is American Indian, or is used by American Indians or owned by American Indians, behind a glass case, you only see American Indians as being people who you can't touch, you can't interact with, you can't meet American Indian people. You don't expect to meet Indian people unless you go somewhere like a museum. (Interview transcript, April 25, 2010)

When museums and school curricula focus on pre-contact cultures and Indian Removal, one tribal member explained, non-Indigenous people "don't hear about the people who found ways to stay here and how they did that" (Interview transcript, April 25, 2010). Because Occaneechi participants viewed themselves as members of a culture that had adapted to survive, they felt that such an image was important to convey on the Homeland Preservation Project site.

The lack of comprehensive knowledge about Occaneechi history and culture affected not only the education of non-Indigenous people but also the identities of present-day tribal members and their immediate ancestors. The fact that tribal members were involved in extensive projects to recover historical knowledge about their tribe and gain recognition of their Indigenous status in the surrounding community was a direct product of a past in which Indigenous people in the region were not free to acknowledge that they were anything other than whatever racial category – Black or White – they were able to "pass" for in the eyes of non-Indigenous people. As one tribal member explained, they were a community "whose race was reassigned" as either Black or White (Interview transcript, April 25, 2010). Recovery from this misrepresentation was ongoing, and at times frustrating, for Occaneechi participants: "The culture was already taken away from us, years back, and we still don't have it" (Interview transcript, January 29, 2010). Politely understating the issue, one tribal member simply summarized that "the whole history of how we got to where we are has been really difficult" (Interview transcript, January 29, 2010). At the same time, however, tribal members viewed the acts of heritage recovery and promotion of awareness of the Occaneechi and their history as a way to correct this difficult past their ancestors lived through. As one tribal member stated, after recalling the frustrations of feeling different from her peers as a child but never being told by her parents that she was American

Indian, "I'm doing this for my mother, because she wasn't able to, and my grandparents because they weren't able to – and they kept it all hush-hush inside their doors" (Interview transcript, January 29, 2010). Increasing awareness of Occaneechi history in the local area allowed tribal members to voice a previously taboo identity as they constructed it from fragments of experience, heritage, and history. To counteract dominant representations of the history of the local area's Indigenous population, the Occaneechi people made personal interaction with visitors a priority. By providing personal interaction with Indigenous people, the Homeland Preservation Project "takes things outside of the box," as one tribal member put it; in doing so, Occaneechi people have created a local Indigenous identity that expanded upon historicized notions and worked against received images and stereotypes of Indigenous people. Occaneechi people expressed the desire to not only restore the contemporary reality of Indigenous people to the education that their non-Indigenous community members received, but also to restore the painful aspects of their history. Several tribal members expressed their hope that when the museum building was added, it would illustrate the unique racial politics that existed for Indigenous people in the South (Interview transcripts, December 10, 2009; April 25, 2010).

In teaching both non-Indigenous community members and tribal members about the hidden history of the Occaneechi people, participants hoped to restore pride in their Indigenous identity and regain recognition and respect. One tribal member explained that the site was important in affirming for Occaneechi people that "we're proud to say we're Indians now instead of having to hide" (Interview transcript, January 25, 2010). A main goal for many of the tribal members was to educate tribal youth and the adults who embraced their Indigenous identity only later in life "to be proud that they're Occaneechi" (Interview transcript, January 22, 2010). Embracing an Indigenous identity also required Occaneechi people to actively deal with stereotypes and preconceived notions of Indigenous people, however, and so the Homeland Preservation Project served as a space for tribal members to confront some of these stereotypes. One tribal staff member explained how the historic reconstructions themselves dispel some stereotypes: at the Homeland Preservation Project, visitors encountered Occaneechi *ati* buildings in the palisaded village rather than "teepees, which a lot of people expect when they see Indians" (Interview transcript, December 10, 2009). The tribal historian expected the farm reconstructions to also give pause to visitors who only "think of Indianness being wrapped up in the non-European tradition" (Interview transcript, December 10, 2009). Finally, participants felt that interacting with visitors helped make diversity visible to children who had "maybe heard about Indians, or seen them on TV, but they didn't really know that the person that may be sitting beside them in class, they could be Native American" (Interview transcript, February 4, 2010). As another tribal member explained, "they realize Indian folks walk among them ... and they don't necessarily all have to wear feathers to be recognized as Indians" (Interview transcript, January 25, 2010). Recognition came out as another key component of the self-representations that Occaneechi people constructed on the Homeland site. Tribal members used the site to continuously reinforce their

37

legitimate Indigenous identities after a difficult state recognition process and so many years of having to hide their heritage. In order to assert contemporary Occaneechi identity, tribal members actively worked against common stereotypes to gain recognition as "real Indians" in their community, while in order to represent Occaneechi history, tribal members actively worked against the dominant conception that the local Indigenous people were completely removed or completely assimilated. Discussing the Indian Removal Act of 1830, one tribal member summarized his motivations for educating non-Indigenous visitors about these issues: "I want people to know that we're still here, we ain't gone nowhere. And it ain't what Andrew Jackson said – we're still here" (Interview transcript, March 30, 2010).

The historical preservation activities of the tribe included an important revitalization project for the Tutelo-Saponi language, once used as the lingua franca in the Carolina-Virginia area where the Occaneechi dominated inter-tribal and European trade in the 17th century. Through linguistic and historical research, tribal members were able to create a dictionary of the language and a curriculum for teaching the language to others. The tribe held language classes primarily for tribal youth, but at which older tribal members were also welcome; one tribal member involved in teaching these classes commented that learning the language was valuable for youth and adults alike because it "validates their identity" (Interview transcript, April 25, 2010). Indigenous language is closely related to issues of identity and cultural survival (Lomowaima & McCarty, 2006). Just as prohibiting the use of Indigenous languages was central to the campaign to assimilate American Indian children during the period of off-reservation boarding schools in the United States, recovering language is central to rebuilding culture: "once you destroy a person's language, you destroy their identity and cultural identity. And understanding a person's language helps you understand their worldview" (Interview transcript, February 19, 2010). Thus, even a revitalized language can be used to redefine the worldview of those who learn it. As one tribal member observed, "we have no word for 'need' because we understand that the creator gives us all that we need" (Interview transcript, February 19, 2010). As another tribal member noted of his experience conducting language classes, "It became a community event. People who maybe didn't have a strong Occaneechi identity and pushed away the tribe started to come out of nowhere to learn about [the language]" (Interview transcript, April 25, 2010). Several tribal members confirmed that access to the revitalized Tutelo-Saponi language enhanced their sense of community through the ability to speak to one another using a unique set of vocabulary shared with their ancestors (Interview transcripts, January 29, 2010; February 19, 2010; March 30, 2010; April 25, 2010).

Having visitors recognize one's cultural identity as distinct and legitimate was an exercise that also took on racial overtones in the American South. Recovery of Occaneechi identity was especially important to Occaneechi tribal members whose families were misclassified on census reports and birth certificates. Correcting these birth certificates was one of the primary goals of the reorganized tribe. One tribal member described the type of situation that numerous others confirmed: "I grew up being pushed into a box down South ... and not fitting in" (Interview transcript, February 19, 2010). Having learned to survive in a biracial world, many tribal members placed removing imposed racial definitions first and foremost among the goals of any educational endeavor. While this goal responded to a local situation, it indicated a broader issue. As one tribal member explained, "We're trying to let folks know that it's not just a two-ethnicity culture ... everything is not always just black and white" (Interview transcript, January 22, 2010). The metaphorical significance of this tribal member's statement is clear: binary racial constructs are just one faulty binary in a diverse and complex world. A similar historical and social situation played out in different ways for numerous groups elsewhere in the United States and around the world; the tribal members' goal of asserting cultural distinction was part of a larger purpose – teaching visitors to understand the historical and social realities of a multicultural world.

Another purpose Occaneechi participants expressed related to achieving recognition of a distinct cultural identity was achieving a sense of belonging within the local area. While tribal members asserted the importance of being recognized as "real Indians," they also wanted to be recognized as "real people" (Interview transcripts, January 29, 2010; March 30, 2010). Thus, another goal of the Homeland Preservation Project and related educational programming was to show the Indigenousness of the Occaneechi – that they had longstanding ties to the local area established across hundreds of years – and to illustrate that the result of this established history was present-day Occaneechi people who contributed to contemporary society. Tribal members found it deeply important that visitors to the site understood not only that the area's Indigenous people continued to exist, but also that they participated in the everyday life of the community (Interview transcripts, January 25, 2010; January 29, 2010). Despite their local context, these assertions of belonging in the community also spoke to Occaneechi participants' goals of changing visitors' broader worldviews. Tribal members hoped that visitors would walk away with the understanding that *everywhere* – not just in Alamance County, North Carolina – diverse peoples existed outside of preconceived notions, and Indigenous identity continued not only in museums and artifacts, but in the lives of real people.

Revising Identities and Redefining Community

In navigating these historical and social issues, Occaneechi tribal members used the Homeland Preservation Project to increase the overall visibility of Indigenous peoples and to mobilize tribal members on multiple levels of active social and political participation. Although the imposed borders of racial constructs and colonial and state lines made recognition difficult for the Occaneechi, tribal members actively redefined their own communities and spaces of social participation. In making Indigenous peoples more visible in the local community, tribal members wanted to dispel myths about American Indians and help visitors attain the awareness that present-day Indigenous peoples can live modern lives that are in keeping with authentic cultural identities. As one tribal member, who was involved with the tribe's youth group and in economic development initiatives to aid Indian-owned businesses in the state, asserted, "Native American people can do a lot more than just shoot bows and arrows ... there are Indian folks that are just like everybody else" (Interview transcript, February 4, 2010).

Tribal members not only wanted to make visitors aware of the ongoing lives of Indigenous people, however – they also wanted to ensure the ongoing relevance of Indigenous histories by inclusively sharing cultural knowledges with a mainstream audience. As one tribal member noted, "I have the responsibility of ensuring that our culture is passed on, not only to my people, but to the world" (Interview transcript, February 19, 2010). One reason why passing on Occaneechi cultural knowledge to a broad, mainstream audience was significant was because tribal members saw themselves as part of broader levels of community. Tribal members reminded me that they had been active local community members and interacted with the non-Indigenous residents of the area for centuries, that the Homeland Preservation Project continued to serve the community as a tourism draw and community improvement initiative, and that tribal members filled many vital roles as professionals, church members, and parents (Interview transcripts, December 10, 2009; January 25, 2010; February 4, 2010). As one tribal member described, recognition was important to showcase not only the fact that Indigenous people still existed in the community, but also that they were an integral part of it: "the tribe is still here and still alive, and our tribal members contribute to the betterment of society" (Interview transcript, January 22, 2010).

Yet despite the strong local heritage of tribal members and the ties the Homeland Preservation Project had to the agricultural heritage of the community at large, tribal members also saw themselves as mobilized on several other levels. The tribe participated in statewide events to celebrate North Carolina's diversity of American Indians, and tribal members were active in economic and political organizations to serve every tribe in the state and promote inter-tribal cooperation. In 2010, a series of educational programs for Occaneechi tribal members emphasized the ways in which identifying as an American Indian person applied to a broader Pan-Indian context for activism and political participation. As the tribal member who planned the series stated, "We're teaching the history and the context of what it means to be an Indigenous person in the United States" (Interview transcript, February 19, 2010). Yet tribal members' sense of participation did not stop at the national level; a tribal staff member explained that in 2009 the tribe put together a cultural heritage day to promote trans-national tolerance and understanding based on pride in the Indigenous heritage of the state. The event "emphasized the Native heritage of a lot of the Central American immigrants to North Carolina," encouraging a Pan-American identity and appreciation for international Indigenous cultures as broader iterations of the local (Interview transcript, December 10, 2009).

Perhaps one of the most distinct aspects of the Homeland Preservation Project was its pointed assertion that teaching visitors about Occaneechi people should be a lesson in the changes all Indigenous peoples have experienced over time. While the specific story available to visitors on the Homeland Preservation Project site was a local one about the Occaneechi and their ancestors who came to share many traditions with the non-Indian farmers of the area, the take-away point for visitors was that times change, and so can Indigenous peoples. The historic reconstructions conveyed the message that Depression-era tobacco farmers could also be Indigenous people, and the tribal members who volunteered on the site conveyed the same message with their presence and engagement with visitors. Visitors to the site met tribal members and learned that nurses, businessmen, and scientists – to name a few – can also be Indigenous people. The site was designed to illustrate for visitors the reality that "Indianness" is not historically bound. By creating that understanding, tribal members hoped to foster not only an awareness among visitors of the ongoing multicultural heritage of their own community, but also the possibility of understanding the present realities of Indigenous cultures around the world. The illustration of the simple reality of cultural change over time removed the borders imposed by mainstream representations in museums and textbooks that restricted Indigenous peoples to a particular historical period. The involvement of contemporary Occaneechi people as volunteers taking a day off from their jobs in mainstream society removed the borders imposed by visitors' perceptions of what an American Indian person should look like or do.

DISCUSSION AND CONCLUSION: REMOVING THE LOCAL BORDERS OF EXPERIENCE

While many underrepresented groups continue to work towards recognition of their ethnic and cultural identities, these local struggles compose a mosaic of international experiences and remove imposed state and national borders to create new forms of solidarity and community on local and global levels. Contributors to the Occaneechi Homeland Preservation Project envisioned preservation and education initiatives as important to themselves and to others on state, regional, national, and international levels, and were active participants in all those social and political spaces. Occaneechi tribal members asserted many points that were echoed in the literature – particularly that traditional Western depictions of Indigenous peoples consistently imply that American Indians are members of a dying race (Hirschfelder & Kreipe de Montaño, 1993; Monroe & Echo-Hawk, 2004), frozen in time (Dubin, 1999). Museum displays often seem to speak more about the way members of the dominant culture view themselves than about the histories and identities of those the exhibits are meant to represent (Cooper, 1997, p. 403; Hirschfelder & Kreipe de Montaño, 1993; Sanchez & Stuckey, 2000). The borders that create segregated histories – in which one historical narrative is told by the dominant culture while competing stories are told by others – have been constructed and imposed by segregated societies like the American South (Davis Ruffins, 2006).

Using any type of museum institution to preserve culture and educate others about it is a complex undertaking, and some Occaneechi tribal members had their doubts about putting objects on display or using the word "museum" to describe any aspect of the Homeland project (Interview transcript, February 19, 2010). As

Cooper (1997) confirmed, "it is not without ambivalence that tribal people [in the Americas] have set up buildings to house collections, launch exhibits, and emulate the very institutions that have so boldly relegated American Indians to the status of flora and fauna of the 'New World'" (p. 403). Yet objects on display do constitute a form of power, and the people who control the mode of display also regulate and legitimate culture (Heumann Gurian, 2004; Kirschenblatt-Gimblett, 1991; Luke, 2002; Weil, 1990/2004); constructing self-representations has thus been a significant exercise for the Occaneechi and many other groups whose identities and cultural knowledges have not always been regarded as legitimate, and whose claims about who they are have had to compete with other people's claims about them. Because of the colonial histories of many of the countries where Indigenous and non-Indigenous peoples now share a home, national borders, systems of governance, and educational institutions have been artificially imposed upon Indigenous groups. Nonformal educational settings provide a model for grassroots ownership of cultural transition and translation for any local community who wishes to redefine their regional, national, and global participation.

For the Occaneechi people, the sovereign educational space of the Homeland Preservation Project constituted a valuable resource for defining and projecting their identities as Indigenous people in a local community that had often not recognized them as such. These high-stakes identity politics came to involve much more than just establishing evidence to legitimate the identity claims of a local population. Becoming recognized as Indigenous people brought with it a host of broader issues. The ultimate goal of recognition, for many Occaneechi people, was being recognized as American Indian people without having to fit into preconceived notions about American Indian people – that is, without having to appeal to stereotypes – to achieve that recognition. Thus, Occaneechi tribal members have had to learn how to dispel stereotypes while remaining open and inclusive of non-Indigenous visitors who may make offensive statements about American Indians and their cultures being extinct. Through the Homeland Preservation Project, Occaneechi tribal members created a rare forum for confronting these issues directly. Volunteering as educators on the site allowed tribal members an opportunity to convey Indigenous identities that were not confined to a single way of life or style of dress. The personal interaction model of education the Occaneechi people used has the potential to provide other Indigenous communities with a means of conveying change over time, directly confronting imposed racial categories, and removing stereotypes that restrict their expressions of Indigenous identity.

By using a combination of multiple historical reconstructions and personal interaction with visitors, the Occaneechi also developed a method for creating social and political awareness in their community. While placing items in a museum display case sometimes seems to imply that the people who made and used those objects are also relics of history, personal interaction with Indigenous people who demonstrate the *use* of objects makes Indigenous people part of a visitor's contemporary reality. For the Occaneechi in particular, but also for American Indian people more generally, the very fact of contemporary existence is the highly politicized product of a painful history that many non-Indigenous people have the luxury of ignoring. Occaneechi tribal members used their educational forum to not only restore the visibility of their hidden history and contemporary Indigenous identities, but also to highlight the painful social and political realities of both. Because Occaneechi tribal members saw the Homeland Preservation Project as an opportunity to heal not only their own people, but also the broader community's heritage of racial oppression, social and political awareness was as central to the project as historical knowledge.

The Occaneechi tribal members involved in the Homeland Preservation Project repeatedly emphasized the importance of being open and inclusive of non-Indigenous people. The Occaneechi people saw themselves as vital members of their local community, and wanted non-Indigenous people to be as excited as they were about the progress of the Homeland Preservation Project. This open and inclusive attitude was an essential characteristic of the contemporary tribal organization, and allowed the tribe to widen its membership to include many people who were previously unwilling to identify as Occaneechi and to recruit supportive partnerships among schools and other organizations. The openness that Occaneechi tribal members conveyed to visitors was also fundamental in the anti-racist education of the Homeland Preservation Project. A staff member welcomed visitors to the site and to the land, and while the visitors may not have recognized the significance of being welcomed onto a piece of land by Indigenous people, this lay the foundation for visitors to overcome any feelings of guilt as a result of gaining social and political awareness of the tribe's history and experience. Visits that began with school children being welcomed to the Homeland often ended with Occaneechi tribal members having children thank them and even express sadness and regret about the painful history of Indigenous people in the United States (Interview transcript, January 29, 2010; Observation field notes, October 8, 2009; October 9, 2009). Hearing children go on to say that they wanted to come back to the site, or that they intended to bring their families to the annual powwow, showed Occaneechi tribal members that their openness to visitors was successful in fostering acceptance of and pride in the Indigenous heritage of the community (Interview transcripts, January 29, 2010; March 24, 2010).

While the findings of the study present interesting new possibilities for community education projects and underrepresented knowledges, more international multiple-case studies of Indigenous groups' successes and challenges in creating self-representations are needed. Additional cross-case comparisons should include analysis of self-representations for the purpose of visitor education as opposed to the edification of in-group members; what the borders between group members and visitors mean to both; the intentions of Indigenous peoples in crafting self-representations as opposed to the ways that such images and texts are received by non-Indigenous visitors; and the contributions that have been made by Indigenous, grassroots, nonformal community education initiatives in partnership or in tandem with formal education systems. Furthermore, the local participants in this study – and the groups and individuals working to orchestrate similar heritage projects around the world – have their own future directions for preservation and education that should play a central role in the scholarship of museums and heritage projects as their own culture-in-transition.

REFERENCES

Ames, M. M. (1992). *Cannibal tours and glass boxes: The anthropology of museums.* Vancouver: UBC Press.

Bennett, T. (1995). *The birth of the museum: History, theory, politics.* New York, NY: Routledge.

Bennett, T. (2006). Exhibition, difference, and the logic of culture. In I. Karp, C. A. Kratz, L. Szwaja, & T. Ybarra-Frausto (Eds.). *Museum frictions: Public cultures/global transformations* (pp. 46-69). Durham, NC: Duke University Press.

Bernstein, B. (1992). Collaborative strategies for the preservation of North American Indian material culture. *Journal of the American Institute for Conservation, 31*(1), Conservation of sacred objects and other papers from the general session of the 19th Annual Meeting of the American Institute for Conservation of Historic and Artistic Works, 23-29.

Buntix, G., & Karp, I. (2006). Tactical museologies. In I. Karp, C. A. Kratz, L. Szwaja, & T. Ybarra-Frausto (Eds.), *Museum frictions: Public cultures/global transformations* (pp. 207-218). Durham, NC: Duke University Press.

Cameron, D. F. (2004). The museum, a temple or the forum. In G. Anderson (Ed.), *Reinventing the museum: Historical and contemporary perspectives on the paradigm shift* (pp. 61-73). Walnut Creek, CA: Rowman & Littlefield. (Original work published 1971)

Clifford, J. (1988). *The predicament of culture: Twentieth-century ethnography, literature, and art.* Cambridge, MA: Harvard University Press.

Cooper, K. C. (1997). Museums and American Indians: Ambivalent partners. In D. Morrison (Ed.), *American Indian studies: An interdisciplinary approach to contemporary issues* (pp. 403-412). New York, NY: Peter Lang.

Davis, P. (1999). *Ecomuseums: A sense of place.* London: Leicester University Press.

Davis Ruffins, F. (2006). Revisiting the old plantation: Reparations, reconciliation, and museumizing American slavery. In I. Karp, C. A. Kratz, L. Szwaja, & T. Ybarra-Frausto (Eds.), *Museum frictions: Public cultures/global transformations* (pp. 394-434). Durham, NC: Duke University Press.

Dickens, R. S., Jr., Ward, H. T., & Davis, R. P. S., Jr. (Eds.). (1987). *The Siouan Project seasons I and II.* Chapel Hill, NC: University of North Carolina at Chapel Hill Research Laboratories of Anthropology.

Dubin, S. C. (1999). *Displays of power: Memory and amnesia in the American museum.* New York, NY: New York University Press.

Duncan, C. (1991). Art museums and the ritual of citizenship. In I. Karp & S. D. Lavine (Eds.), *Exhibiting cultures: the poetics and politics of museum display* (pp. 88-103). Washington, DC: Smithsonian Institution Press.

Ethridge, R. (2010). *From Chicaza to Chickasaw: The European invasion and the transformation of the Mississippian World, 1540-1715.* Chapel Hill, NC: University of North Carolina Press.

French, L. A. (1994). *The winds of injustice: American Indians and the U.S. government.* New York, NY: Garland.

Glesne, C. (2006). *Becoming qualitative researchers: An introduction.* Boston, MA: Pearson Education.

Graybeal, L. M. (2011). *(Re)constructing and (re)presenting heritage: Education and representation in an American Indian Homeland Preservation Project.* (Unpublished doctoral dissertation). The University of Georgia, Athens, GA.

Hazel, F., & Dunmore, L. A. III, Esq. (1995). *A brief history of the Occaneechi Band of the Saponi Nation.* (Available from the Occaneechi Band of the Saponi Nation, P.O Box 356, Mebane, NC 27302.)

Heumann Gurian, E. (2004). What is the object of this exercise? A meandering exploration of the many meanings of objects in museums. In G. Anderson (Ed.), *Reinventing the museum: Historical and contemporary perspectives on the paradigm shift* (pp. 269-283). Walnut Creek, CA: Rowman & Littlefield.

Hirschfelder, A., & Kreipe de Montaño, M. (1993). *The Native American almanac: A portrait of Native America today.* New York, NY: Prentice Hall General Reference.

Hoxie, F. E., & Nelson, J. T. (2007). *Lewis & Clark and the Indian country: The Native American perspective.* Urbana, IL: University of Illinois Press.

Kirschenblatt-Gimblett, B. (1991). Objects of ethnography. In I. Karp & S. D. Lavine (Eds.), *Exhibiting cultures: the poetics and politics of museum display* (pp. 386-443). Washington, DC: Smithsonian Institution Press.

Kratz, C. A., & Rassool, C. (2006). Remapping the museum. In I. Karp, C. A. Kratz, L. Szwaja, & T. Ybarra-Frausto (Eds.), *Museum frictions: Public cultures/global transformations* (pp. 347-356). Durham, NC: Duke University Press.

Lavine, S. D., & Karp, I. (1991). Introduction: Museum and multiculturalism. In I. Karp & S. D. Lavine (Eds.), *Exhibiting cultures: the poetics and politics of museum display* (pp. 1-9). Washington, DC: Smithsonian Institution Press.

Leask, A., & Fyall, A. (2006). *Managing world heritage sites.* Amsterdam: Elsevier, Ltd.

Lomowaima, K. T., & McCarty, T. L. (2006). *"To remain an Indian": Lessons in democracy from a century of Native American education.* New York, NY: Teachers College Press.

Loukaitou-Sideris, A., & Grodach, C. (2004). Displaying and celebrating the "Other": A study of the mission, scope, and roles of ethnic museums in Los Angeles. *The Public Historian, 26*(4), 49-71.

Luke, T. W. (2002). *Museum politics: Power plays at the exhibition.* Minneapolis, MN: University of Minnesota Press.

Monroe, D. L., & Echo-Hawk, W. (2004). Deft deliberations. In G. Anderson (Ed.), *Reinventing the museum: Historical and contemporary perspectives on the paradigm shift* (pp. 325-330). Walnut Creek, CA: Rowman & Littlefield.

Oakley, C. A. (2005). *Keeping the circle: American Indian identity in Eastern North Carolina, 1885-2004.* Lincoln, NE: University of Nebraska Press.

Occaneechi Band of the Saponi Nation. (n.d.). *The constitution of the Occaneechi Band of the Saponi Nation.* Retrieved October 5, 2009 from http://www.occaneechi-saponi.org/downloadables/Constitution.pdf.

Occaneechi Band of the Saponi Nation. (n.d.). Homeland Project. Occaneechi Homeland Preservation Project: Bringing the past and future together. Retrieved December 6, 2011 from http://www.occaneechi-saponi.org/homeland_project.html.

Patton, M. Q. (2002). *Qualitative research and evaluation methods.* Thousand Oaks, CA: Sage.

Payne, G., & Payne, J. (2004). *Key concepts in social research.* London: Sage.

Peltomaki, K. (1999). "Cooperation and conflict": Images of the Seneca at the Rochester Museum. In J. N. Brown & P. M. Sant (Eds.), *Indigeneity: Construction and re/presentation.* Commack, NY: Nova Science.

Rectanus, M. W. (2002). *Culture incorporated: Museums, artists, and corporate sponsorships.* Minneapolis, MN: University of Minnesota Press.

Ross, T. E. (1999). *American Indians in North Carolina: Geographic interpretations.* Southern Pines, NC: Karo Hollow Press.

Sanchez, J., & Stuckey, M. E. (2000). The rhetoric of American Indian activism in the 1960s and 1970s. *Communication Quarterly, 48*(2), 120-136.

Silva, N. K. (2004). *Aloha betrayed: Native Hawaiian resistance to American colonialism.* Durham, NC: Duke University Press.

Stocking, G. W., Jr. (Ed.). (1985). *Objects and others: Essays on museums and material culture.* Madison, WI: University of Wisconsin Press.

Tuhiwai Smith, L. (1999). *Decolonizing methodologies: Research and Indigenous peoples.* London: Zed Books.

Vogt, F. (2002). No ethnography without comparison: The methodological significance of comparison in ethnographic research. *Debates and Developments in Ethnographic Methodology, 6*, 23-42.

Ward, H. T., & Davis, R. P. S., Jr. (1999). *Time before history: The archaeology of North Carolina.* Chapel Hill, NC: The University of North Carolina Press.

Weil, S. E. (2004). Collecting then, collecting today: What's the difference? In G. Anderson (Ed.), *Reinventing the museum: Historical and contemporary perspectives on the paradigm shift* (pp. 284-291). Walnut Creek, CA: Rowman & Littlefield.

Weil, S. E. (2004). Rethinking the museum: An emerging new paradigm. In G. Anderson (Ed.), *Reinventing the museum: Historical and contemporary perspectives on the paradigm shift* (pp. 74-79). Walnut Creek, CA: Rowman & Littlefield. (Original work published 1990)

Wittlin, A. (2004). A Twelve Point Program for museum renewal. In G. Anderson (Ed.), *Reinventing the museum: Historical and contemporary perspectives on the paradigm shift* (pp. 44-60). Walnut Creek, CA: Rowman & Littlefield. (Original work published 1970)

Yin, R. K. (2009). *Case study research: Design and methods* (4th ed.). Los Angeles, CA: Sage.

Lesley Graybeal
Wake Technical Community College

PART II

INTEGRATION AND DOMINATION OF ETHNIC MINORITY GROUPS

ÉVA FÖLDESI

CLASSMATES

Critical Analysis of School Integration of Roma Children in Nyíregyháza, Hungary

INTRODUCTION

The struggle of Roma people is to challenge the history of citizenship as 'minoritization.'

Though this essentialist but wise assumption of Engin F. Isin (2008, p. 8) refers to the history of citizenship, I suggest that analogically the struggle for integrative education of Roma children should also be seen as a challenge against stereotyped ethnic relations. There is a huge gap between Roma and non-Roma people both in material and cognitive spaces, which is reflected in the drastic problems of Roma people: massive and long-term unemployment, under-education, historical marginalization. Familiarity, knowledge, contact, and a common identity are almost entirely absent from the web of (non)relations between these two groups; rather they are dominated by neurotic, fearful and unstable approaches. Integrative education may be able to recast these properties of ethnic relations, bringing together the hitherto separated groups, which were consequently invisible to one another. Relying on the legacy of Allport, in this chapter I assume that the rupture between different ethnic groups could be reduced by interactions (Allport, 1958; Braddock, 1980; Sigelman & Welch, 1993; Bouma & Hoffman, 1968). Due to integrated classrooms Roma and non-Roma can meet and interact with each other; interactions may challenge the socially embodied stereotyping norms. This supposition is the central tenet of this chapter. The analysis was based on the experience of two integrated schools' in Nyíregyháza, in East-Hungary. The schools had been selected to receive those Roma students who were attending the city's largest Roma-only school which had closed. This segregated Roma school was closed due to legal pressure in 2007; nevertheless, the case is all the more current since recently the local government announced it was considering reopening the segregated Roma school. This caused exaggerated and heated debates locally, reflecting political and social discourses on a national scale. Regarding the sphere of politics, there is a visible turn toward advancing minority education (which often leads to segregation) via supporting churches to take over public educational responsibilities from local governments, who were and are primarily the maintainers of schools. Historically, churches in Hungary run schools for talented and middle class children, focusing less on the education of

D.B. Napier & S. Majhanovich (eds.), Education, Dominance and Identity, 49–64.

disadvantaged and Roma children. As a case in point, the Roma school – which formerly had been closed, and which is situated in the heart of the Roma settlement was offered to the Church to maintain, once again resulting in segregation, since the inhabitants of the ghetto, i.e. Roma children, returned to attending the school.

The educational advantage of integration, its equalizing power and the legitimacy of positive discrimination are the focal points of the current ethnic and national debates. The *raison d'être* of this paper was to analyze the mainstream discourses (general approaches and opinions) of teachers and of non-Roma parents vis-à-vis integration in order to contribute to the heated debates on integrative measures. To this end, the paper set up two operative assumptions.

One assumption was that integration was able to produce more receptive and less antagonistic relations between Roma and non-Roma people. In addition, my concern was related to the fact that integrated education was realized because of the closure of the homogeneous Roma school in the heart of Nyíregyháza's largest Roma ghetto. I was interested in how the fact that these pupils live in a ghetto affects their accommodation in schools. Also, my intention was to map whether the ghetto-image influences the exclusion of Roma people. The second assumption therefore was that spatial segregation has a significant impact on the way Roma children are perceived in schools; as well as Roma people at large.

I made some preliminary evaluation regarding these assumptions. Concerning the first assumption following one month of fieldwork, the findings suggested that contact as such does not reduce stereotypes, but rather it enhances them. The visibility of Roma children became translated into the visibility of problems and conflicts, characteristically along ethnic lines. Nevertheless, there was also a de-ethnicized discourse (that is, that the dominant perceptions about Roma children and families were not controlled by ethno-centred, stereotyped explanations) articulated often in relation to those Roma children whose parents were already integrated to a certain extent to the body of the mainstream Hungarian society. This phenomenon, in turn, provides an answer to the second operative assumption. The ethnicized and stereotyped discourse regarding particular Roma children was produced due to their identification with the ghetto. Therefore, I suggested that indeed, spatial segregation as such has a significant impact on the way Roma children and families are identified. In many interviewees' narratives, the Ghetto had become the symbol of difference and the focal reference of problems. It was therefore often interpreted as a reason for the failure of integration, being a socio-culturally poor, separate and ultimately low Roma space.

In the following two sections I describe first the methodology and analysis, and then a brief description of the field site, the particular context of desegregation. Then I describe the case study data analysed through three different lenses: the image of integration, general concerns, and the dichotomy of school and of home.

METHODOLOGY

After the closure of the homogenous Roma school in 2007, six schools were involved in the integration of Roma children. The reason behind selecting two schools as the focus of analysis in my research was that due to time limitations visits to all schools could have potentially reduced the quality of the field work, which lasted for a month in the spring of 2009. Besides, my previous experiences in the field – spending the winter of 2007 in Nyíregyháza for the same reason, but with a different focus – suggested the benefit of choosing these schools due to their richness in terms of a wide variety of opinions of teachers and Roma parents. In 2007 I was able to focus on the perspectives of Roma mothers regarding their children's accommodation in the new schools. In addition, one school did not respond to my request for access, the same one, whose principal had refused to let me in the school in the winter of 2007. Moreover, another (the most respected) school was dropped from the potential sites of research since from fall of the 2009/2010 year they stopped the integrating process of accepting children from the ghetto.

For understanding the social perspective of integration, I chose to examine the perceptions of teachers and non-Roma parents because they are principal actors of integration: their approach toward integration is decisive. The assumption (see for example Kertesi and Kézdi, 2004) is that the teacher is at least as important in the development of children as the father or mother. The disposition of teachers toward Roma children could have a meaningful impact on their development and educational progress; at the same time they shape the quality of integration. Secondly, the choice of parents about schooling is decisive in sustaining or failing integrative education. Studies such as that of Zolnay (2005) show that in schools where the ratio of Roma students has reached 10-15%, integration falters because non-Roma parents remove their children from those institutions. In the literature (most notably see for example Coleman, 1966) this process is often called "white flight." Therefore, majority parents' perceptions about integrated education are influential in sustaining or undercutting that educational model.

I refer to the two selected schools as *school 1* and *school 2* instead of using their official names, to respect confidentiality. Like all of the six schools, the selected ones enjoyed a good reputation in the city. More precisely, the second one was said to be one of the best schools in the local education system.

School 1 is situated at the edge of the city in a poor environment, being surrounded by some family houses, and more block houses. In contrast, the "inside" life of the school was vivid and energetic as evidenced by the posters in the hallways which advertised various events and competitions, and as the colourful and creatively arranged venues and class-rooms indicated. Its teachers stated that characteristically middle class children, but also those from working class families attend the school. The total number of children in the fall of 2009/2010 was 650. The number of Roma children who arrived after the closure of the ghetto school (from the fall of 2007 till the study period, the fall of 2009/2010) was 22. I calculated these numbers from my 2007 research and on the estimations school principals provided.

School 2 is situated in the centre of the city, within a noisy and busy environment; however, it is characteristically dull and uninviting inside. In addition, a quasi security service was employed in the school, consisting of two men. In *school 2*, generally, middle and upper class children were said to attend. The total number of children was 665 and the number of Roma children who were relocated following the decision was 17.

In order to explore the effect of classroom integration on the alienated ethnic relations in Nyíregyháza, I used a social constructionist and interpretive approach that regards each social act as an outcome of social interactions and interpretations, as something constructed through social processes. On those grounds, ethnic perceptions and social distances reflected in interactions and meetings were regarded as subjects of change, rather than as stable and fixed. In this spirit, I conducted semi-structured, open-ended interviews with the two target groups: with teachers and non-Roma parents, for a total of 13 in *school 1*; and 10 in *school 2*; in addition to several spontaneous discussions that took place. In each school I interviewed the school principal as well. I developed a separate interview-guide for use with the teachers' and principals' interviews, where questions focused on the following main themes: general representation of the integrative measures, educational and social achievement of new-comer children, frequency and subject of contact between interviewee and Roma children/families, and class-room effect of integration. I recorded and transcribed all interviews. The majority of the 25 interviews took place in a pre-scheduled time in the school building; nevertheless, some were carried out in the school building before or after the classes spontaneously. Generally, the individual interviews lasted 40-60 minutes each. The goal of interviews was to find those instructors who teach classes with newly-arrived Roma children, as well as to balance the number of teachers from lower- and upper classes.

The discussions with some 30 parents in the schools were less structured and shorter since they mainly took place before or after the school when they were dropping off or picking up their children. I noted and transcribed these discussions as well. In this chapter I often refer to the outcome of the interviews and discussions as narratives, referring to the expressed opinions and views of interviewees. In analyzing the transcribed narratives I used edge-coding, schematized along the main themes that emerged in the interviews, which were the following: school- vs. home values, cultural distinctiveness, invisibility of children, racial discourse, parental integration, self-reflections and teacher – role, 'guszev' [ghetto] vs. town differentiation, and critique of positive discrimination.

Furthermore, I engaged in some participant observation by visiting 10 lessons and also two parental meetings. In both situations I was observing except in two classes, where I participated more. Once I was allowed to sit next to a student in an upper grade and help him, whereas in another class I was engaged in handicraft activities with lower grade children. I recorded these experiences in fieldnotes and transcribed them.

The strategy of analysis in the paper was to employ quotations from the informants, selected due to their representativeness in the sense that their message (in various forms, but identically in substance) appeared in many narratives. During the analysis I did not separate the experiences of the two schools, because there were more similarities than differences vis-à-vis their experiences, but I did indicate from which school each quote originated.

CASE STUDY

The Field Site: A Brief History And The Case Of Integration In Nyíregyháza

The integration of Roma children in Nyíregyháza was the result of a Roma NGO's de-segregation litigation against the Local Government for maintaining a homogenous Roma school, named the "Huszár, ("Cavalrymen") school. This school was situated in the centre of the town's biggest ghetto or "Guszev," as the inhabitants call it.

Approximately one thousand Roma live in the "Guszev" ghetto. The living and infrastructural conditions are poor: there is a high unemployment rate among these Roma people; poverty is tangible. The usually one-room dilapidated houses are often without proper electricity or water supplies; in addition, roads are muddy and hardly useable in winter by car. The buildings had been transformed from 19th century military-officers' houses and stables.

In 2006, 119 Roma students attended the ghetto school, which was a Roma-only school. Being a segregated school it had all those shortcomings which generally characterize these institutions: the infrastructural and pedagogical conditions were worse compared to the two neighbouring counterparts (Zolnay, 2005). For a long period only the Russian language was taught there and it had no computer facilities, but surveillance cameras and security service were employed. The educational curriculum of the schoo – as in other segregated schools – was significantly lower than in the neighbouring "mixed" schools shown in numerous research studies including Kertesi and Kézdi (2004) and Havas and Liskó (2002, 2005) who also underscored that segregated schools suffer from significantly lower pedagogical and infrastructural factors compared to their counterparts, which reduces the overall quality of education, and that in turn has notable consequences on children's progress and learning perspectives.

In December 2006, a Roma NGO, the "Chance for Children Foundation," initiated a legal suit against the school, and as a result the school was closed by the end of March 2007. From September on, all the children were relocated in six heterogeneous, typical downtown schools, designated by the Local Government. The rapid decision and its consequences produced wide protests on the part of both Roma and non-Roma parents; the socio-political climate therefore was far from positive.

In the following section I describe my analysis of the two selected schools' experiences and views on integration. The focus is on the perceptions and evaluation of teachers and non-Roma parents. The analysis is structured around three themes: Image of integration, general concerns, and a summary explanations of interethnic relations.

Image of Integration: Common Perceptions, Different Approaches

During the interviews and spontaneous discussions, usually the first thing which was articulated was a consistent disagreement with integration; however, the explanations provided for that varied on a wide scale. Some teachers and non-Roma parents saw integration as not being in the interest of Roma children and parents emphasized its inadequateness due to extremely high expectations which they would have to meet. Indeed, as described in section one, both schools, that accepted children were regarded as extremely good schools; besides, children are specialized to either language or gym subjects. Consequently, their curriculum was demanding and their reputation was strong, which was implied and confirmed in many interviews and conversations. In this competitive context, as informants emphasized, Roma children could not easily succeed, producing unnecessary hardship for them. One teacher summarized the situation through a powerful analogy:

> Integration is like when we expect a ladybird to fly like an eagle, but it can fly only 3 metres and not 3000, what as an eagle can (sic). In that form, integration should be banned. (Teacher, school 2)

This quotation implies another often mentioned critique of integration, which is more of a policy-oriented assessment than a phenomenological one. It claims that the nature of the decision itself was wrong and violent, according to a young mother. Respondents believed that only first grade children should have been integrated, or at maximum, the junior classes (from the 1st to the 4th grade); while seniors should have finished their education in the "Huszár" ghetto school. The educational, social and psychological advantage of that more careful implementation of integration was sometimes interpreted as the chance for easier assimilation. This way of expressing the situation may imply that the difference between integration and assimilation by definition is unclear. On the other hand, it may also imply a preference for complete cultural incorporation, of assimilation.

The hope of teachers that small children might be accommodated/assimilated more smoothly could be viewed in light of Bourdieu and Passerons's (1990) concept of "habitus," which expresses the way particular dominant ideas and beliefs are transmitted implicitly. These internalized norms and beliefs constitute habitus, the embodied disposition which has practical implications and also which organizes and reproduces the given order in such a way that it remains at the level of the unconscious. This is what Bourdieu called "symbolic domination" or "symbolic violence" (1990, pp. 1-2). By the same token, junior children, due to their young age and receptivity, can more easily internalize the norms of school ensuring a more fluent adjustment to it, and the reproduction of the dominant norms of schools. Although, indoctrination in schools is a conscious, politically defined and institutionalized "project," it is also socially inscribed in a way that it is sustained by individual and unconscious practices.

A different framing of integration emerged in the interviews, pointing to an inverse explanation. All those indicators – segregation, negative discrimination, and separation – which often characterize the situation of the Roma people, took a semantic turn and became the focal points of self-positioning of the non-Roma people. It usually meant that the benefits the Roma people enjoyed were viewed negatively by the non-Roma. In other words, all the perceived advantages which Roma people had – like separate buses for the children, financial relief in terms of schooling expenses – were seen as unfair to non-Roma people. All of these frustrations are shown in the following citation:

> We are now negatively discriminated [against]. Irritating. They have their own bus, don't pay for food. I raise my child alone, but don't have these benefits. Millions of insults and discrimination is a result of integration. (Teacher, school 1)

Other opinions that rejected the idea of integration were based on nostalgia for past educational practices, such as for separated classes and harsher pedagogical means, which can discipline and order the life of schools, ensuring morality and good conduct.

Nevertheless, there were a few respondents who clearly attached a positive image to this form of integrated education. These teachers and parents usually emphasized that integration benefits society, immediately (through equal access to quality education) as well as in the long run (ensuring better occupational chances for Roma people). Also, the proponents highlighted the fact that it does promote cultural sensitivity through addressing differences and by allowing Roma and non-Roma people to get to know one another.

Having highlighted the prevalent approaches and arguments for and against integration, in the following part of the paper I present the frequent concerns and challenges schools face, which explain the image of integration drawn above. To do so, I analyzed the junior classes and the middle/upper classes – from the 5th to the 8th grades separately – taking into consideration significant differences.

General Concerns: Perceptions of The Presence Of Roma Children

> To be a better Man, this is the essence of integration, isn't it? (Teacher, school 1)

This unanswered question indirectly represented the essence of the main concerns: the emergence of different problems and difficulties with integration. However, in this question the challenges are formulated constructively in a generalizing and moralizing manner.

Junior classes

Usually the everyday experience of teachers was that even small children have significant educational lags: reading and spelling problems, lacking basic knowledge of orientation and expressions. Besides, behaviour and accommodation problems of Roma children were also frequent. The following quote from a teacher depicted them:

In the beginning of the semester we had many problems. He was fighting with the whole school. He was a small "bellwether." Now he seems more peaceful and relaxed … besides I am surprised sometimes how he knows the answer to difficult questions, but can not write properly. (Headteacher, 2nd grade, school 2)

Behaviour problems and educational lags produced challenges for the teachers, which they regarded as an everyday battle in that teachers should pay special attention and provide extra classes for these children to accomplish as much as their non-Roma fellows; however, regarding the size of the classes – usually 26-30 children per class – these additional "tasks" were demanding and time-consuming. Nevertheless, there were teachers who devotedly emphasized that lags could be compensated for with pedagogical means and extra attention even within these conditions. They stressed the importance of their own teaching role, in this everyday battle against disadvantages.

Middle school
In the upper classes, the problems and gaps presented above were more dominant and significant. Besides, the accumulated educational disadvantages, teenage (and more serious discipline) problems aggravated the accommodation of older Roma children. In addition, teachers identified the lack of motivation and refusal to cooperate as major problems. Some teachers articulated more radically the perceived problems claiming that Roma children have no knowledge, and usually their behaviour is aggressive and ignorant. Therefore, as one teacher explained it, they tend to regard integration as a domain for educating a criminal mob. Some interviewees even talked about a threat, a feeling of insecurity due to the presence of some Roma children. One teacher told me that she felt threatened when leaving the school if she met Roma children gathered in a gang. In order to avoid trouble, as she explained, she usually walked close to the wall and waited for them to pass. Although, she acknowledged that it was likely to be an imagined fear since she admitted that they most probably would not hurt her, still she could not help her feelings.

In contrast to the constructive problem resolution strategy of the teachers of small children, these teachers emphasized that they are not equipped to cope with the problems they faced with Roma children. They did not believe that their own pedagogical means and power were sufficient to handle these educational and discipline problems, therefore they tried to ignore them. The narratives depicted that this perceived helplessness pushed teachers to regard problems as invisible. That is, teachers did not intervene in any kind of activity of the problematic children, even if it was disadvantageous regarding the students' learning achievement, as long as it was not disturbing the progress of the lesson or the order of the classroom; as long as it did not become visible.

These concerns reflect a conflicted and insecure relationship between teachers and Roma children, which produced an ignorant disposition on the side of teachers and withdrawal on that of Roma children. These insecure relations can be interpreted into a different light via the analysis of Braddock (1980), who claimed that unequal power relations in schools could be realized through minority students' rejection of class participation or aggression because of frustration, which in turn explains the teachers' (imagined or real) feelings of insecurity and being threatened. I would add that the behaviour problems of children could be seen as a compensation for asymmetrical power-relations in schools; the rejection of school norms and life, which contains the power of remaining different.

Class participation, spontaneous talks and observations clearly underscored the spatial embodiment and symbolical power of these unequal and insecure relations. Usually Roma children sat alone, rarely able to participate in class-work, with neither material (pens, books, compasses) nor symbolic means (like knowledge and fellow respect) to participate. As a result, some started to talk or act out, provoke classmates, or ignore orders. Others sat at the desk silently, and completely detached from the reality of the classroom, only engaging in some activities such as drawing, arranging papers, daydreaming, just to overcome loneliness. I suggest that the position of these children can be best described as a *stranger* position in the sense that these children are both insiders and outsiders. A stranger is a person who is a member of a group but distant from it too, since both inclusive and antagonistic strategies are applied to him or her. This definition of "stranger" originates from Simmel (1950). He stated that the stranger "is near and far at the same time," trapped "between nearness and distance" (1950, p. 407) in relation toward the "Other" group.

Nevertheless, as was continuously emphasized, there were positive examples too, where classroom relationships were neither antagonistic nor alienating. Rather, solidarity, affiliation and even personal attachment to the Roma children prevailed. As a result, the accommodation of these children was more fluid and the interactions they engaged in were more frequent, comfortable and going beyond ethnic borders, while their school achievement was balanced. This relationship, I suggest, allowed the children to be insiders, to be attached to the social life of the classroom, and to be *fellow classmates.*

Explaining Interethnic Relations: The Dichotomy of School And Home

In this section, I discuss how I looked for more substantial answers to the two questions of the paper: does contact help to overcome prejudice? and to what extent does a ghetto-image influence the teachers' and non-Roma parents' opinions of Roma children, and of Roma people at large? To do so, I list the reasons given by teachers and non-Roma parents for the different, whether successful or failed, accommodation of Roma children.

The most frequent framing of problems was to situate school and home into a dichotomous relation, in which schools were usually presented as the place for bettering; while homes were identified as the source of problems. Both teachers and non-Roma parents tended to emphasize that the education children get in schools are in opposition to the norms of Roma families. This is formulated in different ways: some were stereotyping, while others used an explicit racial discourse to clarify this opposition. By discourse I mean the opinions interviewees frequently expressed and the approaches they often took. Nevertheless, all of the circulating arguments put an emphasis on differences and otherness, demarcating the peculiar properties and particular traits of that group, that are the essence of Romaness. The representation of Roma children and their parents was often constructed through well-known images like reluctance to work, relying on social benefits and the overall cultural inferiority. This was exemplified in more detail in this quotation:

> The Guszev (Roma ghetto) is a very low socio-cultural environment and children see no positive example. They (Roma parents) are undereducated and it causes the low mental capability of these children. Plus, they marry within own kinship system, live on benefits. These all affect the mental status of children. It is in their blood, it is genetic. (Head teacher, 2nd grade, school 2)

We see here that the stereotypical image of Roma families, in turn, influenced the narratives of the children in which low mental capacity was seen as a genetically inherited quality. In addition, the Roma ghetto was seen as a devalued and fearful space although neither teachers nor non-Roma parents had ever been to the ghetto, with the exception of one or two visits. I suggest, that the fear itself to approach the Roma ghetto served as a steady legitimization for the rejection of interethnic actions, whereas, physical and symbolical distance was regarded as a guarantee of security.

The role of the Roma ghetto to define the distinctiveness of Roma people could be interpreted in terms of Isin's (2002) and Caglar's (2001) analyses on the relation of social and material space. Isin (2002) emphasised that the spatial distribution of relations can not be ignored, claiming that each space is a "socially ranked geographical space" (2002, p. 41). A symbolic space in which social relations – through domination, alienation, and unfamiliarity – are produced could be translated into a physical space too. The symbolic space has a cognitive structure, while the physical means a geographical territory. More importantly, this social or symbolic space is in a dialogical relation to the material one; therefore social struggles take place in space, but also space itself shapes them.

In that context, the isolation of Roma people in the ghetto indicated their social isolation. Having no or rare contact with the city resulted in their segregation in the social and cognitive spaces too. Therefore, the mere existence of the ghetto contributed to the bounded social, economic and political position of Roma people. Also, spatial distance characterizes the orientation toward and the perceptions of each other. In the cases reported here, spatial separateness was associated with a cultural distinctiveness, where Roma people were defined as a distinct ethnic group within a bounded territory. Consequently, the demarcated Roma ghetto space deterministically remained a distinctive "ethnospace," as Appadurai (1996) put it.

Bourdieu's (1991) understanding shines a different light on unequal relations. He stated that the power of labelling, naming and categorizing subjects represents symbolic capital, which has practical implications. It is symbolic in the sense that it consists of knowledge, signs, beliefs, thoughts and expressions. Nevertheless, it also has the power to dictate tactics, strategies and acts toward the dominated (Bourdieu, 1991). As he noted more generally: "struggles about the meaning of the social world is power over the classificatory schemes...which are the basis of the representation of the groups and therefore of their mobilization or demobilization" (Bourdieu, 1984, p. 479). The constructed image about Roma people therefore affects every-day ethnic relations, but also locates them in the social and political reality of the city.

Caglar (2001) emphasised the power of ghetto-image as a symbol for influencing the social and political discourse on exclusion and distinctiveness. She wrote about the general discourses concerning Turkish immigrants living in a ghetto in Germany, but her findings are highly relevant in our case. She compellingly noted that the metaphor of the ghetto becomes the basis for ethno-cultural understanding of citizenship of Turkish immigrants. Although in the context within which she was working, this discourse even informed policy making, I would emphasise here its potential was to shape public discourse.

Analogically, we see that the perceived relation between space (ghetto) and traits (low education profile of children) often became ethnicized in people's opinions. To be more precise, the ghetto image attached to the Roma people was mobilized in mainstream discourse which took shape in the interviews, in a way that it emphasised their discounting cultural and ethnic distinctiveness. It is all the more interesting, since the educational lags of Roma children who do not live in the ghetto were less to be explained in ethnic terms.

Having internalized the belief that the educational norm of school is unfamiliar and distant from that of Roma families, teachers tended to underestimate their power to reduce disadvantages; instead a pessimistic, neglectful and desperate approach was produced toward difficulties and toward Roma children. Havas (2008, p. 8) deemed it "pedagogical fatalism." It was often expressed through the dismissive phrase that it is only 8 hours that they spend here but then they go home, to that substandard space, which destroys the symbolical (internalization of dominant norms) and the material (educational) progress of Roma children attained during school time. The underestimation of their own teacher's role is more far-reaching since studies show (see for example Kertesi & Kézdi, 2004) that the role of the teacher in the development of children is as decisive as the role of the family.

Interestingly, other teachers and non-Roma parents explained educational lags and accommodation problems through the critique of positive discrimination, which I analyzed earlier, but from a different perspective. The critics usually emphasized that positive discrimination produced protection for Roma children, which was either not appreciated or was even used by some of them according to their self-interest.

Some interviewees emphasized that all those advantages – like their own bus, extra classes, and special attention – are not appreciated by Roma children, that these were instead perceived either as a given right or as worthless. Positive discrimination therefore became a dichotomous site of the empowerment of Roma people and of the devaluation of the interest of the non-Roma. Through this lens, positive discrimination is a source of furthering the social and political gap between Roma and non-Roma people.

In this context the rationale behind the powerful role of the separate bus in the interpretation of differences, became evident. The bus, in which Roma children travelled back and forth to the ghetto each day, was often interpreted as the emblem of separation. It separated the two groups by providing an advantage to Roma children. But also, it became the symbol of differences because the bus trip was often interpreted as a liminal, but already exclusive feature which detached Roma children from the reality of schools and transferred them to their culturally different home, to the feared world of the ghetto.

In addition, others who criticized positive discrimination usually claimed that some children abused it, misinterpreting and ethnicizing those pedagogical means with which they do not agree. To give an example:

> There is a kind of dark side of integration. Once when I tried to call her into the classroom, she told me: "don't touch me, I will call the police." My husband is a lawyer, he suggested putting not even a finger on these children, since then I could go to court. They say that if we try to keep order with them as well that we are treating them like this because they are Roma. It is not about that. It is about conduct, education and respect. (Teacher 5th grade, school 2)

This story illustrates well that positive discrimination provided a defensive strategy for Roma children, rearticulating the properties of Romaness which became in that way the site of claim-making. This ethnicization of teachers' acts served for some Roma children as a legitimization for their rejection of general rules and overall it provided an excuse for the non-participation in the life of schools. I suggest that this abusive strategy of ethnic-based advantages by some Roma children is in dialogue with the ethnicization of problems by some teachers. Nevertheless, both things – acting out Romaness and stereotyping – indicate as well as enhance separateness. They decrease the chances of successful contacts and also these phenomena obstruct the genesis of a normalized and de-ethnicized discourse where problems and difficulties could be addressed properly. The de-ethnicized discourse would challenge the socially embodied stereotyped relation between Roma and non-Roma, where problems would be examined in their own complexity in a forward-looking manner replacing the biased, ethnic-oriented explanations. Nevertheless, on the other side, we could find more nuanced, self-reflexive and de-ethnicized explanations for the difficulties of integration. They underlined that the lack of kindergarten education, the low quality of education of the closed ghetto school and the embodied biases are responsible for Roma children's hardships. They usually tended to ignore or neutralize any kind of distinction making; be it positive or negative. Rather, they promoted equal demands and standards introducing individual- and skill-based teaching methods as well as treatment. They stressed the importance of positive examples for the demolition of prejudice on two fronts. They addressed the need of the employment of Roma teachers in schools; on the other hand, they also criticized the stereotyping agency of the media. This resonates well with the study of Rabinowitz (2001) on a co-existence project in Israel. This study, although in a differently politicized context and in a critical manner, still underscored the importance of positive examples for the transformation of hitherto generalised fallacies, or at least for the moderation of stereotypes.

In addition, teachers emphasized that good cooperation with parents is a very important factor in solving problems: reducing disadvantages and ensuring better accommodation of children.. The positive disposition was understood as an appreciation of institutionalized norms (either of schools or of working places) and the ambition to break out of the vicious cycle of poverty. Therefore, those students were seen to perform better whose parents have already been integrated, as some teachers stated. This explicates the phenomenon, noted above, that the educational lags of those Roma children who did not live in the ghetto were less prone to be explained in ethnic terms. Therefore, any kind of integration, whether residential or occupational, seems to lessen ethnic-centred representations and fallacies.

Further, the findings showed that cultural differences were less emphasized in relation to Roma children who lived outside the ghetto, and who usually were in the school from the first grade. Moreover, ethnic-centred representation of teachers and non-Roma parents became almost entirely incommensurable in relation to half-Roma students. When I asked a question about the half-Roma children, usually it took time to identify them, but respondents were able to do so. Still, both the Roma who did not live in the ghetto as well as the half-Roma children – but definitely more consistently the half-Roma ones – tended to be seen as *insider* students, or *fellow classmates* entirely belonging to the life of schools in a way that their Romaness was often neutralized and had become irrelevant. Further research may be needed for more substantial analyses of the far more benevolent and de-ethnicized status of half-Roma children.

CONCLUSION

In this chapter I assumed that integration may be able to transform and challenge the ethnic representation, the 'minoritization' of Roma people ensuring interethnic meetings beyond the edge of the Roma ghetto. Nevertheless, as we saw, integration as such can challenge hostile interethnic relations only partly. The research highlighted those obstacles which hamper integration and exacerbate the struggle of Roma people to fend off ethnic stereotyping.

There was an ongoing struggle on the part of teachers for order and for the protection of mainstream norms, inherited pedagogical methods, and for fairly well defined everyday practices in classrooms. These were all challenged through integration; conformity and authority were contested and rearticulated. Sometimes, both teachers and Roma children had no means to react. On the part of teachers the protection strategies were ignorance, imagined invisibility of problems, and avoidance, but also in other instances the responses revealed teachers' hope in their work and belief in integration. On the part of children, the discomfort of the situation may have resulted in silent withdrawal from participation, or sometimes in aggression remaining outside of the realm of classrooms. I suggest that so far there is no equal participation in the life of the school; moreover, there is no real communication, instead there are patronizing or fearful approaches on the part of teachers and non-Roma parents.

Examining the rationale behind the different outcomes of contacts, and venues of participation, I found that the separateness of the ghetto powerfully influences relations. The ghetto as a symbol of cultural distinctiveness informed a stereotyping ethnic-centred perception of teachers and non-Roma parents. This antagonistic ethno-cultural framing still limited the images constructed about Roma people and worked against integration. When teachers and non-Roma parents talked about Roma children, they usually referred to the ghetto Roma children and to the problems. Rather than lessen stereotypes, integration brought to the forefront conflicts and tensions perceived along ethnic lines. The (ghetto) Roma pupils were integrated into the dominant society in schools; nevertheless, they remained separated in the ghetto before and after school and this binary relation between integration and separation has become an everyday experience for them: their social inclusion is a liminal or superficial status taking a *stranger* or *outsider* position.

The analysis also revealed that positive discrimination is another important impetus for the reproduction of hostile relations between Roma and non-Roma people, perceived by the informants as a dichotomous site of the empowerment of Roma people and of the devaluation of their interests. Nevertheless, there were also positive examples, where mutual trust, caring affiliation, successful joint group work characterized the relationship of teachers and students irrespective of origin. This relation I suggested, produces the subjectivity of the *fellow classmates*, or that of the complete *insider*.

This more benevolent approach was more often presented in relation to those Roma children who do not live in the ghetto and those who are integrated from the first grade. Moreover the analysis implied that the perceived ethnic distinctiveness (Romaness) of half-Roma children becomes almost entirely incommensurable. The rationale behind this de-ethnicized discourse (which is not informed by an ethnic-oriented understanding of the other, but by a more universal approach) vis-à-vis some Roma children is that their parents have already been integrated, as many teachers as well as non-Roma parents described. It refers to the fact that they have already participated in interethnic relations, be they occupational, educational or residential. Therefore, frequent and durable interethnic contact seems to have the power to produce a less stereotyped, but a more nuanced social discourse. This supposition is also presented in other studies. Kézdi and Surányi (2008) for example, evaluating the outcome of integrative education in thirty elementary schools in Hungary, concluded that integration can lessen stereotypes. Moreover they found that this form of education can enhance the learning achievement of Roma children in a way that does not have a negative impact on the educational attainment of non-Roma students.

From this perspective, the local government's current initiative to reopen the only-Roma school in the heart of the Roma settlement would reverse the potential benefits of integration. I suggest that in spite of the necessary hardship and challenges that integration may bring, re-segregation would cause more significant harm. It would reproduce the low educational outcomes of Roma and undermine the preparation of Roma children to participate in truly equal inter-ethnic relations, to learn about the other children and to have prospective employment opportunities. In this paper I tried to contribute to the universal dilemmas involved in the segregation and accommodation of oppressed minority students to understand the challenges and properties of classroom integration conveying important messages to the whole society.

REFERENCES

Allport, G. W. (1958). *The nature of prejudice*. New York: Dubleday Anchor Books.
Appadurai, A. (1996). *Modernity at large: Cultural dimensions of globalization*. Minneapolis: University of Minnesota Press.
Bouma, D. H. B., & Hoffman J. (1968). *The dynamics of school integration: Problems and approaches in a northern city*. Grand Rapids: W. B. Erdmans.
Bourdieu, P. (1984). Classes and Classification. In *Distinction*. Paris: Minuit.
Bourdieu, P. (1991). *Language and symbolic power*. Cambridge: Polity Press.
Bourdieu, P., & Passeron, J. C. (1990). *Reproduction in education, society and culture*. London: Sage Publications.
Braddock, I. J. H. (1980). The perpetuation of segregation across levels of education: A behavioral assessment of the contact-hypothesis. *Sociology of Education, 53* (July), 178-186.
Caglar, A. (2001). Constraining metaphors and the transnationalization of spaces in Berlin. *Journal of Ethnic and Migration Studies, 27*(4), 601-613.
Coleman, J. S. (1966). Equality of Educational Opportunity (Coleman) Study (EEOS), 1966 [Computer file]. ICPSR06389-v3. Ann Arbor, MI: Inter-university Consortium for Political and Social Research [distributor], 2007-04-27. doi:10.3886/ICPSR06389.v3.
Havas, G. (2008). Esélyegyenlőség, deszegregáció [Equal chances, desegregation]. In K.-K. Fazekas & J. János-Varga (Eds.), *Zöld könyv a magyar közoktatás megújításáért* [Green book for the innovation of the Hungarian public education]. Budapest: ECOSTAT.
Havas, G., & Liskó, I. (2005). Szegregáció a Roma tanulók általános iskolai oktatásában [Segregation of Roma students in primary schools]. Vol. 266, Edited by C. Zoltán. Budapest: Felőoktatási Kutatóintézet.
Havas, G., Kemény, I., & Liskó, I. (2002). *Cigány gyerekek az általános iskolában* [Roma children in elementary school]. Budapest: Oktatáskutató Intézet-Új Mandátum Könyvkiadó.
Isin, E. (2002). *Being political*. Minneapolis: University of Minnesota Press.
Isin, E. (2008). *Acts of citizenship*. London: Zed Publications.
Kertesi, G., & Kézdi, G. (2004). Általános iskolai szegregáció – Okok és következmények [Segregation in the primary school system – Causes and consequences]. Budapest: Magyar Tudományos Akadémia Közgazdaságtudományi Intézet Munkaerőpiaci Kutatások Műhelye.
Kézdi, G., & Surányi, É. (2008). Egy sikeres iskolai integrációs program tapasztalatai [Experiences of a successfull school integration program]. Budapest: Educatio Társadalmi Szolgáltató Közhasznú Társaság.
Rabinowitz, D. (2001). Natives with jackets and degrees. Othering, objectification and the role of Palestinians in the co-existence field in Israel. *Social Anthropology, 9*.
Sigelman, L., & Welch, S. (1993). The contact hypopaper revisited: Black-white. Interaction and positive racial attitudes. *Social Forces, 71*(3), 781-795.

Simmel, G. (1950). The stranger. In *The sociology of Georg Simmel*. New York: The Free Press.

Zolnay, J. (2005). Oktatáspolitika és etnikai szegregáció Miskolc és Nyíregyháza általános iskoláiban [Educational policy and ethnic segregation in the elementary school of Miskolc and Nyíregyháza]. Budapest: Európai Összehasonlító Kisebbségkutatások Közalapítvány.

List of Documents

Önkormányzati Közgyűlés beszámolója [Minutes from The Local Government's General Assembly] 25th of June, 2007 E-City Hall of Nyíregyháza. http://www.nyirhalo.hu/index.php?option=content& task=category&sectionid=40&id=195&Itemid=118 (retrieved November 26, 2008).

Az esélyegyenlőséget szolgáló intézkedések támogatása [Support of activities promoting equal chances]. Ministry of Education.
    http://www.okm.gov.hu/letolt/esely/23_2009_okm_rendelet_prez.pdf (retrieved June 4, 2009).

Information about the school opening in Guszev settlement http://mindennapi.hu/cikk/hirsor/ nyiregyhaza-gorog-katolikus-iskola-tobbsegeben-roma-gyerekeknek/2011-05-25/3496(retrieved November 23, 2011)

Éva Földesi
Roma Education Fund
Budapest

KATALIN R. FORRAY & TAMAS KOZMA

SOCIAL EQUALITY VS. CULTURAL IDENTITY

Government Policies and Roma Education in East-Central Europe

INTRODUCTION

Aims and Scope

The aim of this chapter is twofold: a) To describe the situation of the Roma population in Central and Eastern Europe, especially their situation in school and the education systems; and b) to analyse and compare government policies (especially educational policies) which influence the situation of the Romas and which may contribute to their future in those societies.

The twofold aim is reflected in the structure of the chapter. First, we review theoretical and practical literature on government policies of national and ethnic minority communities. Second, we introduce a collection of country case studies and their findings related to Roma schooling and education policies in Central and Eastern Europe. Third, we compare those policies in the light of the theoretical models suggested by the literature. In the conclusion, we comment on the usefulness of the models in understanding Roma education policies of Central and Eastern Europe.

There are some key words and concepts that we use here that require clarification: the people or migrating groups designated as 'Roma' are known by several names, most common being 'Gypsy' (Egyptians). There is a lack of agreement about their own names within the groups. The term 'Roma' was accepted in 1971 when the International Roma Committee organized its first World Roma Congress in London. The word 'Roma' can be used as an adjective but also as a noun. To avoid misunderstanding and to follow the use of the literature we call those people 'Roma' (singular) and 'Romas' (plural). We shall also use the same word as an adjective as well as a noun.

Central and Eastern Europe – sometimes called East-Central Europe – is that part of the European continent which remained "behind the Iron Curtain" after World War II, and was liberated from the Soviet Empire or influence by the 1989/1990 political changes. Sometimes simply called 'Eastern Europe' the region is more complex than that. The region liberated during the turbulent years of 1989/90 is therefore a mixture of both Eastern and Western traditions and values and is called in this paper as East-Central Europe (ECE) (see Johnson 1996, pp. 10-11).

D.B. Napier & S. Majhanovich (eds.), Education, Dominance and Identity, 65–81.

The chapter in its present form is an attempt to approach the 'Roma problem' in a new way. Most of the existing literature analyses the situation of the Romas, its causes and its relations. We try to analyse it in the context of existing government policies which contribute to the present situation of the Romas and which may also improve or alter their situation.

Government Policies

One of the reasons for the situation of the Romas becoming an international issue has been the political transitions of the East-Central European (ECE) countries. The demolition of the Iron Curtain multiplied the number of possible connections between the Roma communities living on the Western and Eastern parts of the Continent, and shocking news about what happened to the Romas served as an alarm for the public in other European countries because of violence and intensifying migration (Bollag, 1994; Costarelli, 1993; Crowe, 1994; Krause, 2000; Liégeois, 1994). Gheorghe (2001) described this situation as the most challenging point in the recent history of the Roma people in the ECE countries.

Guy (2001), after describing the situation of the Romas – "the largest, poorest and most marginalised minority of Europe" (p. 9) – indicated the importance of the government policies. International debates on the Roma problem "has to lead to more pragmatic policies to aid the integration of Romas" (p. 9). Stewart (2001) in the same volume presented an analysis of Roma policy in the Communist government and party showing strong proof of forced assimilation to avoid political unrest and social turbulence. Acton (1997) said that a new Roma policy is urgently needed not only at the country level – in his case the UK – but also at the European level. Government policies connected with civic activities may promise a new future for the situation of the European Romas.

In their collection, Acton and Mundy (1997) described the Roma culture which led to the 'Gypsy identity.' It may be an element of government policy that relies on the cultural identity of the Roma communities. The outstanding collection of Weyrauch (2001) went further in the same line of argument showing how traditional 'Gypsy Law' is in relation to – or in disagreement – with the majority concept of law on which public policies rely. Acton – as early as the 1970s – looked through the history of ideology concerning the Roma population, mostly in the UK. This overview showed how an ethnic ideology under pressure of Victorian reformism would lead to nationalism (Acton, 1974).

The contributors of the volume edited by Vermeulen and Perlmann (2000; see also Kozma, 2003) discussed the new wave of immigrants to Western Europe and the social and political problems that migration caused in the late 1980s and during the 1990s. Their theories suggested two major types of government immigrant politics, one relying on cultural identity, the other built on the social situations of the immigrants. The case studies that follow the theoretical part of the book reflect the realities. The authors did not find model policies in various political situations but a mixture of policies of both models.

On the basis of this short review of the selected literature, two policy models aimed at supporting education of the Romas can be seen. (Fenyes, 1999). Policy Model A deals with Roma communities as cultural minorities and aims at integrating them into the cultural minorities of the respective countries – while Policy B recognises them as groups with social handicaps. Policy A views schools and other institutions as responsible for developing Roma cultural identity by conveying and disseminating their cultural heritages. Policy Model B uses education as a means for socio-economic equality. Both policy models have sought their own means of realisation after the fall of the Soviet Empire and the political transition. Both policies are legitimate, building on real social processes, seeking solutions for discrepancies, trying to find socially and legitimately effective answers to old questions. None of these policies can achieve their goal completely; however, they reflect on an important social group, the Romas, whose demands, opportunities and public appearance have to be considered in Central Eastern Europe.

Methodical Considerations

We tried to test the theoretical models of possible policy making suggested by Vermeulen and Perlmann (2000). We took them as the possible theoretical models of the Roma education policies and studied some ECE countries and their actual policies of Roma education. The question was whether they would be applicable to the actual situation of Roma education in the ECE countries; and if so, which countries apply policy A or B. Further on, we also asked whether Policy A or Policy B would be more applicable to the actual situations of the various countries.

Nine government policies were selected to test our questions. They are the government educational policies of Albania, Serbia, Kosovo, Bulgaria, Croatia, Slovenia, Romania, Slovakia and Hungary. Case studies were conducted longitudinally between 2000 and 2009.

The dominant method of the study was the selection and collection of country cases from the point of view of their Roma schooling and education policies. First, we selected the country- and state-cases on the basis of our former studies (Forray & Szegal, 2000; Forray, 2009). Second, we looked for official data and personal connections; we also visited some countries and collected data and impressions on the spot. Third, we reorganised the collected data and tried to compare them by the help of the international statistical guides (European Roma Rights Center, 2000, *Roma Demographic Table*).

GOVERNMENT POLICIES

Albania

During the communist era governments tried to assimilate the Roma communities to the socialist Albanian society. Overall employment supported this assimilation pressure: our target group was involved in the labour market most typically as unskilled workers. Roma communities had to participate in education, public health and housing as a result of enforced assimilation.

Their situation started to decay apace after the communist era. Today most of the Roma communities live in extreme poverty (World Bank, 2005). They are targeted by discrimination in the labour market: 80-90% of Roma people were unemployed in 1996 (World Vision, 2007). Today 78% of the Romas live below the poverty line whereas only 22% of the non-Romas share the same fate. Ninety-two per cent of our target group reported difficulties with finding a job in the labour market because of lack of employment skills and social discrimination. Many of the Romas live on state or non-state (i. e. church) social aid that is still the most effective support in Albania. The informal sector is a basis for income of others who may work as musicians, construction workers, or those collecting paper or metal ware.

Lack of education also contributes to the difficult situation of the Romas. According to UNDP and UNICEF reports this characteristic is due to the poverty of Roma families (European Union, 2007). Many Roma parents are not educated either; therefore – and because of their poor financial conditions – they do not realise the importance of educating their children.

Serbia

The number of Romas in Serbia is estimated at 100 000 to 500 000 people, which is 1-6.5% of the total population. Most of these people live in city slums; according to research findings 30% of them in extreme poverty, especially around the capital, Belgrade (73%). As registration of Romas is forbidden in the country we need to emphasise that the numbers and percentages in Serbia are merely estimates. Official Serbian documentation of Romas and Kosovo refugees is often missing (Milivojevic, 2008).

Roma is the language spoken by most of the Romas and the majority of them also speak at least one other language (Serbian, Albanian, Hungarian, Romanian) depending on where they live. At first sight, the Roma population of Serbia is successful with regards to the Roma language; however statistics show that at least 70% of children do not finish primary school. According to the 2004 Helsinki report poor children in Serbia are practically excluded from education, health service and social services (Helsinki Committee for Human Rights in Serbia, 2004).

According to the data and analysis published in the report the reasons for substandard education of Roma children are dominantly poverty, negative stereotypes, discrimination and the interpretation of education in Roma communities. Experts say that the self esteem of Roma children is extremely low because of their experience with discrimination from the majority group, and negative evaluation of their own language and culture. Analysis reveals that Roma parents make their children earn money because of their poor financial circumstances. The environment of child labour is outrageous (United Nations Fund for Children, 2007).

The Serbian government has been participating in the program entitled The Decade of Roma Inclusion that was organised by the World Bank in 2005 and declared that it would improve the situation of the Roma minority as one of the priorities of the country. The fact that the presidency of the program was held by a Serb meant a significant step in 2008. In that year Serbia declared and introduced a new strategy: they invested 120 million dinars into the education of the Romas, they called on the support of ministries responsible for health services and education, ratified antidiscrimination legislation, and prepared a new bill of primary education.

The National Action Plan (2009) is the latest programme aimed at raising the status of Roma communities. A part of this plan is the employment of a respondent for Roma issues in every ministry of the government. In 2010, such an employee was working in the ministries responsible for education, health services, environment and economic projections

Kosovo

Kosovo is a partially recognised state in southeastern Europe. When international and NATO forces entered Kosovo in June 1999, the mass exodus of the 'Romas,' 'Askali' and 'Egyptians' (RAE) began. Many of them joined the Yugoslavian army to avoid atrocities. Others had to face expulsion (United Nations Development Program, 2003) and escaped to Serbia, Montenegro, Macedonia, Bosnia and Western Europe. A small group of RAE stayed in Kosovo and were labelled 'Internally Displaced' (IDP) and received permission from local authorities to reside. Ten years after they had been chased away from their homes, hundreds of Romas live in camps in settlements such as in Kosovska Mitrovica where even basic health service cannot be found.

The unemployment rate is quite high in Kosovo and is increasing annually by 10-12% (United Nations Development Program, 2003). Employment in Kosovska Mitrovica is only 22%, the level of education is very low, and the RAE are both socially and politically marginalised. Before the conflict in 1999 most of the Romas lived in Mahalla and lived as day-labourers in construction and agriculture. Some of them found permanent jobs. Traditional working positions vanished due to the decay of the economy in general and the collapse of industries. Jobs that used to be done by RAE traditionally are done by Albanians today (United States Agency for International Development, 2004).

The education level of the RAE population is low. Parents who do not understand the significance of schooling are a huge drawback for their children whose labour and salaries are needed by the family. For girls, marriage typically takes place as early as at the age of 12-14. Due to the lack of teachers with RAE background children speaking Roma languages cannot adapt to schools. School failure results from the limited number of children speaking Serbian and Albanian. The presence of NGOs in this concern is a key to success: regions, where NGOs help schooling, 70% of children who are required to go to school by law do attend schools. We can assume that in regions where NGOs support children, they can prevent girls from leaving school early (United States Agency for International Development, 2004).

Bulgaria

The Roma population of the country can be divided into three larger groups: the 'Bulgarian Gypsies,' the 'Turkish Gypsies' and the 'Vlach' which refers to the Romanian Romas. Within these larger groups the original sub-group identity is still alive to the extent that researchers describe the identity characteristics of the larger Roma group only in the case of Roma intelligentsia (Tomova, 1995).

'The Roma problem' has been an issue throughout the history of Bulgaria. Among reasons for the problem, a few should be emphasised, such as:

– the significant ratio of nomadic, non-settled groups,
– a high toll of assimilation into Muslim Turkish and Tartar communities,
– the organisation of their elite evident in cultural associations, newspapers, some schools and a theatre from the late 18th century on,
– permanent public anti-Romaism sustained by party regulations and media presentations.

The Roma Settlement Programme started only in 1954 and lasted for more than a decade. In the first phase of the programme housing estates for around 20 000 Roma families were built on the outskirts of assigned settlements. This segregated, ghetto-like settlement was shifted into the Settling into the Bulgarian Neighbourhood program in the late 1960s, prescribing the number of Roma families that could be settled in a street (Tomova, 1995).

Until the end of the 1980s the purpose of the Bulgarian government has been the creation of the united Bulgarian nation – the Turks and the Romas who had opted to identify themselves as Turks were seen as major obstacles to these intentions. The requirement to change names to make Turks seem more Bulgarian, was mandatory for the Romas as well. For example, cultural clubs and football teams were ordered to take a name of a Bulgarian hero and there was a campaign against Roma musical bands in 1984. This programme, which mainly aimed at the assimilation of the Turks has affected the Romas as well and it only stopped because of international objections. Its psychological consequences however still live on and these are articulated in spontaneous social anti-Roma campaigns, blaming the economic situation that has evolved after the collapse of the Zivkov-regime on the Romas. Crime in particular is seen as the result of nomadic Romas living in the country.

The same contradiction prevailed in the field of education as occurred in the case of settlements. One approach focused on assimilation attempts and pressure while in other cases segregation has taken place. The extremely low education level of the Roma population, the significant number of illiterates, and school age children not attending school are all features that have become more and more striking and troublesome. Three programmes were set up in order to increase the level of education of Roma communities. One involves taking children away from their families so that assimilation can work more effectively: weekday boarding schools have been set up. The other is setting up a system of Roma Schools, i.e. segregated institutions for Roma children that aimed at education at a level lower than general and focused on practising special skills. The third policy is schooling Roma children in institutions set up for the mentally disabled.

After the regime change, masses of people lost their work and became impoverished. These people have suffered mentally and physically as a result of these processes. The educational index of the Roma people is far below that of the Bulgarian and Turkish population. Roma communities live in segregated, ghetto-like settlements even today. This is how Tomova (1995) was able to sample them when she carried out research in neighbourhood circles: their housing and living conditions are far below those of the Bulgarian population.

There are two factors detrimental to the education of school age children: first, the poverty of masses who are unable to buy school equipment, feed and clothe their children properly (school equipment and catering used to be free in Bulgarian schools); and second, objections of the wealthy Vlach, especially Lovari and Keldarashi groups against pressures for assimilation, their intentions aimed at keeping their traditions.

In order to solve the educational problems the Ministry of Education and the Ethnic and Demographic National Cooperation Committee, a state organisation responsible for minorities initiated a project with UNESCO and PHARE (Poland and Hungary: Assistance for Restructuring their Economies) support. They published school books written in the three most widely spoken Roma dialects, and introduced facultative Roma language teaching or multicultural education projects in some schools.

Croatia

There are contradictory estimates regarding the total number of the Roma population in the country: it varies between 6 000 and 150 000. Unusually, the Roma Priests' Committee of the Croatian Bishops' Conference carried out its own research and found that one sixth of the Romas are Muslims. They live in the Northern region of Croatia, especially in Medjimurje County, Osijek and Baranja County, Sisak and Moslavina County and Zadar County. The most significant number of Romas living in Croatia is the so called Boyash.

The Croatian Constitution and the minority act ratified in 1991 bestowed equal rights on each national community who are allowed to be represented in parliament as long as the number of the community members reaches a certain number. In the case of the Romas the number is not high enough to enable them to send representatives to the parliament on a community basis.

In Croatia there has been no research on the living conditions, the Romas' attitudes towards the majority group or that of the majority group towards the Roma. Experts report that wealthy Romas assimilate and identify themselves as Croats while amongst the poor there are people who apply for social aid and identify themselves as Romas even if they are Croats (Forray & Szegál, 2000).

Living conditions and housing of the Romas is worse than the general level in the country; most Romas live in settlements. On the other hand they rejected the suggestion of the Croatian government that they move into the villages of expelled Serbians. Their educational index is very low: they do not attend kindergarten or pre-school, they start school at the age of 7-8 instead of the age 6, they live far away from schools, so due to the lack of proper clothing and other reasons they attend school irregularly until they become teenagers – and at this point their education is most likely over as they start their own families at an early age. Earlier endeavours aimed at organising kindergarten or schools in their settlements had not led to success and today they reject these kinds of initiatives because they suspect racism behind these efforts. Unsolved problems related to the schooling of the Romas cause real conflicts. Teachers report that most Roma children do not speak Croatian and they can hardly understand a word in Croatian because they speak "the Roma Language" at home. In their opinion this is the root of their failure at school. In spite of this factor, the number of Roma youth – probably not amongst those who live in settlements – going to secondary education is increasing slightly.

Numerous projects, initiated by the Roma Alliance in cooperation with the Ministry of Culture and the Roma Priests' Committee of the Croatian Bishops' Conference, primarily aim at developing Roma literacy and introduction of the Roma language in schools. Summer camps and schools represent another type of initiative that focuses on secondary school students, the future intelligentsia of the Roma. Organisations dealing with educational, cultural issues of the Romas lack connections to international groups. That may be the reason for the lack of multicultural and intercultural projects set up with other countries facing similar challenges (Szilágyi, 1996a).

Slovenia

There are about 6,000 to 7,000 Romas living in this country who belong to subgroups. Most of them live in the Mura Region; they speak Roma or Hungarian. In the North-West of Slovenia the Sinto settled and there are new waves of Romas moving from Kosovo and Macedonia to the region of Maribor and Ljubljana. Most of them are settled but we can also find traditional travelling Romas in Slovenia (Szilágyi, 1996b).

Since 1960 the social, cultural and legislative situation of the Romas has been a burning issue. Although a single act has not been ratified, several action plans and programmes have been developed aimed at supporting social, health and cultural conditions of the Romas.

Only one quarter of registered Roma children attend school regularly, one third of them do not go to school at all, while others go irregularly and rarely. When explaining these features, Roma families talk about traditional family occupations related to agriculture, along with poverty, early marriage, inappropriate knowledge of Slovenian, school discipline, or lack of teachers to adapt to the Roma children.

Although the social status of the Slovenian Romas is worse than that of average Slovenians, according to the action plan regarding education, social status is not the factor that causes the biggest challenge but rather language (Szilágyi, 1996b). Most Roma children do not speak Slovenian; therefore, year long language kindergartens have been organised aimed at developing children's Slovenian and other skills. One year has proved to be a short time to overcome shortcomings. The challenge is even more serious in multi-lingual regions of the country where Slovenian, Hungarian, Croatian and Roma are spoken. Therefore bi- or tri-lingual learning groups are created. Although this practice is often given as a positive example, as far as Roma children are concerned it causes extremely serious challenges. Children, whose mother tongue is Roma and who speak Roma only at home have to acquire two foreign languages at a time (Slovenian and Hungarian) and consequently they are not able to express themselves appropriately and are not able to understand transmitted information. As in these classes there are fewer Slovenian or Hungarian children – because parents register their children elsewhere – learning groups turn into "Roma classes" where education is trilingual.

Romania

Social status, including education of national communities in Romania and of the Romas is described in a report from the Romanian Institute for Human Rights (1994). According to this book the Romanian government does not find the status of the Romas problematic. They emphasise the important results as follows: The Romas in Romania received 'national minority' status and in this way they can claim the same rights as any other minorities; representatives of the Romas are involved in the work of state organisations and offices; and work has started in the field of education. As an illustration of this latter phenomenon is reporting of three schools where Roma language teaching has been introduced (EU, 2000).

Although so far only 55 pupils have participated in this programme the mere organisation of such a project is quite important considering that before 1989 Roma was not taught in Romanian schools at all. The ministry has a 'Roma issues expert' in every county, and financial support focusing on minority projects has been increased. The ministry mainly supports anti-discrimination actions. Also, the idea of setting up a research centre focusing on national and ethnic minorities was presented. Political articulation of the Romas is quite significant, Nicolae Gheorghe, the well-known representative of European Romas fights for their cultural and political rights on the European level (Gheorghe, 2001).

Slovakia

Before separation in 1991, the Slovakian government accepted a document entitled "Governmental policy concerning the Romas," which proposed several ways to improve the conditions of the Romas (Gallová-Kriglérová, 2006). This document consisted of projects regarding education, employment and housing. Although some of the projects had started the following year, after the separation, realisation of every program related to the Romas stopped because of financial problems.

73

More projects have been introduced focused on developing the situation of the Romas since 1998 (Socio-graphic mapping of Roma ..., 2004), but we cannot report significant results. Billions of Euros have been invested into building houses that should have solved housing problems of the Romas but this project led to even greater segregation. The flats were built two to three kilometres away from towns and villages in areas that do not have any connection to public services, or in the case of children – schools. The most important sponsors have been the Ministry of Construction and Regional Development and the European Union, PHARE Poland and Hungary: Assistance for Restructuring their Economies). In 2004 the government invested 200 million Euros into building low comfort social blocks of flats in towns where there is a large population of Roma. Fourteen micro regions with 134 000 inhabitants were identified. In 2006 they used 170 million Euros for renovating 24 blocks that consist of 432 low comfort flats. (Gallová-Kriglerová, 2006). These flats were built for the Romas – and problems started the very moment they were settled. They had to settle outside the town in a strange environment surrounded with new and alien neighbours without any public services. School was very far from this area, children did not even attend when the weather was bad. In the district of Presov for instance, 176 flats were built for 1236 (un-officially 1700) residents with the support of the Ministry of Construction and Regional Development. This district has become the second largest ghetto of Slovakia. The first one is situated in Kosice with almost 4400 official and another 900 un-official residents. Many of those living here do not have money so they have started to steal from neighbouring gardens. Presov is planning to build a wall around the district.

In education the traditional practice continues: Roma children are sent to special education classes without any prior psychological examination, classes where the level of education is very low and children are targets of discrimination. Today 59% of Roma pupils attend special classes. In Pavloce nad Uhom 99.5% of Roma children attend special classes. Parents often agree with schooling their children in such circumstances because they are not aware of the consequences of this kind of education. These special education institutions are maintained with a greater financial support; therefore they are ready to accept as many Roma children as they can regardless of the real skills of the pupils. "Roma children regularly face disadvantages because of inappropriate monitoring, non-transparent financial controlling, legislation deficit and enforcement" (Tichy, 2009). The Slovakian National Action Plan that is being prepared for the Decade programme declares that "the number of Roma children learning in special education classes has to be reduced" but it does not define indicators and criteria to contribute to realising this purpose. Another suggestion is creating boarding schools. Some Roma parties as well as Amnesty International argue against this kind of institution: "Deepening the segregation of Roma children beside the general education system would contribute to infringing on their basic human rights" (Tichy, 2009).

There have been successful programmes carried out between 2002 and 2006, mostly with PHARE support and that of the Roma Educational Centre in Presov. The secondary grammar school with eight grades (the Gandhi School) that was introduced for talented children in Zvolen is well worth mentioning although later on they wanted to close it due to financial problems and lack of pupil interest. A similarly successful experiment is the Hronca Secondary School in Bratislava in existence since 2004 which offers courses in English and Roma. Training Roma educational assistants is also a remarkable programme. These assistants help Roma children at school to overcome language and other barriers.

Hungary

It has been primarily the Romas who paid the price of the regime change in Hungary because of the implosion of the planned economy and slow development of the market economy. According to one study (Forray, 2009) a high unemployment ratio corresponds to a great extent to low education levels and the lack of skills. The main channel of young people's vocational education in vocational schools at the secondary level has become much narrower and in this way access to secondary education was denied to many. The Roma community is far behind the majority of the society regarding their educational and vocational index. However, compared to other countries of the region, the country can report very positive results. About three quarters of young Romas remain in the compulsory education system for eight years. The most significant challenge in 2009-2010 was education at the secondary level, the remaining four years of compulsory education.

One of the main goals of the Hungarian education policy is to prepare as many Roma children as possible for a successful start of institutionalised education because a good start can ensure the completion of the eight primary classes. There are typical programmes aimed at fulfilling this goal – a kind of streaming of Roma children either based on failures (catch-up programmes) or success (gifted education). Another intention of Hungarian education policy is to direct as many young people as possible to secondary education to train them to take the matura/GCSE exams – a prerequisite for entering tertiary education in Hungary. State and non state or partial state, so-called 'public foundational' grants support those who continue their education successfully (Dezső, 2009).

The second priority of educational policies is to treat the Roma communities as a national minority. The 1993 minority act ratified Roma communities as national minorities, the two Roma languages – Roma and Boyash – spoken in Hungary have become recognised languages as well as any other languages of national minorities living in the country. Institutions of public education receive nominal support based on educational programmes organised for Roma children. These programmes include Roma folklore and culture or are articulated as gifted education projects – tutorials for talented Roma children (Forray, 2009).

Teaching Roma languages is an on-going goal, although due to lack of teachers there are hardly any schools where the languages could be introduced. Kindergartens and schools, which aim to satisfy special educational needs of the Roma population at a quality level, are notable. In most teacher training institutions, courses on particularities of the Romas can be studied. A specialisation in Roma Studies is being organised both in elementary teacher training and at the bachelor's level.

DISCUSSION

The initial question we raised was the following. Are the two models of minority policy making applicable to the educational policy making of the selected ECE governments? And if so, which model is chosen by whom? Can the governments' Roma educational policies be modelled with the help of those theoretical types? On the basis of the government cases we look for relevant answers.

Answer 1: Common Grounds

The ECE government policies have many features in common. From a certain point of view they may be seen as very similar (see the historic analysis of Stewart, 2001). There are two reasons for this.

During the decades of state-socialism, the situation of the Romas had been shaped differently in these countries from European democracies where market-economies had flourished. The ideology of a class free society and the practice of a planned economy placed the Roma communities under strong pressure to assimilate. Bottom up community organisations were forbidden, caravan sites were illegal, employment and education was mandatory. Consequently an important proportion of Roma communities of these countries affiliated into the class of unskilled workers of heavy industry and large-scale agriculture. Counter-balancing this situation, relative social welfare of the Romas was guaranteed. Regime change caused serious problems with the introduction of representative democracy and the so called liberal market economy. The Roma communities who had just started their assimilation process during the previous 30-40 years were left with no support. Demolishing planned economies had to get rid of unskilled workers first and previously available social welfare started to disappear together with employment. The collapse of the Ceausescu regime in Romania generated an exodus among the Roma of Romania and shocked the rest of Europe. Mass petitions for asylum of Czech and Slovakian Romas in the early nineties warned the old continent that a time bomb was tickling due to the collapse of the Soviet Empire.

These post-Soviet government states were "ordered" to find solutions for the challenges represented by Romas as a prerequisite to join the European Union. Because of this and in spite of regional similarities, it is reasonable to conduct a comparative analysis of the country peculiarities.

Answer 2: Applicable Policy Models

The second answer to the initial question is that the theoretical models of minority government policies can be applied to the situation of the Romas in the ECE region. It can also be used to distinguish among government Roma education policies that seemed otherwise to be very similar because of their 'common grounds.' On the basis of the case studies the policies can be characterised as follow.

Policy A built on the concern that the Roma community is one of the national and ethnic groups: its culture, traditions and language differ from those of the majority and the other minorities as well. Being representatives of such a community, their own nationality education has to be organised according to relevant legislation. This fact reflects the demand that the culture of the Romas deserves the same level of attention and respect as any other folk groups in a country; language and every other aspect of a culture represented by its people have to be assumed, cultivated and developed. Consequently education has to be developed in a way that can serve the demands aimed at regular teaching of Roma languages and culture.

Policy B focuses on those with social handicaps. According to this policy, school has to be developed so that students who cannot get on with their studies in general circumstances could progress together with their peers. Students who are targeted by this policy are those with heavy social handicaps whether they be Romas or subjects of special education. The challenge is to guarantee equal chances for students at risk of failure because of social reasons and personal peculiarities in school: these students must have the same chance for development and progress as their peers who do not struggle with the same drawbacks. Most of the Romas in this sense belong to the category of those living with social handicaps or even more challenging: heavy social handicaps. The central task is catch-up education: finding the most appropriate ways that support these students to achieve more favourable results and more valuable school certificates.

These policy types have long traditions in the region. Both of them represent important values. The first one (Policy A) emphasises sustainability and development of Roma culture – it reveals the significance and equality of Roma culture and its components compared to other cultures. The second one (Policy B) aims at achieving equal social inclusion regardless of the nature of the social and cultural group targeted. Policy A understands the Romas as a group that can be distinguished from others by substantive cultural values and aims at ensuring individuals belonging to this group with equal social positions through cultural legislation. Policy B characterises the Romas as a group of people with social handicaps and therefore it aims at enabling them to achieve equal social positions through social justice measures. Both policies can be argued pro and contra. If Policy B prevailed, would it let the Romas be understood as a culturally different group of people? If Policy A is followed, what remains to the Romas living on the margins of our societies? Or should we instead understand the two policies as ones equally supporting our target group?

Answer 3: Combined Policies

Although our models are applicable to the ECE region and Roma policies of its governments, none of the governments follow one type of policy or the other exclusively. Rather, governments in the ECE region – as elsewhere – are combining elements of Policy A and B, as is quite common on the political scene. It is unusual that all of them prefer Policy B to A. An initial comparison of the government policies shows the following.

Both policy models are applied; the only question remaining is to what extent. Schools and education for the youngsters of Roma communities can focus on social mobility or strengthen their cultural identity. Languages can be taught in order to provide someone with skills that will give them a better chance in the difficult labour market or could steady one's community consciousness. There are policies of course that are exclusively typical of either Policy A or Policy B. For example building new housing estates in Bulgaria or Slovakia has a social nature primarily so they can be classified as a feature of Policy B. Different ways of protecting cultural inheritance on the other hand can be described as features of Policy A, even if surplus education facilitates finding one's place in the labour market.

These policies are characteristically interwoven, their pattern is coherent both historically and considering international affairs. Policy A usually appears in states where national consciousness has started to be re-formulated vigorously after the transition. It is not surprising – this kind of cultural and political atmosphere reflects the community consciousness. Policy B is typical in periods of times when one state or another is poised to join the European Union. In this case states are trying to meet the regulations of the European Union so they start to apply different forms and versions of Policy B almost irrespective of the readiness of targeted Roma communities and the achievability of results. Some leaders from the Roma communities in our case studies reject those applying Policy B because the support of the European Union has been obtained by aiming at integration and catching up. This is the case of the governments within the EU (Hungary, Slovakia, Romania, Bulgaria, Slovenia) and outside of it (Serbia).

This condition is typical of governmental policies considering Roma communities in the region. All of them are top down policies where bottom up initiatives do not fit in or fit in slightly. Bottom up policies – although we have not investigated them in the present treatise – always appear as an element of the governmental policies such as the case of the Gandhi Secondary School which exists in both Hungary and Slovakia. The more the European Union supports top-down practices, the narrower latitude is left for bottom up initiatives resulting in fewer chances to observe such policies. Because of these circumstances, governmental policies are mostly contradictory and counterproductive. Policy B intends to raise Roma communities socially; however, this intention requires discrimination, even if it means affirmative action such as building new housing estates. Policy A focuses on strengthening the cultural identity of Roma communities, although it can lead to legitimising behaviour that is not acceptable to the majority of the society; e.g. the negative relationships of Roma communities to education and culture. The government policies of Serbia, Romania and Bulgaria show these features.

The contradictions above can be traced back to the same reason. Governmental policies of the region do not aim at supporting the challenges of Roma communities – or do not exclusively target them, but rather support those of the majority group. Furthermore – and this has been typical of governmental policy of the region, especially during the period of joining the European Union – these policies are articulated in order to ease the problems of the earlier member states of the European Union. Consequently the preference for Policy B can be observed everywhere where experts from the European Union arrive who usually lack information considering the particular local Roma communities. Their reports are formulated with foreign concepts based on earlier experience in other countries. These diagnoses do not focus on the needs of local Roma communities as much as on those of the sponsors who finance the programmes.

Every society in the region has an interest in the establishment of her own Roma middle class. Without any doubt the way towards establishing Roma middle classes can be reached by Policy B. At a certain point of development however governmental policies have to recognize the benefits of Policy A, even if this concept is foreign to European communities who would prefer homogeneous political nation states. A Roma middle class supported by Policy A will necessarily require their own positions at political forums so that they can contribute to formulating their issues. In some countries – in the case of Hungary, for instance – we can already trace this process. We cannot foretell if the Romas of the region would identify themselves as national-cultural communities – as it can be observed in the case of several governments of the Balkan Peninsula (language teaching, multilingualism, ethnographical research) – or as a political entity, such as in Hungary.

To Sum Up

Two types of government policies towards Roma education have been discussed in this paper. Policy A deals with Roma communities as cultural minorities and aims at integrating them to the cultural minorities of the respective countries, while Policy B recognises them as groups with social handicaps. Policy A uses schools and other institutions to develop Roma cultural identity by conveying and disseminating their cultural heritages. Policy B employs education as a means for socio-economic equality. The two policies are partly complementary, but partly contradictory. Their representatives have been competing from the political transition (1989-93) on, and can also be connected to political ideologies and party politics. The years 2004-2010 proved to be a period of the domination of Policy B in the new EU countries of the region. Various socio-economic government projects have been launched; they have proven to be partly successful, but partly not. Policy A emphasises the outstanding importance of formal and non-formal roles of educational institutions. In this case it is hoped that the higher level of schooling would result in better chances to participate in the labour market and improved living conditions of the Roma population.

ACKNOWLEDGMENTS

The authors owe special thanks to Azra Kacapor-Nurkic and Lucia Balog-Curejova for their valuable contributions.

REFERENCES

Acton, A. T. (1974). *Gypsy politics and social change*. London: Routledge, Kegan Paul.
Acton, A. T. (1997). *Gypsy politics and traveller identity*. Hatfield: University of Hertfordshire Press.
Acton, A. T., & Mundy, G. (Eds.). (1997). *Romany culture and gypsy identity*. Hatfield: University of Hertfordshire.
Bollag, B. (1994). Roma studies on the move. *The Chronicle of Higher Education*, August 3, 37-38.
Costarelli, S. (1993). *Children of minorities: Romas*. Firenze: UNICEF.
Crowe, D. M. (1994). *A history of the Romas of eastern Europe and Russia*. New York: St. Martin's Griffin.
Dezső, R. A. (2009). Minority nationality education: A true marker of democracy. In I. Tarrósy & S. Milford (Eds.), *Regime change and transitions across the Danubian region, 1989-2009* (pp. 103-126). Pécs: Publicon Publishers.
EU. (2000). *Schools, language and interethnic relations in Romania. State policies toward Roma communities in candidate countries to the EU*. Strasbourg: Printing Office of the EU.
EU. (2007). *The CARDS programme for Albania: Needs assessment survey on minority groups in Korca and Tirana districts*. Strasbourg: Printing Office of the EU.
European Roma Rights Center. (2000). *Roma demographic table*. http://www.errc.org (03.04.2010).
Fényes, Cs. (Ed.). (1999). *Multicultural education: Policy, planning and sharing*. Budapest: Open Society Institute.
Forray, R. K. (2009). Roma children at school. *Educatio, 18*(4), 25-36 [in Hungarian].
Forray, R. K., & Szegál, B. (2000). Roma students in Central and Eastern Europe. *Educatio, 8*(2), 25-36 [in Hungarian].
Gallová-Kriglérová, E. (2006). *The impact of measures to improve the situation of Roma children in education*. Bratislava: Slovak Governance Institute [in Slovak].
Gheorghe, N (2001). *The Romas in the twenty-first century: A policy paper*. http://www.eurozine.com/articles/2001-03-12-mirga-gheorgh-en.html (03.05.2010).
Guy, W. (Ed.). (2001). *Between past and future: The Roma of central and eastern Europe*. Hatfield: The University of Hetfordshire Press.
Helsinki Committee for Human Rights in Serbia. (2004). *National minorities in conflict with a state ethnic identity*. Policy Paper. Beograd:Helsinki Committee for Human Rights in Serbia.
Johnson, L. R. (1996). *Central Europe: Enemies, neighbors, friends*. New York/Oxford: Oxford University Press.
Kozma, T. (2003). Immigrants, schooling and social mobility. *International Sociology, 18*(4), 730-733.
Krause, M. (2000). *The essential prerequisite between Romas and educational institutions*. www.romnews.com/s/perspectives1.htm (14.03.2010).
Liégeois, J- P. (1994). *Romas, gypsies, travellers*. Strasbourg: The Council of Europe.
Milivojevic, Z. (2008). *The position of the Romas in Serbia*. Beograd: Government Printing Office.
National Action Plan. (2009). Beograd: Government Printing Office.
Romanian Institute for Human Rights. (1994). *The legislative and institutional framework for the national minorities of Romania*. Bucharest: Romanian Institute for Human Rights.
Sociographic Mapping of Roma Communities. (2004). Bratislava: IVO.
Stewart, M. (2001). Communist Roma policy 1945-89. In W. Guy (Ed.), *Between past and future: The Roma of central and eastern Europe* (pp. 71-88). Hatfield: The University of Hetfordshire Press.
Szilágyi, I. (1996a). A romák helyzete Horvátországban [The situation of the Roma people in Croatia]. *Régió 1996, 3*, 69-80 [in Hungarian].

Szilágyi, I. (1996b). Romák Szlovéniában [Romas in Slovenia]. *Régió 1996*, *2*, 81-95 [in Hungarian].

Tichy, B. (2009). *The influence of the Amnesti International to the state budget of Slovakia.* http://www.sme.sk/c/3347510/branislav-tichy-na-reziu-ai-ide-cez-50-rozpoctu.html (05.05.2010) [in Slovakian].

Tomova, I. (1995). *The Romas in the transition period.* Sofia: International Center for Minority Studies and Intercultural Relations.

UN Development Program. (2003). *Kosovo factsheet on unemployment.* New York: UN.

UN Fund for Children. (2007). *Breaking the cycle of exclusion: Roma children in south east Europe.* New York: UN.

US Agency for International Development. (2004). *Early warning system Kosovo.* Washington DC: Government Printing Office.

Vermeulen, H., & Perlmann, J. (Eds.). (2000). *Immigrants, schooling and social mobility.* London/New York: MacMillan, St Martin's.

Weyrauch, W. O. (Ed.). (2001). *Gypsy law: Romani legal traditions and culture.* Berkeley/Los Angeles: University of California Press.

World Bank. (2005). *Romas and Egyptians in Albania.* Washington DC: World Bank.

World Vision. (2007). *Situation analyses of the Romas.* Rome: World Vision.

Katalin Forray
University of Pecs, Hungary

Tamas Kozma
University of Debrecen, Hungary

NATHALIE THOMAUSKE

CHILDREN'S HOME LANGUAGES IN EARLY CHILDHOOD EDUCATION SYSTEMS: HANDICAP OR ASSET?

A Comparative Study of Parents' and Early Childhood Practitioners' Attitudes

INTRODUCTION

The question of how to deal with minority children whose families have recently migrated has been central in scientific and political debates in Germany and France since the beginning of the first 'guest workers' immigration after the Second World War and following the independence of some French colonies in the 1950s and 1960s (Mecheril, 2004). In Germany, the debate about the 'integration' of so-called children with migratory background is ongoing. The focus has been on the role of the national language and, in particular, the children's competencies in speaking it as a key to school success. The pressure has steadily risen on early childhood education to teach German as early as possible whereas the children's home languages have been pushed to the background. In France, the debate on the question of language has taken a different shape. Instead of debating about how and when is best to teach French, as it is clear that in the kindergarten or preschool (*école maternelle*), the children learn French, whether or not they speak it as a first or a second language. The focus has instead been on how French is spoken in the *banlieues* (suburbs) and how it has deleterious effects on the national language. Nevertheless, the national language is also seen as a key to school success and a strong vector of the French identity and a marker of citizenship.

In the following chapter, I will focus on how children's home languages are perceived or (de)valued in the early childhood education systems by plurilingual and monolingual parents and by early childhood practitioners.

National Contexts

Since the formation of nation-states, the understanding of belonging to the nation is linked to the 'perfect' master of the 'common' national language. Although, for example in Germany and France, there was a diversity of regional languages, the idea that a nation and its territory are united by one people and by a single common language succeeded. During the process of nation building, ideologies which saw some languages as, for example, more superior or more rational than others were constructed and as a consequence the value of the national language increased over

D.B. Napier & S. Majhanovich (eds.), Education, Dominance and Identity, 83–99.

regional and minority languages (Thomauske, 2009). But as Adrian Blackledge noted: "Ideologies of language are not about language alone, but are always socially situated and tied to questions of identity and power in societies. [...] language ideologies are often contested, and become symbolic battlegrounds on which broader debates over race, state and nation are played out" (Blackledge, 2005, 31f.). Hence, alongside this linguistic assimilation, social dominance structures were established in which certain social groups were given more symbolic and material power than others; thus, distinguishing between those that belong to the nation and those who are excluded. The effects of this language ideology promoting dominance relationships is also reflected in the systems of early childhood education today, in particular, in areas such as the professionals' training or the educational content itself (Hélot, 2007, pp. 141-156; Varro, 2008).

Another important historical influence for the present-day language policy was the process of Europeanization from the 1970s onwards (Hélot, 2007). One result of this Europeanization was the creation of the European Charter for Regional and Minority Languages (1998) which recognizes languages other than the national ones as heritage languages and thus aims to revalue them. Even though, the charter was signed by France on 7 May 1999 it has still not been ratified, having instead provoked a debate about the threat which this shift to diversity could have on national unity and hence to the idea of French Republicanism and Universalism (Moise, 2008).

It could be argued that as a result of the aforementioned processes, the general acceptance in Germany as in France of the importance of multilingualism for the construction of Europe and the integration of foreign languages in the education system is limited to only a few selected global languages, such as English, German, French or Spanish (Hélot, 2007). Thus, bilingualism of élites finds a place in school and becomes valorized whereas bilingualism of the marginalized groups is not legitimized in school but is relegated to the private space and is thus made invisible. Consequentially, the home language(s) of minority children are being problematized as being a handicap for the future.

Due to their unique historical developments, the two early childhood education systems in France and Germany are quite different. The French early childhood education system is anchored in the centralist school system, in which the *école maternelle* is a part of primary school. Early childhood practitioners are teachers trained at the university. Due to republican values such as *liberté, égalité, fraternité* (freedom, equality and fraternity) every child is treated equally on the basis of a standardized educational policy. The monolingual rhetoric and the explicit assimilationist approach, based on the legacies of the nation-state formation processes and colonial language policies, have led to a language policy where the main objective is the acquisition of French. Home languages are excluded from the school domain and relegated to the private domain (Bertucci & Corblin, 2004). The idea behind this is that in order for children to have an equal starting ground they need to be freed from private influences such as family background, or group relations such as religious, cultural or linguistic backgrounds. The children are removed from their home context and are reduced to "pupils" with the primary function being to form them into French citizens and equipping them with the necessity being for them to participate in the democratic processes (Schiffauer et al., 2002; Raveaud, 2006).

The German Kindergarten (*Kita*) is organized on a federal basis in which each 'Land' (Federal State) has its own educational and social policy. Early childhood education is not part of the school system but is an element of the social system responsible for young people. Most of the Kitas are not state-run but belong to a variety of agencies depending on *Länder* (federal states) and municipalities enforcing the Child and Youth Welfare Law (Kinder- und Jugendhilfegesetz). Private agencies or organizations – such as the AWO (workers' welfare), parents' initiatives, independent agencies, the Catholic or Protestant church, or mosques – are responsible for the implementation of the law. Regarding professional training, educators or professional social workers do not receive university education but are trained in vocational schools for two to three years (Wahl, 2006). Due to decentralized nature of the education system, there is no stringent curriculum concerning the language policy or educational policy, but rather guidelines that practitioners should orient their work on which may vary from 'Land' to 'Land.' One example is the great variances in the implementation of the 'Situationsansatz' (an approach acknowledging the child as an individual and integrating its lifeworld). Since every Kita can decide how the children's lifeworlds should be integrated there are vast differences in approaching a child's plurilingualism, as a comparison between the guidelines in Berliner Bildungsplan (Preissing, 2004) and those in Thüringen (2010) shows, with the former valuing plurilingualism as part of the child's family background and as a resource for every child and the latter restricting multilingualism to its importance for the acquisition of the second language.

Since the publication of studies such as PISA (OECD-Programme for International Student Assessment) in 2001 or IGLU (International survey/inquiry of literacy competence in the primary school / elementary school) which revealed a huge discrepancy between the results of pupils with and without migration background, there has been a boom of language support measures (Deutsches PISA-Konsortium, 2001). For an overview of language support approaches in the Kita, see Brockmann (2006); Lengyel et al. (2009); Bainski and Krüger-Potratz (2008); and Maas (2008). The measures were founded on the premise that the reason for the poor performance of children with a migratory background is due to their lacking lingual skills to progress in the school system. Hence, the learning of German has been delegated to early childhood education, even if their practitioners are not trained to teach German as a second language

The discourse on plurilingualism as being either a handicap or an advantage for a successful school career varies in France and Germany. So does the degree of research into it. The extent to which the discourses can affect the domain of early childhood education has so far lacked substantial contributions. In particular, this chapter addresses the question of how the discrimination of plurilingual children is constructed, justified or explained and what (language) ideologies and discourses are hidden behind practitioners' and parents' voices. Hence, this chapter aims to establish whether and how the political discourse on plurilingualism as being a handicap or as being an advantage for a successful school career affects the practice of early childhood education.

Research Project

This study is part of a larger research project called 'Children Crossing Borders' (CCB), a research-cooperation between partners in five countries: U.S.A., U.K., Italy, France and Germany. The choice of these particular countries is based on their similarity of being democratic countries but also because of their differences in Early childhood education and care (ECEC) systems and approaches and notions of citizenship, nation, federalism, public services (Mantovani & Tobin, forthcoming). The focus of this research paper is on two of the five countries: Germany and France.

The primary goal of the project is to "give voice to hopes, beliefs and concerns of parents recently migrated about the education and care for their children" (Mantovani & Tobin, forthcoming). The interest in a comparison is not to find a 'one size fits all' solution but to learn from other examples, and therefore to be able to reflect better on the taken-for-granted daily practices. I participated in this research for two years during the end of the data collection. In the CCB project a complex video cue was used to stimulate a multivocal conversation following a polyphonic ethnographic method which was developed by the principal investigator Joseph Tobin for his study *Preschool in Three Cultures: Japan, China, and the United States* (Tobin et al., 1989; see also 2009). In order to be able to stimulate a conversation about early childhood education, the video material is richer, better contextualized, and less abstract than verbal questions asked in an interview. Another advantage is that the researcher avoids directing questions in a certain way by using certain words and terminologies which have certain political connotations. However, it is clear, that the situations in the videoclips selected for the discussion also provoke certain perspectives on the practice but maybe not as much as with specific verbalized interview questions. It is important to note that the video itself is not used as data but only as a stimulus for the focus group discussions. The sites selected for the taping of the video were comparable in demographic characteristics such as the composition of the children's group: more than 20% immigrant children, low to middle class or the location in an urbanized area. It was important to show a site which was known for its good but not extraordinary practices. The videos were taped within one week so that the children could get used to the cameras and the visitors, and to permit the researchers to get to know the children and practitioners and the typical routine of a day to be able to select four or five key children for filming also know which scenes could be typical for this setting. At the end of the week, the videotapes were shown to practitioners and parents who were then filmed themselves, or whose children were filmed, in order to get their feedback on whether they felt comfortable with what they saw. This negotiation continued in a general team meeting during which the team discussed which scenes were to be selected for the 20 minute videoclips. In this meeting the insider- outsider effect was used to select typical scenes for the national context (insider perspective) but also provoking discussions about themes which could be interesting to stimulate audiences from other countries, such as pedagogical approaches, language issues, religious concerns (outsider perspective). Some of the editing guidelines were: the sense of physical layout, sense of routines, shots suitable to provoke discussions of key issues: pedagogy, classroom management, the use of both home and second languages at school, interaction between parents and early childhood practitioners (Kurban, Rayna, & Bove, forthcoming). After that, early childhood practitioners and parents were asked again whether they felt comfortable with the edited version. The goal was to produce five videotapes which were similar in style and content and thus had common events such as the arrival, departure, morning and afternoon activities, routines, etc. but also national specifics. For example, in the German video there is a group of girls having a conflict about a hair clip and speaking or mixing Turkish and German. One example in the French videotape concerning language was that during a break the early childhood practitioner helped a minority child to fulfill the task. In this situation she tried to explain the parts of the body in French, so it became clear that there was a monolingual approach but it was not clear if the child understood French or not.

The data collection was divided into two phases: During the first phase, homogeneous parents' groups speaking the same language and coming from similar cultural backgrounds, and heterogeneous focus groups with parents from a variety of cultural and linguistic backgrounds, were organized. The national videotape was shown and the participants of the focus groups, usually between four to ten parents, were asked whether what they saw was typical for a preschool setting / practice. The ongoing discussion was provoked by open questions or follow-up questions, if themes were raised which were not in the video. The groups were facilitated by native speakers (Arabic, Turkish or Russian) so that the parents were given the choice in which language they'd like to speak. This had political and ethical implications because it acknowledges the linguistic backgrounds and it encourages building trust in the conversation (Vaughn, Schumm, & Sinagub 1996). Separately, we organized focus groups with early childhood practitioners of between four to ten participants in each country.

In a second phase, we showed videotapes made in two other countries to the same focus groups. Each country in the study was matched with two others for this step, for example, German and English and sometimes American tapes were shown to French participants, while in Germany the French and English clips were shown. Their comments about what they found attractive and repugnant in the practices of other countries served to clarify and highlight their own beliefs and values. In a cross-national study the video clips provide the same set of images to which different voices from different national contexts can react.

Analysis of the Data

Since a comparative approach was chosen comparing the language policies or language practices of two countries, several aspects needed to be considered. In the discipline of comparative education (Adick, 2008; Cowen & Kazamias, 2009; Bray, Adamson, & Mason, 2007) the first step is to determine the comparison criteria based upon which the focus groups are to be compared. Criteria for comparison, developed inductively in the research logic of grounded theory (Strauss & Corbin, 1998). Hence the criteria were developed from analysis of the literature and from the data.

In the analysis of the focus groups I followed Duchesne and Haegel (2008) and grounded theory (Strauss & Corbin, 1998), which assumes that theories can be generated inductively from data. First, data are described and an initial thematic analysis of all focus groups is made, in this case with the help of the computer-based qualitative data analysis program 'Hyperresearch' (Tobin, 2012). This description of data allows systematic treatment of data according to themes or codes that are relevant for answering the research questions. This is followed by the second step, where selected focus groups (approximately four per country) are analyzed in greater depth with sequences to generate codes and categories. With the in-depth analysis, the patterns of interpretation with respect to the language policy or language practice are identified.

RESEARCH FINDINGS

Languages Spoken at Home

The study findings revealed that parents in Germany and France feel responsible for the maintenance of their home languages. The majority of parents in both countries spoke quite often about the fear of losing their home languages and the intention to use these language a lot when speaking to their children in order to prevent them from forgetting them.

> Most of the parents are afraid that their own uh the mother tongue [will get] lost/ uh that the children won't learn the mother tongue ... they won't speak with my parents at all, with the aunts and so forth. When they are on vacation visiting somewhere, then they won't understand anything at all. Also uh, it's gone through my mind that once they get/ they'll never know where their parents' grave is, for example, ya know. They can't read ... but in the main the German language will always win. ... I believe the German language [is] everywhere: on television, the children's channels, with the girlfriends on the telephone, in kindergarten, in the schools, on the street. (Berlin, Arabic father)

In contrast to Germany, however, in France some plurilingual parents talked about the shame their children feel when they communicated in their home language:

Others look, if I say "Kwo" when my son, I speak Comorian, if we go out "Kwo" "mom, it's embarrassing" [the French expression has a familiar and stronger tone, more like, "shame on us"] [...] "What's going on?" I speak "Binthou ... [familiar way to call someone] oh, oh," there are people who look at us, there are people who look at me. And my child "mom, it's embarrassing." I told him "I don't understand French." (Marseille, Shikomor mother)

It seems that the idea of Universalism is so internalized in French society that even children get the impression at an early age that they are different when they or their parents speak their home language in the public space. Since they want to be like the mainstream monolingual French-speaking people and do not want to feel different, they are embarrassed when their parents communicate with them in a language other than French.

In Germany, the idea of early linguistics findings was that children ought to have knowledge of the basics of their first language in order to learn a second language such as German/French more easily. This approach was employed by many parents; hence, most of the parents are convinced that children need to learn their home language properly in order to be able to learn a second language:

SO: Well, she [Hayel] thinks that the mother tongue is quite important, that once the children have learned the mother tongue, well, have fundamentals in the mother tongue, that they then also learn another language much better. (Berlin, Turkish mother)

But parents seemed to agree that this acquisition takes place in the private domain and does not need to be encouraged in early childhood education.

Early childhood practitioners in Germany and France did not talk a lot about home languages in the private space. But if they did they differed in their view of the language capacities of parents and children, with early childhood practitioners in Germany tending to emphasize that home languages should be spoken and taught 'correctly' at home:

Whereas we always preach, at home the native language. (Berlin, female early childhood practitioner)

In contrast, French early childhood practitioners advised parents to speak their second language French at home and not their home languages in order to help their children to learn the dominant language more easily:

So I asked that at least one of the parents speak French at home, and then in the classroom, uh, because she came into the little section, so this was a student who began her school life early. [...] Because I think there should be a link between school and family and this link should be constructed by at least one of the parents. (Franqueville, female early childhood practitioner)

They tended to delegate the task of connecting to the early childhood educational institution to parents and do not see the necessity of contributing to this. In comparison to Germany, the private domain is more separated from the public domain. Everything that belongs to the individual's background or identification is relegated to the private domain. Initially the idea was to free the people from their religious dependence but today it serves the monolingual majority which is in a position to define what a legitimate or an illegitimate difference may be: the Christian cross is accepted but the Muslim headscarf is not. The children's linguistic background is thus denied or devalued since it is relegated to the private domain. Another problem in demanding of parents to speak their second language with the child is that the child's further language development could be in danger because he/she would learn neither the home language nor the second language properly but would be kept in an inferior position compared to the monolingual child (see Cummins, 2000).

But there were also critical views amongst the early childhood practitioners regarding this aspect:

> What I was told at the IUFM [Institute for teacher training (Institut Universitaire de Formation des Maîtres] and ... what I've tended to verify, is that in general, the child learns to speak French better, if at home ... Let's say, if the parents don't speak the French language well, it's better if they don't speak it. Because otherwise, there is a mixture of both which is not good at all. What I tell the parents, is: "if you don't know, the children ... (inaudible), he will learn at school. Speak to him in Arabic, if he masters his mother tongue well ..., his mother, yes, mother tongue, he will learn better that way". (St Gilles, female early childhood practitioner)

It seems to help some of the early childhood practitioners to get a linguistic formation in vocational or further training which can be verified afterwards in practice and change their opinions about language acquisition.

Home Languages in Early Childhood Education Institutions

Influenced by national discourses on learning deficits of plurilingual children, parents in Germany said that the main task of the Kita is to teach their children German. They understand that it is important to be able to speak German well in order to obtain the best chances for a good school career and for their future life.

> I'm not worried about the mother tongue, they'll speak that anyway, I'm always worried about the German, because that is the future for our children and their life here, they need German. They don't get that from nature, like the mother tongue, they have to learn that. (Berlin, Arabic mother)

Parents did not see the necessity of learning or speaking home languages in the Kita because they think this would happen at home naturally; although, there seems to be some ambivalence about his. On the one hand they feared that home languages will get lost but on the other hand when it comes to integrating home languages in the school system they feared that the presence of home languages in the Kita will be a handicap for learning the national language. One father phrased it thus:

I had said earlier, in Germany, German is the biggest need, more so than money, clothing. (Berlin, Turkish father)

This belief has been called the "time on task" theory of language learning (García, 2002), which leads parents to think that if early childhood practitioners are supporting home languages in the classroom they are diluting instructional time needed for second language acquisition (Gill et al., forthcoming).

Another argument for the necessity to teach German as early as possible is, as one mother pointed out, that the school system advantages children who speak the national language as good as a first language:

Discriminating the German, or non-German, or nothing like that happens, it's just that in terms of language Turks start school losing 0-1, we don't want our kids to be in that position. We send our kids to German Kindergarten so they can be educated as them, so they can talk as them. We don't want them to start school losing 0-1. (Berlin, Turkish mother)

She thought that for example children whose first language is Turkish have lost already when they enter school and that is why she expected the Kita to teach her child to speak German very well in order to avoid starting school in a worse position than first-language German speakers. This shows that parents understand very well the relations of power in society concerning their status compared to those of 'monolingual' speakers. That is also the reason for some parents to go even further and wish for early childhood practitioners to forbid speaking home languages in the Kita even amongst children.

Only some parents approved the presence of home languages in specific situations, for example, when children enter the Kita the first time:

For example one of my children doesn't speak German, that's how it was for us, since she had a Turkish educator she didn't struggle at all. But my other children struggled quite a bit because they didn't know a word of German, suddenly they're immersed in German, the first four five months were nice, until they understand German, but after that I'd personally prefer German. (Berlin, Turkish mother)

Parents in France were more ambivalent when they talk about home languages in the école maternelle. On comparing the monolingual and the multilingual approaches, parents recognized that integrating home languages in the institutions would show an acceptance and an appreciation of their plurilingual children. The following extract shows how a mother reflects about the French system:

Facilitator: In the United States, two languages are spoken by adults in the classroom.

A: They adapt to the children! We don't find that here in France, unfortunately. I said that in France there's no tolerance. They don't tolerate [foreign] origins, they don't tolerate culture, they don't tolerate difference, quite simply. Are we different because we have a different religion? We're not different because of religion, we're all similar people! But on the other hand, there are people who see that. For example, to wear a headscarf, well oops, that's a problem. It's a bad image immediately, isn't it, unfortunately. But in America, it's not like that, there's, they are really tolerant. (Mantes-la-Jolie, Arabic mother)

An additional socio-political reason becomes apparent behind the wish of integrating home languages in early childhood education: this mother was aware of the fact that her home language has a lower status in society but she wishes to integrate Arabic in a 'normal' school in order to change people's minds about this language and its value for children to learn languages that differ in their perceived social status like for example English as a high status language as well as 'low status' Arabic. Here again she spoke about the relevance of her home language as a symbol of identity and of the connection to her roots and her family:

Facilitator: And if your children had Arabic or Berber spoken at school, would you have enrolled them in the mosque to learn Arabic?

Mother 4:   No, why would I need to? They would already have the school. Why take them to the mosque then? We pay there, it's not free. […] I would really like them to go to the normal school. […] It's a language like my other language, it's more important for us (inaudible). It's the roots, like the parents, like the grandparents. (Mantes-la-Jolie, Arabic mothers)

Other parents, however, doubted the applicability to the French school system based on the idea of French Republicanism and its Universalist conception of society and the school system. They seem to have internalized this concept so deeply that they often do not see that there could be ambivalence in wishing their children to be a competent bilingual in their home language and in their second language:

It's not good to teach the mother tongue, because it creates differences between the children, and the school should be like a common mold for everyone. (Paris, Arabic mother)

Here the aspect of Universalism which rejects differences becomes clear; the mother appeared convinced that any differences made visible between the children would hinder community-building processes amongst them. This idea is possibly based on the assumption, that her child is in an inferior position compared to monolingual ones and by accentuating this difference through the attribution of the home language to the child, the relations of power between the children would become even more apparent. There seems to be a strong belief, that if the linguistic differences are made invisible, the different social positions in the society also become invisible. There is, however, an issue with this line of thought. Even though the collection of data for national statistics based on racial, ethnic or linguistic differences is prohibited and thus structural discrimination or racism is made invisible, it does not address the issue of discrimination in gaining access to workplace or apartments in wealthier areas as research has shown (Guénif-Souilamas, 2006; Perrin 2008).

Another line of argumentation for giving preference to German early schooling education was that home languages in the Kita would undermine the early childhood practitioners' ability to understand the children or hinder the ability of the children to communicate amongst themselves or with practitioners. Other early childhood practitioners who feared a loss of control if they did not understand what is going on tend to forbid speaking home languages instead telling them to speak German:

> At home the mother tongue and here German. Almost no day goes by where we don't [tell] the parents, don't just really quickly in the cloak room quickly a conversation in passing, when they have any questions, too, and such (whispers) at home native language, please, here you speak German now, yes, yes (firmly). (Berlin, female early childhood practitioner)

Concerning teacher training in questions of multilingualism, most early childhood practitioners in France and Germany were reportedly influenced by common-sense concepts of language acquisition rather than aware of recent research literature on language acquisition. They lacked adequate preparation for the task of working with second language learners. In the responses of practitioners, such as that bilingualism or a bilingual environment in the Kita or the école maternelle would lead to language confusion and to 'semilingualism,' feature prominently. The latter was perceived as a considerable risk for educational prospects.

> And if they just don't have command of their mother tongue or their first language, then they'll never learn the German. Well, if the grammar doesn't stick there (shrugs shoulders). Then it's also important that the parents then mostly only speak in the first language and not additionally try to teach broken German. And (to Galina, Franka) that then becomes twice half a language. (Berlin, female early childhood practitioner)

In order to avoid this, early childhood practitioners were generally against the presence of home languages in the institution as an obstacle to the acquisition of the national language. They saw themselves as having the task to help the children become fluent in the national language before they enter primary school in order to avoid the risk of educational failure.

> Well yeah, one can understand that, too, because especially in school the children come under a lot of pressure. There's/ there everything's done in German and if they don't have a command of German and don't properly grasp assignments, no matter in which subject, they could be very good in math, if they can't read the assignment instructions, they've lost. (Berlin, female early childhood practitioner)

But often they did not know how to support language acquisition, saying that they talk a lot but that they lack a linguistically based language approach.

One difference between early childhood practitioners' attitudes in both countries was that some practitioners in Germany were in favor of integrating home languages in order to encourage the child's identity and their roots:

> Facilitator: And how important do you [all] find that, well, that the first language/the mother tongue is also considered in the kita? Should it be considered, is that the task of the kita? How do you see that?

> Early childhood practitioner: That is totally important, that's very important, because they identify themselves by way of their mother tongue – the children, that is the/ the language that they speak at home, that's their family, that's their country, ... well that must absolutely be considered and that has to be dealt with with respect and esteem and appreciation. (Berlin, female early childhood practitioner)

When it comes to the needs of the child, early childhood practitioners thought that it is important to comfort the plurilingual child in their home language, especially when it is not able to understand German:

> Early childhood practitioner: we did try with the/ especially when they came really new into the group, always to somehow still get a little across in the national language, so that they feel at ease. But with/ is that enough!?

> Facilitator: Do you then mobilize your Russian?

> Early childhood practitioner: Yes, well, just a little bit. So that first of all the child hears that language again. And I notice that it also did help the child.. (Jena, Russian female early childhood practitioner)

This line of argument to integrate the home language of the child was also highlighted in France:

> To have a transition a bit too ... difficult for the children, I mean, I ... [...] I imagine that for the child, it's still easier to make it ... I mean, additionally the children in general have never been to school, they don't know what school is, they come, no one speaks their language. (St Gilles, female early childhood practitioner)

Early childhood practitioners in France saw the integration of home languages in the école maternelle as an opportunity for giving voice to children who are not able to speak any French. For those children a multilingual approach is seen as a possible solution.

In addition to that, the dominant discourse was that it is enriching to be able to speak many languages, but as it was shown above, this bilingualism is often restricted to the one of the élites:

> A: I think that it is actually enriching, with regards to ... [...]

B: Yes, by practicing different languages, one develops different capacities to make phonemes, to pronounce, to ... It also helps to be open to // To also be open to the mental structure of the language, one should better learn other languages. And then, personally, I find that it's enriching to be able to speak plenty of different languages. Then, it's true, maybe from country to country,

culturally, there are things that are sometimes difficult to go through ... (Mantes-la-Jolie, female early childhood practitioner and Arabic male early childhood practitioner)

CONCLUSION: HOME LANGUAGES – HANDICAP OR ASSET?

As the results of this study have shown, the public discourse in Germany as well as in France does not recognize the plurilingual competencies of minority children but in contrast portrays these children (and their parents) as being deficient and handicapped since they speak home languages and do not master the national language sufficiently, as this citation of a politician with education expertise shows:

> *leur insuffisante maîtrise de la langue française, orale et écrite, constitue un handicap pour un parcours scolaire réussi* (Children's insufficient control of the national language constitutes a handicap for a successful school career). (Lang & Bonnisseau, 2007, p. 127).

The research shows that Germany and France have got 'linguicistic' education systems, because as Skutnabb-Kangas explained:

> If the education system is organized in a way that migrant children don't achieve a high level of bilingualism and education in order to be able to claim their just part of power and resources [...] then the system operates linguicistically. (Skutnabb-Kangas, 1992, p. 49)

In order to gain access to societal resources despite their linguistic backgrounds, parents aware of this discourse and this linguicism try to adapt or even assimilate to it as they prepare their children as well as possible to these dominance structures. They understand that in Germany and France, the national language as linguistic capital plays a decisive role in and is intrinsically linked to getting access to other forms of capital such as symbolic capital (good education) and economic capital (getting highly qualified jobs) later on (Bourdieu, 1982). They differentiate between the types of languages which should be taught or integrated in early childhood education: High status languages such as English or even Chinese are therefore seen as an additional competence or capital which is likely to increase the chances on the labor market. Home languages however constitute an inferior role in the school system. A large majority of parents and early childhood practitioners think that integrating or letting the children speak in their home languages would take the time needed for the acquisition of the second language which is why they are even against using them in the early childhood education setting. Practitioners in early childhood education should be aware of theories on language acquisition and learning which have shown in contrast to common belief that children can learn several languages easily and it is even most beneficial cognitively as in the development of a 'metalinguistic competence' as well as in questions of identity in the recognition of their plurilinguistic repertoire (Cummins, 2000; Kosonen, 2007).

As was shown earlier, the discourse on plurilingualism as an asset only applies to global, colonial languages; parents do not value their languages themselves as being an important language and as an asset in the public domain. They do not see the need for the home languages to be supported by the educational system and even fear that if their children were encouraged to learn the home language, they could be made visible as 'foreigners' preventing them from being on an equal footing with the mainstream children and hence, from having equal chances later on. Home languages however play a major role in the private domain as a means of communication and they are very important for identity construction and the connection to the family and the parents' or grandparents' country of origin. Even though most of the parents do not think that it is possible to integrate the home language in early childhood education without hindering the acquisition of the national language, they would idealistically be in favor of an integrative approach, with multilingualism being seen as a benefit to their children.

As the deficit view of multilingual children persists and children are unable to develop their bilingual competencies in the school system, there are no 'Linguistic human rights' for minorities. As Skutnabb-Kangas developed in the universal declaration of linguistic human rights, which should guarantee at an *individual* level, in relation to

the mother tongue(s) (MTs), that everybody can

- identify with their MTs (first languages) and have this identification accepted and respected by others
- learn the MTs fully, orally (when physiologically possible) and in writing. This presupposes that minorities are educated through the medium of their MTs
- use the MTs in most official situations (including schools)

Other languages,

- that everybody whose mother tongue is not an official language in the country where s/he is resident, can become bilingual (or trilingual, if s/he has 2 MTs) in the MTs and (one of) the official language(s) (according to her own choice).

The relationship between languages,

- that any change of MT is voluntary, not imposed. This presupposes that alternatives exist, and enough reliable knowledge about long-term consequences of the choices.

Profit from education,

- that everybody can profit from education, regardless of what her MT is. (Skutnabb-Kangas, 1998, p. 23)

I think it is politically important to recognize that everyone should have the right and the opportunity to develop his or her plurilingualism as an asset but this should not lead to a "'sauvetage' linguistique à outrance car la langue ne vit que si elle sert" (excessive language "rescue" as the language lives only if it serves) (Felici, 2000, p. 361). As the parents stated, they do not want their children to be 'othered,' for example, with the introduction of segregated language courses. I believe it is important to avoid patronizing the parents in telling them what is the best for their children and by institutionalizing the home language or 'mother tongue' language education in such a way that choice is taken away and relations of power are reproduced. An alternative approach is taken in the Berliner Bildungsplan (Preissing, 2004) as one of the concepts of language awareness approaches where plurilingualism is integrated for everyone equally. Without forgetting the dominance of the market law or other dominance relationships, it could serve to deconstruct or reflect language hierarchies and value the individual linguistic repertoires, thus making it necessary to "instaure d'autres modes d'évaluation, d'autres valeurs que «marchandes»" (Encrevé, 2007, p. 18) (develop other methods of evaluation, values other than "commercial"). In addition, children should also be prepared to deal with racism or linguicism in order to be able to understand power relations and be able to recognize them. As the linguist Pierre Encrevé noted "L'école n'est pas là pour changer la structure inégalitaire de la société, mais peut-être pour la rendre plus supportable" (Encrevé, 2007, p. 18). (The school is not there to change the unequal structure of society, but perhaps to make it more bearable.)

REFERENCES

Adick, C. (2008). *Vergleichende Erziehungswissenschaft. Eine Einführung.* Stuttgart: Kohlhammer.

Bainski, C., & Krüger-Potratz, M. (Eds.) (2008). *Handbuch Sprachförderung.* Essen: Neue-Dt.-Schule-Verl.-Ges.

Bertucci, M.-M., & Corblin, C. (Eds.). (2004). *Quel français à l'école? Les programmes de français face à la diversité linguistique.* Paris: L'Harmattan.

Blackledge, A. (2005). *Discourse and power in a multilingual world.* Amsterdam/Philadelphia: John Benjamins Publishing Company.

Bray, M., Adamson, B., & Mason, M. (Eds.). (2007). *Comparative education research. Approaches and methods.* Hong Kong: Springer.

Brockmann, S. (2006). *Diversität und Vielfalt im Vorschulbereich: Zu interkulturellen und antirassistischen Ansätzen.* Oldenburg: BIS-Verlag.

Cowen, R., & Kazamias, A. M. (Eds.). (2009). *International handbook of comparative education.* Heidelberg, London, New York: Springer.

Cummins, J. (2000). *Language, power, and pedagogy: Bilingual children in the crossfire.* Reprinted. Clevedon, New York, Ontario: Multilingual Matters.

Deutsches PISA-Konsortium (Ed.). (2001). PISA 2000. *Basiskompetenzen von Schülerinnen und Schülern im internationalen Vergleich.* Opladen: Waxmann Verlag.

Duchesne, S., & Haegel, F. (2008). *L'enquête et ses méthodes. L'entretien collectif.* Barcelone: Armand Colin.

Encrevé, P. (2007). Entretien Pierre Encrevé. *Diversité Ville Ecole Intégration, 151,* 13-19.

European Charter for Regional and Minority Languages. The convention was adopted by the Committee of Ministers of the Council of Europe. It entered into force on 1 March 1998. http://languagecharter.coe.int/docs/Translations/German_2c_off.pdf.

Felici, I. (Ed.). (2000). *Bilinguisme -- Enrichissements et conflits. Actes du colloque organisé à la Faculté des Lettres et Sciences Humaines de l'Université de Toulon du Var les 26, 27 et 28 mars 1999.* Toulon: Presses de la Faculté des lettres de Toulon / Honoré Champion.

Garcia, O. (2002). Teaching language minorities in the United States: From bilingualism as a deficit to bilingualism as a liability. Comments to Eugene Garcia, Bilingualism and Schooling in the United States. *International Journal of the Sociology of Language, 155/156,* 125-130.

Gill, D., Fuster, T., Thomauske, N., & Zaninelli, F. (forthcoming). The multiple meanings of language: Exploring language and identity through the reflective accounts of parents and practitioners. In J. Tobin, *Children crossing borders.*

Guénif-Souilamas, N. (Ed.). (2006). *La république mise à nu par son immigration.* Paris: La Fabrique.

Hélot, C. (2007). *Du bilinguisme en famille au plurilinguisme à l'école.* Paris: L'Harmattan.

Kosonen, K., Young, C., & Malone, S. (2007). *Promoting literacy in multilingual settings.* Bangkok: UNESCO Bangkok.

Kurban, F., Rayna, S., & Bove, C. (forthcoming). The video method. In J. Tobin, *Children crossing borders.*

Lang, A.-C. & Bonnisseau, J. (2007). Le programme « Réussite pour tous » de la Région Île-de-France. In: *diversité ville école intégration n° 151,* 127-128.

Lengyel, D., Reich, H. H., Roth, H.-J. & Döll, M. (2009). *Von der Sprachdiagnose zur Sprachförderung.* Münster: Waxmann. Reihe: FörMig 5th Edition.

Maas, U. (2008). *Sprache und Sprachen in der Migrationsgesellschaft. Die schriftkulturelle Dimension.* Schriften des Instituts für Migrationsforschung und Interkulturelle Studien (IMIS), Band 15. Osnabrück: Universitätsverlag Osnabrück bei V&R unipress.

Mantovani, S., & Tobin, J. (forthcoming). Introduction. In J. Tobin, *Children crossing borders.*

Mecheril, P. (2004). *Einführung in die Migrationspädagogik.* Weinheim und Basel: Beltz.

Moise, C. (2008). Protecting French: The view from France. In M. Heller, & A. Duchêne (Eds.), *Discourses of endangerment. Ideology and interest in the defence of languages* (pp. 216-236) (Advances in Sociolinguistics). London, NY: Continuum.

Perrin, E. (2008). *Jeunes Maghrébins de France. La place refusée.* Collection: Logiques sociales. L'Harmattan.

Preissing, C. (2004). *Das Berliner Bildungsprogramm für Kinder bis zum Schuleintritt.* Senats-verwaltung für Bildung, Jugend und Sport Berlin & INA. Berlin: Verlag Das Netz.

Raveaud, M. (2006). *De l'enfant au citoyen. La construction de la citoyenneté à l'école en France et en Angleterre.* Presses Universitaires de France. Éducation et Société.

Schiffauer, W., Baumann, G., Kastoryano, R., & Vertovec, S. (Eds.). (2002). *Staat – Schule – Ethnizität. Politische Sozialisation von Immigrantenkindern in vier europäischen Ländern.* Münster/ New York/München/Berlin: Waxmann.

Skutnabb-Kangas, T. (1992). Mehrsprachigkeit und die Erziehung von Minderheitenkindern. *Deutsch Lernen. Zeitschrift für den Sprachunterricht mit ausländischen Arbeitnehmern, 1,* 38-67.

Skutnabb-Kangas, T. (1998). Human rights and language wrongs – A future for diversity. In P. Benson, P. Grundy, & T. Skutnabb-Kangas (Eds.), *Language rights.* Special issue of *Language Sciences, 20*(1), 5-27.

Strauss, A. L., & Corbin, J. (1998). *Basics of qualitative research: Techniques and procedures for developing grounded theory* (2nd ed.). Newbury Park: Sage.

Thomauske, N. (2009). *Biographien mehrsprachiger Menschen am Beispiel Französisch-Deutscher Bilingualer.* Oldenburg: BIS.

Thüringer Ministerium für Bildung, Wissenschaft und Kultur. (2010). *Thüringer Bildungsplan für Kinder bis 10 Jahre.* Berlin: das Netz.

Tobin, J., Wu, D. Y. H., & Davidson, D. H. (1989). *Preschool in three cultures – Japan, China and the United States.* New Haven: Yale University Press.

Tobin, J., Hsueh, Y., & Karasawa, M. (2009). *Preschool in three cultures, revisited.* Chicago: University of Chicago Press.

Tobin, J. (Ed.). (forthcoming). *Children crossing borders.*

Varro, G. (2008). Le bilinguisme dans le contexte scolaire français: Déficits de reconnaissance et mixités. In C. Hélot, B. Benert, S. Ehrhart, & A. Young (Eds.), *Penser le bilinguisme autrement* (pp. 175-184). Frankfurt am Main: Peter Lang.

Vaughn, S., Schumm, J. S., & Sinagub, J. (1996). *Focus group interviews in education and psychology.* Thousand Oaks: Sage.

Wahl, S. (2006). *Bildung von Anfang an/Les premiers pas.* Dohrmann Verlag.

Nathalie Thomauske
University of Bielefeld / University of Paris 13

RENÉE DEPALMA & CATHRYN TEASLEY

CONSTRUCTING SPANISH

Discourses of language hegemony in Spain

INTRODUCTION: LINGUISTIC IDEOLOGIES AND LANGUAGE HEGEMONY

How has the Spanish language come to be constructed as hegemonic in a multilingual Spanish State? While other historic Iberian languages such as the Catalan, the Galizan (or Galician), or the Basque survived, despite all odds, nearly forty years of repression during the Franco regime (1939-1975), how does language policy play out in contemporary Spain, 35 years after the fall of the dictatorship, and specifically in the country's educational system? The challenges posed to Spain's minority languages continue to this day, albeit through combined forces of transnational origins both within and beyond State boundaries. We examine language policy in Spanish schooling with an eye on such forces.

By means of comparison, we will look briefly at the role of Spanish in schooling in the United States, now home to the second largest Spanish-speaking population of the world (Ruiz Mantilla, 2008). This trans-Atlantic point of contrast will hopefully serve to further situate our conviction that language policy is, fundamentally, a power issue based on historically arbitrary social and political conditioning factors, and not so much on "rational," "viable," or "common-sense" arrangements for institutional communication, especially where schooling is concerned. In the global context of an ever-growing volume of human movement across borders, we are witness to the reactive reinforcement not only of physical borders (European Union/North Africa, US/Mexico, Israel/Palestine), but of symbolic borders as well. The development of restrictive language policies represents one such symbolic move.

Some of the same kinds of social processes involved in Spanish becoming a hegemonic language in Spain have, ironically, rendered it minoritized in the US. What these related but divergent historic processes share is the social construction of "the natural order of things" or "common sense," which paves the way for domination through intellectual social control (hegemony) rather than coercion (Gramsci, Hoare, & Nowell-Smith, 1972). Common sense in this context is a social and political construct, a set of value-laden assumptions that come to be taken for granted. The ideologies and practices of the more powerful social group become associated with status and success and are converted into cultural capital (Bourdieu, 1986), and accordingly, the language or dialect that is used by a powerful group becomes part of this cultural capital. In this sense, "free" choice can become an unwitting instrument of hegemony, as speakers of minority

D.B. Napier & S. Majhanovich (eds.), Education, Dominance and Identity, 101–118.

languages, whether Spanish-speakers in the US or speakers of other languages in Spain, may become convinced that rejecting their minority language is the most expedient path to acquiring the more powerful and promising majority language, including all the cultural capital that is thought to come with it.

Our understandings of languages and their speakers are informed by language ideologies, which Pomeranz (2002) defined as:

> constellations of people's assumptions and expectations about language and language users. They differ from beliefs in that they are shared across individuals and implicated in power relations. Whereas beliefs are often characterized as existing within peoples' heads, ideologies are seen as a social production, constructed within and through everyday linguistic practice. (p. 280)

These ideologies tend to have racist and/or xenophobic elements: popular attitudes towards certain cultural groups shape the ideologies we form concerning the languages they speak. Nevertheless, a more insidious process takes place when these speakers themselves begin to accept these ideologies in response to market forces which cast certain languages as less useful or less beneficial to future generations.

Since language status is socially constructed, Spanish has come to be associated with particularly low cultural capital in the US and other English-speaking countries, while at the same time it is hegemonic in other sociopolitical contexts, such as in most Latin American countries and Spain. In Spain, regional languages such as *Catalá* (Catalan), *Euskera* (Basque), and *Galego* (Galician/Galizan), although currently legally recognized as "co-official" with Spanish, have been marginalized both explicitly and implicitly for centuries. The language that has come to be widely recognized as Spanish actually originated in the ancient Kingdom of Castile, which came to dominate the rest of the Spanish territory by the end of the 15th Century when the Kingdom of Spain was established (Ramallo, 2007). More recently, in the 20th Century, the overt repression of Spain's minority languages that characterized Franco's dictatorship has given way to the more subtle hegemony of Spanish fostered by neoliberal discourses on educational choice, flexibility and competition, and by the lingering prejudices about languages that are conditioned by attitudes towards their speakers. A closer look at the case of Spain will provide some initial insights into how this is so.

SPAIN: THREE APPROACHES TO NORMALIZATION OF AUTONOMOUS MINORITIZED LANGUAGES

More than 40% of the Spanish population lives in areas where languages other than Castilian Spanish are spoken and protected by law. Because this protection has not always been the case – in fact, historically, these "other" languages had long been legally prohibited, persecuted and maligned – the current situation in Spain shows that (Huguet, 2007):

1. There are virtually no monolingual speakers of these minority languages.

2.   There are monolingual speakers of Castilian Spanish.
3.   While very few people are unable to understand the minority language, many report that they cannot speak it, or that it is not their habitual language of use.

Spanish is the only language whose knowledge is required by the Spanish Constitution (1978) and, indeed, there are at least 54 other current regulations that require knowledge of Spanish, and only Spanish, in order to access or carry out particular activities. One example is the requirement that packaging and instructions for all medicines be provided in Spanish (Ley 29, 2006; Plataforma per la Llengua, 2009). In each autonomous community of Spain where another language enjoys co-official status with Spanish, the rights of the minoritized language are guaranteed by statutes and implemented by various Language Planning Acts, which include:

- the Catalan Language Planning Act (passed in Catalonia 1983 and in the Balearic Islands in 1986)
- the Valencian Act (passed in Valencia in 1983)
- the Euskera Act (passed in the Basque Country in 1982)
- the Galician Act (passed in Galicia in 1983)

The legally recognized languages of Spain are Galizan (in Galiza), Catalan (in Catalonia and in the Balearic Islands), Valencian (in Valencia), Aranese (a variety of the Occitan language spoken in Catalonia), and Basque (in the Basque Country and in Navarro). In addition, some of these languages are spoken but not legally protected in other regions of Spain, such as Galizan in western Asturias. Some are also spoken outside the Spanish territory; for example, Catalan enjoys official status in Andorra, and is also spoken in parts of France and Italy. Finally, there are minoritized languages in Spain which are considerably more marginalized because they do not enjoy official status in any context; these include Asturian, Aragonese, and Caló (Spanish Romani).

It is important to keep in mind that while knowledge of the co-official languages of Spain is not legally required, as is Spanish, Article 3 of the Spanish Constitution does recognize their official status in their respective autonomous communities and acknowledges the linguistic richness of multilingual Spain as a cultural heritage that should be afforded particular respect and attention. Furthermore, all of Spain's Language Planning Acts share the expressed goal that children emerge from schooling with equal competence in both majoritized and minoritized languages. In this sense, along with the media, political policy and discourse, etc., the school is recognized as a crucial vehicle for the development of linguistic competency in the minority language.

As this brief overview suggests, the linguistic terrain of Spain is considerably more rich and complex than is usually understood (see Lewis, 2009, for an online version of Ethnologue's linguistic map of Spain and Portugal). Despite their co- of Ethnologue linguistic map of Spain and Portugal). Despite their co-existence in the modern Spanish state, there are significant cultural and historical differences among Spain's 17 autonomous communities. The three autonomous communities that we have chosen to examine here, Catalonia, the Basque Country, and Galiza, differ widely in terms of linguistic attitudes, proficiencies, preferences, and language planning policies. In the following sections we will provide a summary of key aspects of the sociolinguistic realities and educational responses in each.

Catalonia

Catalonia's co-official language, Catalan, shares a common romance language heritage with Castilian Spanish, and therefore has a relatively high degree of mutual comprehensibility with Spanish, Galizan, Portuguese and other peninsular and non-peninsular Latin-based languages (but see Penny 2000, p. 14, for a discussion of the subjective and situated nature of mutual comprehensibility). It is perhaps the community that has had the most successful language planning programs in the Spanish State, in part due to a historical connection between Catalan language rights and the resistance to repression from Franco's dictatorial regime (Beswick, 2007). Spanish and Catalan have strong associations with class, political struggle, power, and belonging, which combine to provide a strong framework for language revitalization: "Catalan, far from being heard as public or unclassed, is associated with an elite … [that] had the gateway to socioeconomic success and upward mobility during the 1950s" (Sabaté Dalmau, 2009, p. 40). While this elite never comprised the very highest echelons of society reserved for the largely Spanish-speaking upper class, Catalonia has a historically powerful Catalan-speaking mercantile class. Thus, when early waves of middle-class immigrants arrived from South America, particularly from Argentina, they were faced with a largely unanticipated need to learn Catalan in order to participate in the local finance and business markets (Puigcercós, 2010). As Spanish-speaking working-class immigrants from other regions of Spain and from other Spanish-speaking countries have tended to settle in Spanish-speaking enclaves (in the 1960s and 1980s, respectively), the association of Catalan with the business class, as well as with the anti-Franco struggle, have strengthened its role as a marker of prestige and community identity.

As with all of Spain's autonomous communities, Spanish was the only permissible language for schooling during the Franco dictatorship. In 1978, when the formation of the Catalan government marked the end of the dictatorship, the use of Catalan became obligatory in school (Decree 2092/1978), and the normalization process began with the introduction of three hours of Catalan per week. With the Linguistic Normalization Act of 1983, School Boards were free to choose from three basic language models:

- Normalization Model, where Catalan is the medium of instruction throughout the schooling process, with the exception of Spanish as a subject area.
- Immersion Model, where schooling begins in Spanish and Catalan is gradually introduced until parity with Spanish is attained.

– Minimum Catalanization Model, where Spanish is the medium of instruction throughout the schooling process and Catalan is used only as legally mandated.

By sheer force of demand, the Minimum Catalanization Model practically disappeared over the next decade, while the immersion model fell to 10% and the Normalization Model increased from 45.1% in 1984 to 88.8% of schools in 1993 (Pradilla, 2001). With later educational reforms (Decree 75/1992 of 9 March and Decree 94/1992 of 28 April) these different models were eventually replaced with what can be considered the current model, where children learn predominantly in Catalan regardless of their family language, and Spanish as well as English are studied as separate subjects. As of 2001, 75% of all public schools at the nursery and primary levels were taught entirely in Catalan, while 30% of secondary schools were taught entirely in Catalan and 70% were taught in both languages. A comparison of the 1991 and 1996 census reveals that the strong language revitalization efforts in Catalonia have not gone unrewarded: reported comprehension levels have gone from 93.76% to 94.97%; expression levels have moved from 68.34% to 75.30%; and writing proficiency has increased from 39.94% to 45.84% (Huguet, 2007). Most interestingly, knowledge of Catalan is at its peak among the younger generations schooled in the language, whereas the lowest proficiency levels are reported by those from 55 to 64 years of age. Nevertheless, despite the strong emphasis on the minoritized language in schooling, children in Catalonia do not seem to suffer diminished capacity in Spanish; reading comprehension in Spanish, for example, is comparable with that of children from the rest of Spain (Huguet, 2007).

The education system in Catalonia favors the minoritized language with clearly demonstrated linguistic advantages, illustrating that providing extra schooling support for the minority language does indeed foster a balanced bilingualism more than programs that appear more "balanced" in their distribution of languages. Nevertheless, there are detractors; in 2007 a group of 50,000 Catalonian citizens proposed that Catalonia replace the schooling system with one based on the US Two-Way Immersion, or TWI model (in Spanish "inmersión recíproca") program which, they claimed, offered equal balance of instruction in the two languages and resulted in "perfect bilingualism" (Asenjo, 2007). Actually, these TWI programs often favor the minoritized language in the early years just as the current Catalonian system does (Howard & Sugarman, 2001; Quintanar-Sarellana, 2004), but they seem to be taken up here strategically (and inaccurately) as a language planning model that provides equal instruction in both languages without compensating for language hegemony. The proposal was rejected, but reveals that the commonsense logic of balance – despite sociolinguistic realities and research evidence to the contrary – constitutes a compelling discourse in the public and political imaginary.

The Basque Country

Euskera, the language spoken in the autonomous Basque community, enjoys co-official status as well in neighboring Navarra, but not in France, where it extends throughout the western half of the French Département of Pyrénées-Atlantiques. Basque is not a romance language like Catalan and Galizan, and is vastly different from Spanish in terms of vocabulary and grammar. Basque literary culture has tended to prioritize oral language over written. A written form of the language was not historically incorporated at the institutional level, where most official documents were written in romance languages; nevertheless, an oral literary tradition has survived in a form of extemporaneous oral poetry known as bertsolaritza (Cenoz & Perales, 2001).

Despite this scarce literacy tradition, as well as the effective elimination of Basque from public functions until the end of the Franco regime in 1975, the language has been making a good recovery, even considering the added difficulty of learning two such disparate languages as Spanish and Basque. According to the most recent sociolinguistic survey (2006), 30.1% of the 1,850,500 inhabitants of the Basque Autonomous Community over the age of 16 reported that they speak both Basque and Spanish well. A further 18.3% are passive bilinguals, who understand but do not feel they speak the language well, and just over half (51.5%) consider themselves to be non-Basque speakers. The outlook is even more positive when taking into account time and age factors: the percentage of self-reported competent bilinguals rose from 24.1% to 30.1% in the last 15 years, and the percentage of passive bilinguals has grown from 8.5% to 18.3%. Furthermore, the government estimates that the population of people under 16, who were excluded from this study, are actually the fastest growing bilingual population, with over two-thirds bilingual (Basque Country Administration Department of Culture, 2008). This success does not mean, however, that Basque as a minoritized language no longer needs protection and revitalization efforts given that Spanish remains dominant in most areas of the Basque country; there is often no communicative need to use the language; it is quite difficult for adult Spanish-speakers to learn; and, while Basque proficiency is one of the most influential factors in its use, most of those who have learned the language continue to use more Spanish (Cenoz, 2009).

There are six main Basque dialects, but the common form used in official language interactions (government administration, schools, etc.) is the standardized *Batua*, developed by the Basque Language Academy in the late 1960s. Since 1983, the Basque Community Department of Education and Culture has organized schooling according to three different models:

(1) Model A: All subjects, except Euskera, are taught in Castilian. Euskera is taught as any other common subject, with a weekly dedication of four to five hours.
(2) Model B: Both Castilian and Euskera are used for teaching other subjects. Castilian is used for reading, writing and mathematics, and Euskera is limited to the remaining curriculum subjects. Euskera and

Castilian are taught as subjects also, and for the same amount of hours as in model A for both of them.

(3) Model D: All subjects, except Castilian language are taught in Euskera. Castilian is taught as a subject from the beginning, for the same amount of hours as Euskera in model A. (Huguet, 2007, p. 78)

Model B, which was originally only available at the primary level, is now available at the secondary level as well. Interestingly, while the models were originally chosen with family language in mind, so that Spanish-speaking children might choose the Spanish-dominant Model A or the gradual introduction of Euskera/Basque in Model B, the vast majority of Basque parents have elected the two more Basque-dominant models B and D.

While Model A is still the most popular at the secondary level, in the 20 years after the 1982/1983 school year, the distribution changed:

- The number of pupils following model A (Spanish dominant) decreased from 79.34% to 30.85%.
- Those following model B (Spanish/Basque) increased from 8.49% to 22.41%.
- Those following model D (Basque dominant) increased from 12.17% to 46.74%.

In summary, 90% of students in primary education study either mostly in Basque (Model D) or in Spanish and Basque (Model B) (Huguet, 2007). This overwhelmingly popular movement on the part of Basque parents to ensure that their children are educated, at least in part, through immersion in the Basque language, is coherent with 2006 statistics showing a high percentage of support for the government's overall linguistic revitalization efforts: Almost two-thirds (64.7%) of people above the age of 16 support the promotion of Basque language usage (24% are neutral and 11% are opposed) (Basque Country Administration Department of Culture, 2008). Nevertheless, these efforts are not entirely unproblematic, as might be expected. It has been argued that the tendency for Basque speakers to opt out of Model A might be connected to the tendency of new immigrants to select this model, which could lead to insider/outsider groupings divided across language lines (Huguet, 2007). Furthermore, the tendency for Basque identity to be constructed in a particular ethnic and gendered fashion can serve to exclude some residents of the Basque Autonomous Community, including Basque women, from this collective sense of cultural and linguistic belonging (Echeverria, 2010).

Galiza

The Galizan language is indigenous to the autonomous community of Galiza, as well as parts of Asturias, Castile and León, and Extremadura. Like Spanish and Catalan, it is a romance language and, in fact, shares common origins with Portuguese. Although there is a movement in Galiza to recover these historical Portuguese connections by adopting a similar orthography (reintegrationism; see

Álvarez Cáccamo, 1999), the Autonomous Government has chosen to adopt a more Spanish-style orthography in the current normative version of the language, which was established in 1983 (with some minor modifications in 1995 and 2003). Galizan was included, along with Basque/Euskera, in the 2001 edition of UNESCO's Atlas of the World's Languages in Danger, but in the 2009 edition Galizan was eliminated due to its proximity to Portuguese, a move that reflects a methodological shift rather than a real improvement in the sociolinguistic condition of the language (Freixeiro Mato, 2010).

According to Autonomous Government statistical surveys from 2003 and 2008, Galizan remains the language of preference for the majority of speakers (56.4%, while 42.6% now prefer to speak Spanish). While Galizan in Galiza may not be in immediate danger of extinction, perhaps the most powerful threat is its very low social status, even in the eyes of many Galizan people. The strength of the prejudices against the language and its speakers is illustrated by the Royal Spanish Academy (Real Academia Español) dictionary definition of *gallego* (the Spanish word for both the language and the person): the fifth entry is: *tonto – falto de entendimiento o razón* (stupid – lacking in understanding or reason) (Real Academia Español, 2010). As recently as February of 2010, Spanish president José Luis Zapatero was publicly referred to by a political opponent as a "gallego," to which the opponent added, "in the most pejorative sense of the term," demonstrating that prejudice toward Galician persists today (Rosa Díez, 2010).

Like the other minoritized languages of Spain, Galizan was excluded from official use during the nearly 40 years of dictatorship, including as a vehicular language for schooling. But a class-based stratification of language status had already begun centuries before, when Castilian Spanish-speaking nobles of the Trastámara dynasty (1369-1555), along with their clergy, scribes and servants, ushered in a new sociopolitical model:

> From this time on, Galicia's sociolinguistic fate was sealed: in an attempt to recover their lost social prestige, the Galician nobles gradually substituted their language for that of the Castilian nobles, and Galician as a written language vanished once and for all from the official documents after the first third of the sixteenth century ... at the end of the medieval period, Galician had no ruling class of its own to foster the consolidation of its language's social prestige ... (but) continued to be the everyday language of the common classes. (Ramallo, 2007, p. 23)

The recent rates of decline in language use and the pattern of this decline among Galizan people are cause for concern. The number of speakers who reported using the language habitually fell from 43% in 2003 to 30% in 2008, and the numbers are particularly worrisome for the younger age groups: only among people aged 50 or above are there now more habitual Galizan-speakers than those who usually speak Spanish. And the tendency for Galizan language loss in the cities is profound, as can be seen in the percentage of urban families whose members consider themselves habitual Galizan speakers as follows: Ferrol 3.93%; A Coruña 5.34%;

Pontevedra 6.74%; Lugo 10.45%; Santiago de Compostela 10.62%; and Ourense 13.59% (Instituto Galego de Estadística, 2010).

Students who complete compulsory schooling have been found to have slightly less oral competence in Galizan than in Spanish, while their written competence was found to be "clearly superior" in Spanish ("A competencia en galego," 2010). A recent study of Galizan teacher trainees found that while most of them reported Galizan as their mother tongue, only 55% considered their Galizan competence to be good, as opposed to 76.8% who considered themselves to be competent in Spanish. While most of these students were bilingual, this shift in competence within one generation is striking (Loredo Gutiérrez, Fernández Salgado, Suárez Fernández, & Casares Berg, 2007). While the current situation is not hopeless, the increasing apathy on the part of the Galizan government is nevertheless worrisome (Freixeiro Mato, 2010). This is particularly striking given the data for the Basque and Catalan languages, which seem to have enjoyed considerable revitalization at the hands of proactive autonomous government initiatives, including education policies.

The Galizan Linguistic Normalization Act (Ley de Normalización Lingüística, 1983) stipulated that educational authorities were to develop measures to promote the progressive use of Galizan in teaching; nevertheless, Galiza has recently undergone a restructuring of its educational system that actually loosened previously modest protections of Galizan instruction. The Language Law of 2007 (Decree 127), which had until 2010 regulated more closely the use and promotion of Galizan in the educational system, recalled that the ultimate objective of the schooling system is to produce children who are competent speakers of both languages, and, to this end, dictated the following measures:

- At the early childhood education level, teachers should use whichever language is predominant among the children, but, in Spanish-speaking areas, Galizan should have the same degree of presence as Spanish.
- For primary education, Galizan must be the vehicular language of instruction for a minimum of 50% of the time, and mathematics, cultural, social, cultural and natural environmental studies and education for citizenship and human rights must be taught in this language.
- For compulsory secondary education (until age 16 in Spain), Galizan must be used for at least 50% of instruction, and this must include mathematics and citizenship education.
- For post-compulsory secondary education (the final two years of pre-university schooling) the percentage of Galizan cannot fall below 50%, but there are no further restrictions in terms of assigned subject areas.

The Plurilingualism in Non-University Education Decree of 2010, which became official on 20 May, 2010, constitutes a step backward in several respects (Nova Escola Galega, 2010):

- At all levels the specific minimum requirement that 50% of the teaching should be in Galizan has been removed, although there is still an overall statement that the languages should be present in balanced proportion throughout the schooling process. This is undermined, however, by the mandatory presence of a foreign language ("mainly English"), whose use in schooling is now protected alongside Galizan, a turn that further weakens a language policy originally enacted in 1983 to serve – if only rhetorically (Álvarez Cáccamo, 2005) – the revitalization of the autonomous minoritized language. Following parental approval, English can become the vehicular language for as much as one third of the children's schooling.

- At the early childhood level teachers are still expected to try to make sure that children reach some level of competency in both languages, regardless of their home language. However, there is no longer any specific mention that Galizan must be maintained at 50% in Spanish-speaking areas, and home language is now determined by consultation with individual families, rather than by the school administration's analysis of the school's linguistic context.
- At the primary level, parents are to be consulted every four school years about the vehicular language of instruction for the various subjects, although, as a general rule, cultural, social, and natural environmental studies should be in Galizan and mathematics is to be taught in Spanish (note that mathematics had been assigned to Galizan in the previous Language Law of 2007, and it was not negotiable).
- At the secondary level, parents are to be consulted every four school years about the vehicular language of instruction for the various subjects, although, as a general rule, social studies and natural sciences are to be taught in Galizan and mathematics, technology, and chemistry/physics are to be taught in Spanish.

Particularly curious is the complete disappearance of any mention of "linguistic normalization," a term which the current General Secretary for Linguistic Policy has described as "a concept from the 1960s that is so semantically devalued that I prefer to leave it to the specialists, to give lectures and to write articles in specialized journals" (Puñal, 2010, our translation from the Galizan). Moreover, the assignment of Spanish to subjects generally judged to be the most important: mathematics, chemistry, and physics, does little to enhance social perceptions of Galizan as a socially relevant language – a goal established in the recently overridden legislation ("Normalización," 2010).

The term "plurilingualism" is appropriated for the title of the law, but this kind of multilingualism loses its meaning as it is incorporated into a popular discourse that functions more as a slogan to justify further marginalization of an indigenous language than it does as a sound sociolinguistic and educational principle (Silva, 2010). Indeed, the president of "Galicia Bilingüe" (Bilingual Galiza), a group opposed to Galizan normalization through schooling, has made it clear that it is the option to remain monolingual that they are fighting for: "We are not campaigning for bilingualism. We call ourselves Bilingual Galicia; this means that Galiza is a territory with two languages, and every Galizan will be whatever he or she wants, bilingual or monolingual" (Lombao, 2010, our translation). Nevertheless, if monolingual Spanish speakers who live in bilingual regions of Spain remain unable to converse in the minority languages, speakers of these languages will be forced to address the former in the hegemonic language; thus, the only way to ensure the language rights of the bilingual minority language speakers is to require minimum competency levels (Huguet, 2007).

DISCOURSES OF BALANCE AND CHOICE: FROM NEOLIBERAL DISCOURSE TO HEGEMONIC LANGUAGE POLICY

Endemic to the current rhetoric of linguistic planning in Galiza are discourses of balance and individual rights to choose languages as if they were personal commodities. With Franco's dictatorship well behind us, and despite the current co-official status of the three minority languages described here, utilitarian concerns have convinced large numbers of Spanish people living in historically bilingual areas that monolingualism in the majority language is a right worth campaigning for, and the Galizan autonomous government has essentially legislated that campaign into action by converting schools into a free-choice market, where parents can opt out of bilingualism for their children.

Perhaps not surprisingly, this neoliberal discourse in Galizan educational politics resonates very closely with educational policy discourse circulating on the other side of the Atlantic, where Spanish has been constructed as a minoritized language with respect to English. Given that the United States has no official language at the national level, Spanish (an indigenous language in some parts of the country) as well as indigenous languages such as Navajo and Hawaiian can be seen as being replaced by a particularly hegemonic immigrant language (English). Colonial practices such as punishing children for speaking their native languages in schools have given way to neoliberal processes that construct (English) monolingualism as power. Despite large concentrations of Spanish-speakers in some areas of the USA, controversial campaigns such as "English for the Children" (1997), responsible for California Proposition 227 that was passed in 1998, and Arizona's Proposition 203 that was passed in 2000, sought to eliminate first-language instruction (Onenation, 1997; see also Proposition 227, 1998 & Propositon 203, 2000). These kinds of policies are supported by dominant discourses, both popular and elite, that propagate deficit views of bilingualism and (certain) bilingual speakers, and construct the dominant language as the only legitimate form of cultural capital. Parents, and even children sense that the dominant language provides greater access to opportunities (i.e. power) in society (Nuñez-Janes, 2002). In the US, many Spanish-speakers have been convinced of the alleged utility of monolingual English instruction; a sentiment echoed famously by Richard Rodriguez's (1982) renowned phrase "the loss implies the gain."

Such language ideologies transform the neoliberal discourse of individual choice into an instrument of hegemony. In the two US propositions mentioned above, for example, important and complex pedagogical issues pertaining to language of instruction were submitted to popular vote. As a result, bilingual education was abruptly abandoned in favor of "English Only" programs, and this despite declarations from leading sociolinguists specializing in linguistic diversity

111

in learning, such as Lily Wong Fillmore (1998), who has strongly opposed such approaches in the US, as well as similar research by international scholars (Baker, 2000; Cummins, 2000; Skutnabb-Kangas, 2000). Sound research findings on language learning are now similarly disregarded in Galiza, where current language policy relies on consultation with parents rather than professional educators or language specialists to determine the vehicular language of instruction for their children.

The claim made by the current General Secretary for Linguistic Policy that recent language policy reforms are based on the "idea of balance between Galizan and Spanish" contradicts an assertion he himself made in an earlier school guide on language that drew upon empirical research. In that publication, he asserted that, "This willingness to convert Galizan into the vehicular language of instruction, in light of what has happened over the past 25 years, is a necessary condition for education to guarantee acquired competency in the two co-official languages, as it is Galizan competency that requires specific action" (Fernández Paz, Lorenzo Suárez, & Ramallo, 2008, p. 156, our translation). The new principle of family choice, particularly around a minoritized language of historically low social prestige, is also called into question by this same earlier text: "Certain prejudices and stereotypes surrounding Galizan are maintained, to varying extents, within families. [I]n certain areas the level of Spanish-ization is so high that, in many cases, parents are not motivated to transmit Galizan to their children" (Fernández Paz et al., 2008, p. 128, our translation).

Indeed, the Council for Galizan Culture has argued that the notion of balance perverts the sociolinguistic understanding of language hegemony by conflating ends and means:

Sociolinguistic research demonstrates that the hegemonic language in Galiza is Spanish (although it is not the language of the majority of the population), from the perspective of social value as well as in terms of the students' lived worlds. Therefore, the objective of bilingual competency cannot be based on a philosophy of language balance in schools ... [The 2010 Decree on "plurilingualism"] relegates the notion of balance to the means rather than the end, confusing 'the equitable presence of two languages' (a qualitative notion) with the identical division of school time between them (a quantitative notion). (Consello da Cultura Galega, 2010, our translation)

Similar discourses can be seen in the failed proposal for TWI-style "balanced" bilingual education in Catalonia mentioned above: while a successful process of language revitalization involved using predominantly Catalan as a compensatory measure, opponents considered this to be "social exclusion" and "inequality" for Spanish-speakers: "[I]n this aberrant linguistic immersion system, Spanish-speaking children are denied by this monolingual system the possibility of an adequate knowledge of Spanish" (Asenjo, 2007, our translation). Like the strategically-named "Bilingual Galiza" campaign, these protestors ignore the legacies of historical linguistic domination and adopt a victim discourse for speakers of the currently hegemonic language (Spanish). Invoking the rhetoric of "reverse discrimination," they claim that their individual language rights are being denied by the "imposition" of the minoritized language in schools (see the official website for Galicia Bilingüe, 2010).

Similarly, a recent mandate requiring some government workers to attend Basque language classes (at government expense) was described in the US newspaper The Wall Street Journal as a "Basque Inquisition," a term particularly laden in this context, given the historical burning at the stake of those Basques deemed witches, at the hands of the Spanish Inquisition (Echeverria, 2010). The article also portrayed the language as "an ancient language little suited to contemporary life," offering as evidence that there are 10 different words for "shepherd," while words like "airport," "science" and "democracy" have been newly minted (Johnson, 2007). Similar popular associations with rural lifestyles plague the Galizan language: a recent campaign initiated by three major universities uses the slogan "In Galizan you can do science, too" to disrupt hegemonic language policies that "seek to relegate the use of Galizan to talking with chickens, pigs and dogs" ("As universidades," 2010).

IN CONCLUSION

We began this analysis by briefly reviewing contexts in which Spanish has been constructed as a low-status language, particularly in the US, where political struggles to exclude certain immigrant groups have coded "immigrant" as "Spanish-speaker" and resulted in an extremely low status for Spanish and its speakers. Proposition 227, which banned bilingual education in California, was cleverly titled the "English for the Children Initiative" and successfully marketed immigrant assimilation by playing upon Spanish-speaking parents' fears that Spanish language instruction might deny their children the "tools they needed to succeed in the American economy" (Salomone, 2010, p. 153). In the Galizan/Spanish context, the Bilingual Galiza campaign employed similar strategies to construct Spanish, alternatively, as the language of success in a very different socio-political framework.

By focusing here on a political context in which Spanish has been imbued with high cultural capital – as opposed to being cast as a deficit in California and, most recently, in Arizona – this analysis serves to highlight the socially constructed nature of this capital. Furthermore, as Pennycook (2001) pointed out, Bourdieu's concept of cultural capital is open to criticism on the basis that it can be a purely reproductive notion that fails to consider the potential of agency coming from the ranks of the marginalized to effect change. Drawing upon Judith's Butler's postmodern understanding of performativity (Butler, 1997), Pennycook defined a critical applied linguistics as one that can "escape overdeterministic, overtotalizing critical analyses ... [R]ather than the deterministic view of culture that suggests that it is merely a representation of social difference and therefore a means by which social inequality is reproduced, we can now start to develop a notion of cultural difference and struggle" (Pennycook, 2001, pp. 127-128). By exploring the ways in which Spanish has come to be constructed so differently in the US and

113

Spanish arenas of language and power, by examining the discourses and counter-discourses that play across these transnational struggles for language rights, we hope to contribute some cross-cultural insights that support the ideological struggle for minoritized language rights.

The Universal Declaration of Linguistic Rights (1996) recognizes not only individual rights (for example, belonging to a speech community and using one's own language in both public and private spheres) but also "collective rights of language groups," which include the teaching of languages and cultures and an equitable presence in communication media. Furthermore, this important declaration recognizes the myriad ways in which prejudices, colonialism, and neoliberal market forces co-construct linguistic hegemony, as evidenced by the list provided of sociopolitical factors that affect language situations, including:

- The age-old unifying tendency of the majority of states to reduce diversity and foster attitudes opposed to cultural and linguistic pluralism.
- The trend towards a worldwide economy and consequently towards a worldwide market of information, communications and culture, which disrupts the spheres of interrelation and the forms of interaction that guarantee the internal cohesion of language communities.
- The economicist growth model put forward by transnational economic groups, which seeks to identify deregulation with progress, and competitive individualism with freedom, and generates serious and growing economic, social, cultural and linguistic inequality.

Unfortunately, such sociolinguistic insights are undermined by the concession that acculturation is acceptable as long as it is on the basis of free choice. The declaration insists that acculturation, or the substitution of minority cultural characteristics with those of the majority cultural group, "must on no account be forced or induced and can only be the result of an entirely free choice" (Universal Declaration of Linguistic Rights, 1996). In its uncritical evocation of free choice, this document fails to protect against sociopolitical processes of language hegemony such those described in this chapter.

By contrast, the European Charter for Regional or Minority Languages, signed by 24 member states since it was implemented in 1992, focuses not on individual language rights but on the responsibility of states to safeguard the historical regional or minority languages of Europe throughout all aspects of schooling. The languages of "migrants," however, are expressly excluded under this cultural framework (Salomone, 2010, p. 215). According to one of the Committee members responsible for the drafting of the charter, this emphasis on language as cultural heritage rather than collective linguistic rights for minority groups was a necessary concession to ensure the signing of countries who might have been reluctant to allow language rights violations to be pursued in court (Gramstad, 2010).

In fact, in the case of languages such as Galizan, Basque and Catalan, it may be more effective to draw upon cultural heritage arguments rather than invoke the linguistic human right to "mother-tongue" instruction, as legitimate and just as this right may be (Skutnabb-Kangas, 2000). For we have seen how in the Galizan context this individual-rights argument has been appropriated by organizations such as Bilingual Galiza to invoke "the right of the student to receive early instruction in their mother tongue" ("Galicia Bilingüe," 2010). After all, they campaign under the slogan "It is people who have rights, not languages."

Interestingly, the Right Honorable Terry Davis, Secretary General of the Council of Europe 2004-2009, relates that the Council chose the Basque Country for their April 2009 conference because of Spain's "outstanding" record on promoting its minoritized languages:

Spain has an outstanding record in the protection and promotion of its regional or minority languages, since some of them have official status. We should also note that the autonomous communities, notably the Basque region, have done extremely well in the implementation of [the Charter]. (2010, p. 7)

That said, our comparative and historical analysis of three different Spanish Autonomous Communities nonetheless demonstrates that Spain's record is more complex and uneven than is represented by the Basque situation, and that its progressive policies are far from stable or protected.

The Center for Applied Linguistics (CAL) in the US recommends that teachers explicitly address with children the unequal status of languages. One of their criteria for exemplary practice is that "issues of language status are frequently discussed, and particular consideration is given to elevating the status of the (minority) language" (Howard, Sugarman, Christian, Lindholm-Leary, & Rogers, 2007, p. 84). Ignoring these historical processes can leave us open to neoliberal discourses of personal choice, equal balance, language as personal commodity and, in some political arenas, to protest-rhetoric involving reverse discrimination and imposition.

REFERENCES

Álvarez Cáccamo, C. (1999). O "galego" frente ao "português," ou a lógica social da diferença. In C. Fernández (Ed.), *A lingua e a literatura galegas nos alicerces do Terceiro Rexurdimento (1976-2000) / La llengua i la literatura gallegues als inicis del Tercer Ressorgiment (1976-2000)* (pp. 43-49). Terrassa: Xunta de Galicia/Amics de les Arts i Joventuts musicals de Terrassa/UNED-Terrassa.
Álvarez Cáccamo, C. (2005). Final de sequestro. Sobre o "Plan Xeral de Normalización da Lingua Galega." In Novas de Galiza (Ed.), *O país na janela* (pp. 23-25). Lugo: A Fenda Editora.
As universidades acusan á Xunta de "castrar" o idioma galego. (2010, 03-06-2010). *Xornal de Galicia.* Retrieved 4 June, 2010 from http://www.xornal.com/artigo/2010/06/01/politica/universidades-acusan-xunta-castrar-idioma-galego/2010053123572806901.html.
Asenjo, M. (2007). 50.000 catalanes exigen el bilingüismo en la escuela para rescatarla del fracaso *ABC.* Retrieved 23 May, 2009 from http://www.abc.es/hemeroteca/historico-27-12-2007/abc/Sociedad/50000-catalanes-exigen-el-biling%C3%BCismo-en-la-escuela-para-rescatarla-del-fracaso_1641518881992.html.
Baker, C. (2000). *A parents' and teachers' guide to bilingualism.* 2nd Edition. Clevedon: Multilingual Matters.
Basque Country Administration Department of Culture. (2008). *Fourth sociolinguistic survey.* Retrieved

23 May, 2009 from http://www.ogasun.ejgv.euskadi.net/r51-341/es/contenidos/informe_estudio/ sociometro_vasco_31/es_soc31/sociometro_vasco_31.html.

Beswick, J. (2007). *Regional nationalism in Spain: Language use and ethnic identity in Galicia.* Clevedon, UK ; Buffalo, NY: Mulilingual Matters.

Bourdieu, P. (1986). The forms of capital. In J. G. Richardson (Ed.), *Handbook of theory and research for the sociology of education* (pp. 241-260). New York: Greenwood Press.

Butler, J. (1997). *Excitable speech: A politics of the performative.* London: Routledge.

Cenoz, J. (2009). *Towards multilingual education: Basque educational research from an international perspective.* Bristol, UK/Buffalo, NY: Multilingual Matters.

Cenoz, J., & Perales, J. (2001). The Basque-speaking communities. In M. T. Turell (Ed.), *Multilingualism in Spain* (pp. 91-109). Clevedon: Multilingual Matters.

Cummins, J. (2000). *Language, power, and pedagogy: Bilingual children in the crossfire.* Clevedon: Multilingual Matters.

A competencia en galego é menor ca en castelán ao rematar a ESO. (2010, 5 May, 2010). *Xornal de Galicia.* Retrieved 5 May, 2010 from http://www.xornal.com/artigo/2010/05/05/politica/estudantes-tenen-menos-competencia-galego-ca-castelan-ao-remate-do-ensino/2010050514294300137.html.

Consello da Cultura Galega. (2010). *Ditame do Consello da Cultura Galega Sobre as "Bases para a elaboración do decreto do plurilingüísmo no ensino non universitario de Galicia."* Retrieved 2 February from http://consellodacultura.org/files/2010/02/ditame_ccg_bases_decreto.pdf.

Davis, T. (2010). Foreword. In Council of Europe (Ed.), *Minority language protection in Europe: Into a new decade* (pp. 7-9). Strasbourg: Council of Europe Publishing.

Echeverria, B. (2010). For whom does language death toll? Cautionary notes from the Basque case. *Linguistics and Education, 21*(3), 197-209.

Fernández Paz, A., Lorenzo Suárez, A. M., & Ramallo, F. (2008). *A planificación lingüística nos centros educativos.*

Fillmore, L. W. (1998). *Declaration of Lily Wong Fillmore.* Presented at the State of California hearing "The Case Against Proposition 227," held on July 15, 1998 in San Francisco. Retrieved 23 May, 2009 from http://www.humnet.ucla.edu/humnet/linguistics/people/grads/macswan/fillmor2.htm.

Freixeiro Mato, X. R. (2010). Perigos, incertezas, e perspectivas de futuro para a lingua galega. In G. Sanmartín Rei (Ed.), *Lingua e futuro.* Bertamiráns: Laiovento.

Galicia Bilingüe (n.d.). Retrieved 11 May, 2010, from http://www.galiciabilingue.es/.

Galicia Bilingüe recurre el decreto "para ganar un poco de libertad." (2010, 04-06-2010). *Xornal de Galicia.* Retrieved 4 June, 2010 from http://www.xornal.com/artigo/2010/06/01/politica/galicia-bilingue-recurre-decreto-ganar-poco-libertad/2010060113043100547.html.

Gramsci, A., Hoare, Q., & Nowell-Smith, G. (1972). *Selections from the prison notebooks of Antonio Gramsci* (1st ed.). New York: International Publishers.

Gramstad, S. (2010). The Chater's monitoring mechanism: a practical perspective. In Council of Europe (Ed.), *Minority language protection in Europe: Into a new decade* (pp. 29-40). Strasbourg: Council of Europe Publishing.

Howard, E. R., & Sugarman, J. (2001, March). Two-way immersion programs: Features and statistics. Retrieved 14 October, 2003 from http://www.cal.org/ericcll/digest/0101twi.html.

Howard, E. R., Sugarman, J., Christian, D., Lindholm-Leary, K. J., & Rogers, D. (2007). *Guiding principles for dual language education* (2nd ed.). Washington, DC: Center for Applied Linguistics.

Huguet, Á. (2007). Minority languages and curriculum: The case of Spain. *Language, Culture, and Curriculum, 20*(1), 70-86.

Instituto Galego de Estadística. (2010). Enquisa de condicións de vida das familias: Coñecemento e uso do galego. Retrieved 5 May, 2010 from http://www.ige.eu/web/mostrar_actividade_estatistica.jsp?idioma=gl&codigo=0206002001.

Johnson, K. (2007, November 6). Basque inquisition: How do you say shepherd in Euskera? *Wall Street Journal.*

Ley 3 (1983). 15 de junio, de normalización lingüística. Retrieved 3 March, 2009, from http://noticias.juridicas.com/base_datos/CCAA/ga-l3-1983.html.

Ley 29 (2006). 26 de julio, de garantías y uso racional de los medicamentos y productos sanitarios. Retrieved 3 March, 2009 from http://noticias.juridicas.com/base_datos/Admin/l29-2006.html.
Lewis, M. (2009). *Ethnologue: Languages of the world*, 16th edition. Dallas, TX: SIL International. Retrieved 15 December, 2011 from http://www.ethnologue.com/.
Lombao, D. (2010, 26 March). Xornal de Galicia. *Gloria Lago: "Se Feijóo non cumpre o que prometeu, podemos darlle moitas sorpresas."* Retrieved 27 March, 2010 from http://www.xornal.com/artigo/2009/09/20/politica/gloria-lago-feijoo-non-cumpre-prometeu-podemos-darlle-moitas-sorpresas/2009092021324779400.html.
Loredo Gutiérrez, X., Fernández Salgado, A., Suárez Fernández, I., & Casares Berg, H. (2007). Language use and Galician attitudes in Galicia. In D. Lasagabaster & A. Huguet (Eds.), *Multilingualism in European bilingual contexts: Language use and attitudes* (pp. 40-64). Clevedon: Multilingual Matters.
Normalización: As teses negacionistas. (2010, 18 March). *Galicia Hoxe*. Retrieved 18 March, 2010 from http://www.galiciahoxe.com/indexSuplementos.php?idMenu=55&idNoticia=527358#abajo.
Nova Escola Galega. (2010). Opina: O borrador da lingua. Retrieved 13 May, 2010 from www.nova-escola-galega.org.
Nuñez-Janes, M. (2002). *I'm Mexican, I'm Mexican-American: Conflicting and oppositional identities in a bilingual school*. Paper presented at the 23rd Penn Ethnography Forum, University of Pennsylvania.
Penny, R. (2000). *Variation and change in Spanish*. Cambridge: Cambridge University Press.
Pennycook, A. (2001). *Critical applied linguistics: A critical introduction*. Mahwah, NJ: Lawrence Erlbaum Associates.
Plataforma per la Llengua. (2009). 500 disposicions impositives del castellà a casa nostra. Retrieved 15 April, 2010 from http://www.plataforma-llengua.cat/media/assets/1583/500_lleis_que_imposen_el_castell_des_2009_DEF.pdf.
Pomeranz, A. (2002). Language ideologies and the production of identities: Spanish as a resource for participation in a multilingual marketplace. *Multilingua, 21*, 275.
Pradilla, M. Á. (2001). The Catalan-speaking communities. In M. T. Turell (Ed.), *Multilingualism in Spain* (pp. 58-90). Clevedon: Multilingual Matters.
Proposition 227 (1998). California primary voters' guide. Retrieved 21 September, 1997 from http://primary98.sos.ca.gov/VoterGuide/Propositions/227text.htm.
Proposition 203 (2000). Arizona Secretary of State election pamphlet. Retrieved 10 October, 2000 from http://www.azsos.gov/election/2000/info/PubPamphlet/english/prop203.htm.
Puigcercós, J. (2010). *A lingua propia nas sociedades multiculturais*. Paper presented at the Universidade de Vigo Facultade de Filoloxía e Tradución, Vigo, Spain.
Puñal, B. (2010, 15 January, 2010). Anxo Lorenzo: "A estas alturas eu xa non teño moi claro que é a normalización." *Tempos Dixital*. Retrieved 15 January, 2010 from http://www.temposdixital.com/?p=2836.
Onenation (1997). Campaign for Proposition 227 (California) and Proposition 203 (Arizona). Retrieved 21 September, 1997 from http://www.onenation.org/.
Quintanar-Sarellana, R. (2004). ¡Si Se Puede! Academic excellence and bilingual competency in a K-8 two-way dual immersion program. *Journal of Latinos and Education, 3*(2), 87-102.
Ramallo, F. (2007). Sociolinguistics of Spanish in Galicia. *International Journal of the Sociolinguistics of Language, 184*, 21-36.
Real Academia Español. (2010). *Diccionario de la Real Academia Español*, 22nd edition. Retrieved 5 May, 2010: http://buscon.rae.es/draeI/SrvltConsulta?TIPO_BUS=3&LEMA=cultura.
Rodriguez, R. (1982). *Hunger of memory: The education of Richard Rodriguez*. New York: Bantam Books.
Rosa Díez (2010, 25 February). Zapatero es gallego en el sentido más peyorativo de término. *El Pais*.
Ruiz Mantilla, J. (2008). Más 'speak spanish' que en España. *El País*. Retrieved 13 December, 2011 from http://www.elpais.com/articulo/cultura/speak/spanish/Espana/elpepucul/20081006elpepicul_1/Tes.

Sabaté Dalmau, M. (2009). Ideologies on multilingual practices at a rural Catalan school. *Sociolinguistic Studies, 3*(1), 37-60.

Salomone, R. C. (2010). *True American: Language, identity, and the education of immigrant children.* Cambridge, MA: Harvard University Press.

Silva, B. (2010). *Un modelo de educación pluralingüe para Galicia.* Paper presented at the Seminario sobre lingua, sociedade, e politica.

Skutnabb-Kangas, T. (2000). *Linguistic genocide in education, or worldwide diversity and human rights?* Mahwah, NJ: L. Erlbaum Associates.

The Universal Declaration of Linguistic Rights. (1996). Retrieved 15 May, 2009 from http://www.linguistic-declaration.org/index-gb.htm.

Renée DePalma & Cathryn Teasley
University of A Coruña

PART III

LANGUAGE, EDUCATION, LANGUAGE OF INSTRUCTION AND IDENTITY

ZELIA BABACI-WILHITE

AN ANALYSIS OF DEBATES ON THE USE OF A GLOBAL OR LOCAL LANGUAGE IN EDUCATION

Tanzania and Malaysia

INTRODUCTION

In this chapter I will discuss and analyze issues related to the theories, policies and practices of language choice in education. The scope will be global, reviewing debates and choices around the world, but will give special attention to two countries, Tanzania and Malaysia. I will explore the relationship of Language of Instruction (LoI) to local debates on cultural identity and employment, as well as the influence of global actors and development discourses. My intention is to contribute to debates on the science and policies of LoI and to contribute new insights on policies concerning the use of language in education. I will give particular attention to three questions: a) Given the strong evidence for superior learning when the medium of teaching and learning is a local language, why are some Asian and African countries choosing a global language (English, French or Portuguese) as LoI? b) What have been the relative influences of governments, development agencies, consultants and educational discourses at both the global and national levels on the formulation of LoI policies? c) What are the implications of these LoI policies for quality learning, local identity, work prospects and participation in the global economy?

The chapter is based on research in Tanzania carried out in 2008 and in Zanzibar carried out in 2009 and 2010. As well as a review of recent literature on Malaysia. In Tanzania, I interviewed government officers, academicians, policy makers, Non Governmental Organizations (NGOs) staff and journalists to elicit their understanding of the aims of language and educational policies and I did classroom observations to see how teaching and learning take place with the focus on LoI. I have extensively reviewed the LoI literature from Tanzania and Malaysia before and after my fieldwork. When it comes to LoI in Tanzania the research has been part of a project named LOITASA (LoI in Tanzania and South Africa), a University of Oslo-based project which has examined educational and language issues in Tanzania and South Africa from 2001 until 2012.

Over the course of the past two centuries, first through colonialism and more recently through globalizing economies and international development, English, French, Portuguese and Spanish had taken the place of local languages in educational programs in many parts of Africa and some parts of Asia. The introduction of "Western education" in the context of schooling or formal

D.B. Napier & S. Majhanovich (eds.), Education, Dominance and Identity, 121–132.

education with specialized curriculum, syllabus and professional teachers, instructors and trainers emerged in Africa in the late 1800s during the colonial era 1885-1960 (Kimizi, 2007). This emergence has continued to the present through globalisation. Geo-JaJa and Yang (2003) describe globalization in the context of Africa in four stages, a) slave trade, which extracted labor and disrupted local societies b) colonialism, which divided the continent without regard to ethnicity and cultural boundaries, c) neo-colonialism, which imposed political and economical pressure, d) the neo-liberal ideology, bringing free trade regimes which shrink space, time and borders through New Information and Communication Technologies (NICT). Furthermore Napier (2011) argued in the education context that many features of globalisation are based on "the global trend of countries lending and borrowing educational policies, English dominance and implications for other languages especially indigenous languages, and elements of creolization, as imported ideas are adopted and variously implemented within a country" (Napier, 2011, p. 59).

In the global context Africa's issues on LoI are not unrelated to China, Russia and many other countries. Africans associate school learning with English and French. When it comes to the choice of language as a medium for teaching and learning, English and French dominance is growing around the world; however, most countries are still using their local language as LoI. Africa is an exception. There is no instance of any secondary school system in Africa which uses a well developed African language in its curriculum. This choice of language is extremely important not only because of the implications for quality learning, but also because of the intimate ties between language and culture. In the global context, English and French are taught as foreign languages in most countries today. This is because a global language is essential as a communication tool and increases the capacity to move from region to region. However, many Africans confuse the importance of learning a foreign language with the choice of LoI. Learning in English may result in improved English skills, but the evidence clearly shows that learning in a non-local language is detrimental to learning and knowledge acquisition (Brock-Utne, 2007; Qorro, 2009; Babaci-Wilhite, 2012).

My focus in this chapter will be on the recent changes in LoI in Zanzibar (in Tanzania) and Malaysia. Both have a British colonial legacy, and both have had a history characterized by debates about language politics and the choice of language in education. Tanzania made an early choice to use Kiswahili as the LoI in primary grades, but that policy has been contested for many years, partly due to pressure from global agents such as the World Bank (Brock-Utne, 2006). Brock-Utne (2011) mentioned that researchers like Crossley and Watson (2003) criticized the uncritical international transfer of educational policy and practice from one country to the other, one continent to the other and that greater attention should be paid to contextual factors. Babaci-Wilhite and Geo-JaJa (2011) argue along the same lines that contextualized curriculum and languages are essential not only for the development of the country but also for the learning process. These universal issues make Tanzania a unique case since Tanzania is one of the few countries in Africa which chose an African language, *Kiswahili* as its national official language.

Today, Kiswahili is the principal means of communication among different ethnic groups in Tanzania and in the government. Nonetheless, the Kiswahili LoI policy in the elementary schools in Tanzania is under threat. Tanzania and Malaysia have both linked the use of their national language to national identity. Tanzania made a political decision to use Kiswahili in schools shortly after independence, but only got as far implementing the policy for primary schools. English is used as LoI from secondary school onwards. In spite of several research projects and evaluations of quality learning in Tanzania, including Vuzo (2007), Mwinsheikhe (2009), Brock-Utne (2007) and Qorro (2009), all of whom recommended continuing Kiswahili through secondary education, a recent decision by the Ministry of Education and Vocational Training (MoEVT) ordered a switch from Kiswahili to English as a LoI for Mathematics and Science studies from grade 5 in primary schools in Zanzibar which will start in 2014. By contrast, Malaysia opted for a change to English in Mathematics and Science education several years ago, but recently reversed their policies and reinstated Bahasa Malaysia as the LoI as of 2010 (Gill, 2005).

HISTORICAL BACKGROUND FOR THE DEBATES ON LOI

Before the colonization of Africa, the usual practice was that each social group educated its children in its own language. Throughout the colonial period (1885-1962), education was formalized and the use of colonial language as a LoI was promoted by both colonial administrations and Christian missionaries (Kimizi, 2007, p. 1). A reaction to this change began in the early 20th century, as African pride and a desire for self-determination began to assert themselves. In East Africa, a movement to promote Kiswahili began in the 1930s. Between 1930 and 1964 an Inter-territorial Language Committee promoted the standardization and development of Kiswahili in Tanzania, Kenya and Uganda. Kiswahili became one of the official languages of the African Union in 2003. According to Brock-Utne (2008), a few years after Tanzanian independence, "in 1967, Kiswahili became the medium of instruction throughout the primary school system in Tanzania" (p. 104). The National Kiswahili Council, in Kiswahili Bakita (Baraza la Kiswahili la Taifa) was founded in 1967 by a government act in Tanzania mainland. In 1983, Bakiza, the Zanzibar Swahili Council was founded in Unguja (Zanzibar) by the Revolutionary Government of Zanzibar. In 2004, a new council was established the Zanzibar Swahili Council Act no.4 of 2004, which strenghened the mandate to promote and encourage the development and usage of the Swahili Language throughout Zanzibar and the United Republic of Tanzania in general and outside Tanzania in particularand other matters which strengthened Kiswahili in the society (Zanzibar Swahili Council Act no.4, 2004).

At the end of the 1970s President Nyerere appointed a Presidential Commission on Education to review the entire education system. The Commission recommended changing the LoI in schools to Kiswahili from January 1985 and in universities from 1991. However, in August 1983 the Minister of Education (MoE) declared that the Ministry was not yet ready for the change. The implementation of Kiswahili was delayed, but in 1997 the government categorically reaffirmed its intention to make the change to Kiswahili (Mulokozi et al, 2008). By 2009, the policy had still not been implemented and in fact was reversed by the Education and Training Policy of 2009 (not yet adopted), which suggests that even government primary schools may choose English as the LoI. In my research in Tanzania, I found that this policy is partially based on a misunderstanding among both government agencies and parents; the belief that using English as a LoI is the best way to improve English skills.

Malaysia shares Tanzania's British colonial legacy. Gill (2005) stated that after independence in 1957, Malaysia chose to reduce the role and status of English and select one autochthonous language, Bahasa Melayu renamed as Bahasa Malaysia which Asmah (1992) explained further that the government of Malaysia at the independence, then called Malaya, chose Malay or Bahasa Melayu as its national language. During that period of strong nationalism, the government did not feel the need to change the name of the language. Later, the racial tensions of the sixties spurred the government to rename the national language as Bahasa Malaysia, the language of Malaysians "these two terms are used interchangeably – Bahasa Melayu to signify that it is the language of the Malays and Bahasa Malaysia, to signify that it is the language of Malaysians" (Asmah, 1992, p. 157). Bahasa Malaysia was made the official medium of government and education as well as the official language to be used in government and as the LoI at all levels. One of the motives behind this policy was to unite the linguistically diverse groups in Malaysia (Heng & Tan, 2006).

However, the government did not attempt to control language use in the private sector, including business and industry, where increasing integration into the global economy contributed to a growing demand for English. In 2003, the government reversed its LoI policy, changing the language used in teaching mathematics and sciences to English in Malaysia (Prah & Brock-Utne, 2009). Six years later, in January 2010, the Malaysian government made a decision to reverse this policy (effective from 2012). The Prime Minister reported to the Parliament that students had not shown significant improvement in these subjects over the six years in which they were taught in English (Zalkapli, 2010). Another factor in the decision was growing protests from residents of rural areas. Representatives of local governments and schools argued that students from rural areas were disadvantaged in national tests because of their lack of familiarity with English.

According to Cavanagh (2009), the pressures to use English in mathematics and science is a reflection of how much attention those subjects are now receiving in the international sphere, and how nations are struggling to balance their desire to gird students for the global job market against issues of national pride and the desire to preserve and promote the use of a native language. Given that Zanzibar in Tanzania and Malaysia are moving in opposite directions on the choice of language in science education, a review of the theories, practices and politics behind these decisions promises to shed light on the broader debates on the consequences for learning, cultural identity and global integration. As Rwantabagu (2011, p. 460) argued "Eurocentric in nature in the sense of ensuring the supremacy of English or French as the dominant channel of communication, knowledge acquisition and cultural production" where he quoted Arnove and Arnove's (1998, p.2) statement that "language policies are central to an understanding of how colonial powers attempted to use schools to assimilate acculturate and control colonized populations." At any rate we can question when African policy makers will revise their language policies according to the realities of today and what is happening in other countries such as Malaysia in the study presented in this chapter.

THEORIES WHICH INFORM THE DEBATES

Foucault (1988) claimed that belief systems gain momentum (and hence power) as more people come to accept as common knowledge the particular views associated with that belief system. Some ideas, being considered undeniable "truths," come to define a particular way of seeing the world (Brock-Utne & Garbo, 2009). This insight is highly relevant in language politics. In order to address claims about the importance of English and other global languages in education, it is important to look at the ways globalizing forces (political and economic) manifest themselves in particular cultural settings. Freire's (1970) theory on formal versus informal learning and the role of schooling in education is important in this context. He views learning as a critical process consisting of reflection, unlearning conventional truths, and relearning, a process in which the valuation of local knowledge is important. This point is also echoed in Chamber's (1997) theory on "Whose knowledge counts?" as well as Sleeter's (2001) related work on changing definitions and interpretations of "knowledge" belief and culture, and their implications for pedagogy. Bishop and Glynn (1999) argue along the same lines that culture and the range of socially constituted traditions for sense-making are central to learning. Since culture, sense making and language are intimately related, there are strong arguments for using a local language in learning. Studies such as those of Odora (2002), Prah (2003), and Brock-Utne (2011) found that the curriculum in many countries in Africa does not reflect local thinking in teaching and learning. As Brock-Utne (2006) pointed out, incorporating local ideas in local languages is urgently needed in order to avoid the "Recolonization of the Mind."

An important consideration in understanding why local knowledge and local languages have been 'subjugated' (in the words of Foucault) to western theory and western science is related to Western-based conceptualizations of 'development,' seen variously as modernization, or even as emulation, as well as discriminatory concepts from Western international relations theories such as "divisible sovereignty" or "semi-sovereignty" (Bull & Watson, 1984, 1995). These global discourses on meaning-making, ways of agreeing, thinking and conversing are brought into classrooms and contextualized in the LoI, as are the full range of ideas about political behaviour, international relations, and diplomatic thinking about language, politics and power. Many educational practitioners continue to ignore culture as a central ingredient in education. Bishop and Glynn's (1999, p. 148) model implies "that it is essential that communities acknowledge their own diversity as they reflect on and develop their knowledge-of-practice." To summarize, important theoretical considerations are often ignored on debates about

LoI: To what extent is valuation of local contexts and cultures dependent on learning in a local language? I address this question in the next section, drawing on research based on interviews with teachers, students governmental officials, NGOs and academics in Tanzania, as well as classroom observation and a review of official documents. During my fieldwork, my research was centered on primary schools in Dar es Salaam and Unguja (Zanzibar). When it comes to Malaysia, my main research was based on a literature review, extented to LoI and teaching and learning Mathematics, Sciences and English within the country and within the area of the country on which the changes were based.

QUALITY LEARNING

Parents are worried about the quality of English that their children are exposed to in school. Learning and learning a language have different objectives. "The objectives of education are different from those for learning English language and as such the two sets of objectives should be set apart and ways to attain each set of objectives should be found" (Roy-Campbell & Qorro, 1997, p. 98). Children taught in any of the language varieties similar to their mother tongue are better off in their learning comprehension than those taught in an adopted foreign language such as English, whose morphology includes regular and irregular structures.

Apparently, this is the thinking behind the latest decision of the Malaysian government to change the LoI from English to Malay. According to Cavanagh (2009) one of the reasons for the change is protests from local governments in both urban and rural areas of the country, where the use of English is less common. Cavanagh added that Ethnic Chinese and Indians in Malaysia argue that mathematics and science should be taught in their native tongues, and in some public schools all subjects are taught in one of these two languages.

Language learning has a chronological sequence according to Skutnabb-Kangas & Phillipson (1995, p. 10) "the mother tongue, the first language, the second language, a second variety, and a foreign languages" (Ngalasso, 1990 quoted in Skutnabb-Kangas & Phillipson, 1995). Furthermore Skutnabb-Kangas (2012) called language as a human right in the education sector and she argues that human righs in education is sustainable. Many studies show that mother tongue is an education in itself and brings quality learning (see Babaci-Wilhite, 2012). The language carries with it a way of thinking, a way of doing and a way of feeling that cannot be obtained in another language. However for economical and political reasons Malaysia and Tanzania decided to use a local language in primary school and to achieve the implementation of a local language versus a colonial language one has to "[l]ess focus on the first best solutions, more on second or third best" (Collier, 2008) and "Beyond pedagogic and psychological reasons ... language is inextricably linked to identity, ideology and power" (Makalela, 2005, p. 163). Whichever context a child is in, s/he can hardly achieve quality learning when there are identity problems. Identity is strongly connected to parents' attitudes, to the language spoken at home and to cultural understanding. If this is ignored, children can become drop-outs or "outsiders" in the society, and on top of that, the society will blame them as being responsible for their own difficulties. Moreover Kosonen (2009) argued that improved quality is substantiated in the better learning results in all school subjects, including the dominant national/official language. He stated further more that improved quality also reduces repetition and dropout. Various researchers have shown that when people feel that they are outsiders, social problems often develop, which means that the cultural identity and sovereignty is important (Prah & Brock-Utne, 2009).

CULTURAL IDENTITY AND SOVEREIGNTY

Kiswahili and Bahasa Malaysia were chosen in Tanzania and Malaysia respectively as the national language to unite the linguistically diverse groups in both countries after the independence. This choice has contributed to the formation of a national identity incorporating these languages. There is evidence that having one common language helps in bridging the gap among people of different ethnic groups (David, 2007). Both Nyerere in Tanzania and the government of Malaysia were congnizant of these cultural identity issues in their choices. As Gill (2005) stated, Malaysia, focused like a number of other countries on the essential which he describes as "educational agendas of nation-building, national identity and unity …" (Tollefson & Tsui, 2004: viii, quoted in Gill, 2005, p. 4).

The use of a local language in the educational system also contributes to self-respect and to pride in local culture. By reinforcing the importance of local languages, one reinforces the interest in local knowledge and culture. Ideally, one would choose a non-dominant local LoI, but in cases in which this is expensive and practically difficult to implement, a local language such as Kiswahili, with local roots and widely used in public spaces is a good second choice (Babaci-Wilhite, 2010). The policy of switching from Kiswahili to English midway through the schooling process, gives the impression that Kiswahili is inferior to English and that the local language is somehow inadequate in engaging with complex concepts. This reinforces the sense of inferiority of local culture and at the same time is disadvantageous for children of the lowest socio-economic strata who have had little exposure to English at home (Babaci-Wilhite, 2010). I agree with Brock-Utne (2006) who wrote "What does it mean for the development of self-respect and identity that the language one normally communicates in does not seem to be deemed fit for a language of instruction in school?" (p. 141). Language is part of one's identity and part of one's culture and should be a right to use in order to develop oneself through schooling. This is consistent with Rwantabagu's (2011, p. 472) argument based on a study in Burundi where he argues that "The possession of one's language and culture is at the same time a right and a privilege and members of the younger generation should not be denied their native rights and advantages, as provided for in article 27 of the Universal Declaration of Human Rights" (UN 1948). Furthermore he pointed out that after a series of education reforms, there is still a debate in Burundi over the use of French or Kirundi as LoI. He argued for the importance of local LoI as a basis for better knowledge acquisition and that policy makers should take evidence research based on language and education into consideration. He also pointed out that African languages will enable African cultures to expand and will ensure the survival of African languages. Referring to Senghor (1976, p. 10) "Culture is growth and this entails that our school systems should aim both at cultural authenticity and openness to foreign influences said "the humanism of the new millennium." Furthermore he concluded that within the context of globalisation "giving prominence to African languages and cultural values could be based on "interdependence and complementarity between cultures and nations" to the challenges of the 21st century.

POLICIES OF LOI

Gill (2005) described the history of Policies of LoI in Malaysia from being the sole medium of instruction in the education system during colonial times. Furthermore he states that English was relegated to being taught in schools as a second language and that the rural areas where there was almost no environmental exposure to the language, English was virtually a foreign language. Moreover Gill (2005, p. 8) quoted Hassan (1988, p. 38) who explained that "The government set up a team of Malaysian and Indonesian language planners and academicians, including scientists who held a total of 6 joint meetings over a period of 16 years from 1972 to 1988."

In Tanzania, the National Kiswahili Council, Bakita was given a budget and a staff with the mandate to develop Kiswahili and make sure the language is used properly in the media. After independence, the work of promoting the language was continued at the Institute of Kiswahili Research (IKR-TUKI) at the University of Dar es Salaam. In the 1980s the government gave consideration to implementing Kiswahili as a LoI, but in the end did not follow through and do it at all levels. The arguments were that Kiswahili was not ready to be a LoI because of a lack of books and terminology. The Chief Academic Officer at the mainland National Kiswahili Council told me in November 5th, 2008, that "In the 1980s those arguments were ok, but now they are using the same argument even if everything is ready." Academicians have tried to convince the government that Kiswahili is mature. Since the 1980s both book publishers and the National Kiswahili Council have engaged in the development of scientific terminology. The Chief Academic officer concluded "We have enough dictionaries now, and we try to convince the government." This raises the question of why a country would not use its language, Kiswahili, when it has two National Kiswahili Council (Bakita and Bakiza) that has developed all the necessary terminology.

Gill (2005) described a similar development in Malaysia. He explained that the development of terminology – about half a million new words had been developed by the mid 1980s – was considered one of the most significant achievements in language planning in the region, showing strong government support in modernizing the language in the post-independence period. Parents are choosing English schools even if neither they nor their children understand English. Most parents do not understand the implications for their children of learning in a language that is not their own (Babaci-Wilhite, 2010). One of the important findings from my previous research is that parental decisions between public versus private schools and between Kiswahili and English are made on the basis of imperfect information about the learning implications of these choices (Babaci-Wilhite, 2012). It is essential that the government provide better information on the role of language in learning and on the advantages of Kiswahili as a LoI. When confronted with this, government officials both in the Ministry of Education and Vocational Training (MoEVT) mainland and in the MoEVT in Zanzibar responded that it should be the parents' responsibility to seek out this information, and that the government should respect parental choices since Tanzania is a democracy. However based on my results, the problem is that the parental misunderstanding about language and learning is based on a myth: They believe that having English as the LoI will improve student's learning abilities and their opportunities in life (Babaci-Wilhite, 2012). The myth has to be deflated in order for parents to make informed choices (Babaci-Wilhite, 2010).

I found resistance to accepting these findings on language and learning in the MoEVT. The resistance is remarkable because of the consensus both within the Tanzanian mainland and in Zanzibar academia and abroad that the choice of a local LoI is important for good learning. For this reason, the latest decision in Malaysia which saw a complete reversal of the role of English, which before the implementation of the 1963 National Language Act was the medium of instruction and administration (Heng & Tan, 2006), is very interesting in relation to the indecisiveness of the Tanzanian government when it comes to switching the LoI in secondary school into Kiswahili and to the recent changes introduced in Zanzibari primary schools by the Revolutionary government of Zanzibar.

CONCLUDING COMMENTS

Learning to read and write in a local language improves students' abilities to think critically about their own conditions and about the world. Retaining local languages as a LoI will provide a sustainable benefit for the country. For the reasons I have outlined, children of all backgrounds will be able to perform better in school. As Napier (2011) concluded, the hegemony of English in many countries seems "unshakeable," even if the language is not spoken at home. She offered larger questions that will enable researchers to continue the work on language in education in order to have a better understanding of why the change is not made in Africa. In line with her conclusions, I further argue that a sustainable investment should be made in LoI not only in primary schools but also in secondary school and the performance of students should be monitored when they finish secondary school in order to assess whether they perform better in school. Based on my findings, the costs of such a policy are exaggerated and the benefits for quality learning underestimated. As Kosonen (2009) argued, students' completion rates can increase if the quality of teaching is improved in primary schools. He added that cooperation should support the development of local languages and that will be economically viable.

Research in the field of economics of education based on cost-effectiveness is needed and my final comment supports Heugh (2006), Kosonen (2009) and Brock-Utne and Nota (2010) when they argued that there is hardly any research, on the costs involved in having millions of school-children in Africa repeating classes or dropping out of school. These cost-effectiveness perspectives are very important since the arguments of most of policy makers claim that costs are the main problem in using Kiswahili as a LoI. However, this cost assessment analysis does not account for the benefits of self appreciation, better learning and increased understanding that come with a local LoI. This narrow view of cost effectiveness is inhibiting the implementation of a right in education, which is a prerequisite for equitable global development.

REFERENCES

Arnove, R., & Arnove, A. (1998). *Issues in post-colonial languages policies: Essentialim vs universalism.* Cape Town: WCCES.

Asmah, H. O. (1992). *The linguistic scenery in Malaysia.* Kuala Lumpur, Malaysia: Dewan Bahasa dan Pustaka, Ministry of Education.

Babaci-Wilhite, Z. (2010). Why is the choice of the language of instruction in which students learn best seldom made in Tanzania? In B. Brock-Utne, Z. Desai, & M. Qorro (Eds.), *Educational challenges in multilingual societies: LOITASA phase two research* (pp. 281-305). Cape Town, South Africa: African Minds.

Babaci-Wilhite, Z., & Geo-JaJa, M. A. (2011). *A critique and rethink of modern education in Africa's development in the 21st century.* Dar es Salaam, The United Republic of Tanzania: Papers in Education and Development (PED).

Babaci-Wilhite, Z. (2012). Local language of instruction for quality learning and social equity in Tanzania. In A. S. Yeung, E. L. Brown, & C. Lee (Eds), *Communication and language: Barriers to cross-cultural understanding* (pp 3-23). Charlotte, NC: Information Age Publishing.

Bishop, R., & Glynn, T. (1999). *Culture counts: Changing power relations in education. Whose knowledge counts? How is knowledge constructed?* Dunmore Press. http://www.instep.net.nz/ knowledge_and_theory/how_is_knowledge_constructed/whose_knowledge_counts (retrieved 18 January 2010).

Brock-Utne, B. (2006). *Whose education for all? The recolonization of the African mind.* South Korea: Seoul: Home Publishing Co.

Brock-Utne, B. (2007). Learning through a familiar language versus learning through a foreign language – A look into some secondary school classrooms in Tanzania. *International Journal of Educational Development, 27*(5), 487-498.

Brock-Utne, B. (2008). The effect of the neo-liberal agenda on education in some African countries. Power, voice and the public good: Schooling and education in global societies. *Advances in Education in Diverse Communities: Research Policy and Praxis, 6,* 91-116.

Brock-Utne, B. (2011). Language and inequality: Global challenges to education. BAICE Presidential Address at the 11th UKFIET International Conference, Oxford, 16 September 2011.

Brock-Utne, B., & Garbo, G. (Eds.). (2009). *Language and power. Implications of language for peace and development.* Dar es Salaam/Oxford/East Lansing: Mkuki na Nyota/ABC/Michigan State University Press.

Brock-Utne, B., & Nota, F. (2010). The economics of language of instruction in Africa – An example from Tanzania. Paper presented at the ASA (African Studies Association) conference in San Fransisco, 10-20 November 2010.

Bull, H., & Watson, A. (Eds.). (1984). *European international society and its expansion.* Oxford: Clarendon Press.

Bull, H., & Watson, A. (Eds.). (1995). *The expansion of international society*. Oxford: Clarendon Press.

Cavanagh, S. (2009). Curriculum matters, Malaysia reverts to teaching math and science in native. http://blogs.edweek.org/edweek/curriculum/2009/07/malayonly_math_and_science.html (retrieved 18 May 2010).

Chambers, R. (1997). *Whose reality counts?: Putting the first last*. London: Intermediate Technology Development Group Publishing.

Collier, P. (2008): IMF seminar, quoted by Olav Lundstøl at Norad Annual conference on Poverty and Development in Oslo, October 15th, 2010.

Crossley, M., & Watson K. (2003). *Comparative and international research to education: Globalisation, context and difference*. London/ New York: Routledge.

David, M. K. (2007). Changing language policies in Malaysia: Ramifications and Implications. Paper presented at the 2nd International Conference on Language, Education and Diverstiy held at the Unversity of Waikato, Hamilton, New Zealand, on the 21-24 November 2007).

Foucault, M. (1988). Power, moral values, and the ontellectual. An interview with Michel Foucault by Michael Bess. *History of the Present, 4*, 1-2.

Freire, P. (1970, Reprinted in 1993). *Pedagogy of the oppressed*. London: Penguin Books.

Geo-JaJa, M. A., & Yang, X. (2003). Rethinking globalization in Africa. *Chimera, 1*(1),19-28.

Gill, S. K. (2005). *Language policy in Malaysia: Reversing direction, 3*, 241-260.

Hassan, A. (1988). *Bahasa Sastera Buku Cetusan Fikiran*. Kuala Lumpur: Dewan Bahasa dan Pustaka.

Heng, C. S., & Tan, H. (2006). English for mathematics and science: Current Malaysian language-in-education policies and practices. *Language and Education, 20*(4), 306-321.

Heugh, K. (2006). Cost implications of the provision of mother tongue and strong bilingual models of education in Africa. In A. Hassana, B. Aliou, B. Brock-Utne, Y. Satina Diallo, K. Heugh, & H. Ekkehard Wolff (Eds.), *Optimizing learning and education in Africa – The language factor: A stock-taking research on mother tongue and bilingual education in sub-Saharan Africa* (pp. 138-156). Paris: Association for the Development of Education in Africa (ADEA).

Kimizi, M. (2007). *Why has the LoI policy in Tanzania been so ambivalent over the last forty years? A Study eliciting views from government policy-makers, international donors to Tanzania, University academics and researchers, and the general public*. Master Thesis. http://urn.nb.no/URN:NBN:no-16663 (retrieved 17 January 2010).

Kosonen, K. (2009). *Cost-effectiveness of first language-based bilingual and multilingual education*. Unpublished paper.

Makalela, L. (2005). We speak eleven tongues. Reconstructing multilingualism in South Africa. In B. Brock-Utne & R. Hopson (Eds.), *Languages of instruction for African emancipation: Focus on postcolonial contexts and considerations* (pp. 147-175). Cape Town, South Africa/Dar es Salaam, The United Republic of Tanzania: CASAS/Mkuki na Nyota.

Mulokozi, M. M., Rubanza, Y., Senkoro, F. E M. K., Kahigi, K. K., & Omari, S (2008) *Report of the 3rd Secondary School Kiswahili Language Textbooks Writing Workshop* [Arts Books Workshop], held at Amabilis Catholic Center, Morogoro, 14-17/11/2008. TUKI/TATAKI.

Mwinsheikhe, H. M. (2009). Spare no means: Battling with the English/Kiswahili dilemma in Tanzanian secondary school classrooms . In B. Brock-Utne & I. Skattum (Eds.), *Languages and education in Africa – A comparative and transdisciplinary analysis* (pp. 223-237). Oxford: Symposium Books.

Napier, D. B. (2011). Critical issues in language and education planning in twenty first century in South Africa. *US-China Education Review B, 1*, 58-76.

Odora, C. H. (2002). Indigenous knowledge and the integration of knowledge systems. In *Towards a philosophy of articulation*. Claremont: New Africa Education.

Prah, K. K. (2003). Going native: Language of instruction for education, development and African emancipation. In B. Brock-Utne, Z. Desai, & M. Qorro (Eds.), *LOITASA language of instruction in Tanzania and South Africa* (pp. 14-34). Dar es Salaam, The United Republic of Tanzania: E & D Limited Publishers.

Prah, K. K., & Brock-Utne, B. (Eds.). (2009). Multilingualism – An African advantage. In *A paradigm Shift in African Languages of instruction Polices*. Cape Town, South Africa: CASAS.

Qorro, M. (2009). Parents and policymakers insistence on foreign languages as media of education in Africa: Restricting acess to quality education. – For whose benefit? In B. Brock-Utne & I. Skattum (Eds.), *Languages and education in Africa – A comparative and transdisciplinary analysis* (pp. 57-83). Oxford: Symposium Books.

Roy-Campbell, Z. M., & Qorro, M. (1997). *Language crisis in Tanzania. The myth of English versus education*. Dar es Salaam, The United Republic of Tanzania: Mkuki Na Nyota Publishers.

Rwantabagu, H. (2011). Tradition, globalisation and language dilemma in education: African options for the 21st century. *International Review of Education, 57,* 457-475. DOI 10.1007/s11159-011-9214-z.

Senghor, L. S. (1976). *Authenticité et négritude*. Kinshasa. Unpublished lecture.

Skutnabb-Kangas, T., & Phillipson, R. (1995). *Linguistic human rights, overcoming linguistic discrimination*. New York: Walter de Gruyther.

Skutnabb-Kangas, T., & Heugh, K. (Eds.). (2012). *Multilingual education and sustainable diversity work: from periphery to center*. London: Routledge.

Sleeter, C. (2001). *Culture, difference, and power* (CD-ROM edition). New York: Teachers College Press.

Tollefson, J. W., & Tsui, A. B. M. (Eds.). (2004). *Medium of instruction policies – Which agenda? Whose agenda?* New Jersey: Lawrence Erlbaum.

UN (United Nations). (1948). *Universal declaration of human rights*. New York: United Nations.

Vuzo, M. (2007). *Revisiting the language of instruction policy in Tanzania: A comparative study of geography classes taught in Kiswahili and English*. Doctoral dissertation. http://www.duo.uio.no/sok/search.html?hits=40&sort=published&start=21&q=phd&absize=2000Norway (retrieved 17 January 2010).

Zalkapli, A. Z. (2010). Government scraps teaching of maths and science in English. *The Malaysian insider*. http://www.themalaysianinsider.com/index.php/malaysia/31709-government-scraps-teaching-of-maths-and-science-in-english (retrieved 18 May 2010).

Zanzibar Swahili Council Act No. 4 of 2004. (2004). http://www.agc.go.tz/pdf/2004-04.pdf (retrieved 17 January 2010).

Zehlia Babaci-Wilhite
University of Oslo
Norway

VUYOKAZI NOMLOMO & MONDE MBEKWA

VOICES FROM THE CLASSROOM

Teacher and Learner Perceptions on the Use of the Learners'
Home Language in the Teaching and Learning of School
Mathematics and Science

INTRODUCTION AND BACKGROUND

South Africa, a country of more than 50 million people, is amongst many countries in the world with a rich cultural and linguistic diversity. The richness of the linguistic diversity in South Africa is acknowledged in its Constitution (1996) which was adopted at the birth of the new democratic dispensation in 1994 as a means of redressing the divisions, inequalities and discriminatory policies of the apartheid government. To accommodate the linguistic and cultural diversity of the South African population, the South African Constitution (1996) conferred official status to eleven languages, nine of which are African languages (namely Sepedi, Sesotho, Setswana, siSwati, Tshivenda, Xitsonga, isiNdebele, isiXhosa and isiZulu) in addition to English and Afrikaans which were the only official languages during the apartheid regime. According to the 2001 national census, of the eleven official languages, isiZulu has the largest number of speakers (23.82%), followed by isiXhosa which constitutes 17.64% of the total population (Statistics South Africa 2004). The rank order of the other official languages in terms of the number of speakers is as follows: Afrikaans (13.35%), Sepedi (9.39%), English (8.2%), Setswana (8.2%), Sesotho (7.93%), Xitsonga (4.44%), siSwati (2.66%), Tshivenda (2.28%) and isiNdebele (1.59%). These languages are spoken across the nine provinces of South Africa, with a large population of isiZulu speakers found mainly in KwaZulu-Natal and Gauteng while isiXhosa is spoken mainly in the Eastern and Western Cape provinces. The Western Cape has a total population of more than 5 million with the majority being Afrikaans speakers who constitute 55.3% of the total population in this province. isiXhosa speakers constitute approximately 23.7% of the population while English is spoken by approximately 19.3% of the total population residing in the Western Cape.

According to the 2011 statistical estimates African language speakers constitute 79.5% of the total South African population, which is estimated at 50.6 million. The whites and people of mixed ancestry (formerly classified as Coloureds) each form 9% of the total population while Indians/Asians constitute approximately 2.5% of the population. Although the majority of South Africans speak African languages as home languages, ironically none of the African languages are used as languages of instruction after the third grade of schooling. English and Afrikaans speakers constitute 20.05% of the current South African population, and these

D.B. Napier & S. Majhanovich (eds.), Education, Dominance and Identity, 133–149.
© 2013 Sense Publishers. All rights reserved.

languages are still used as languages of instruction from primary to tertiary education in South Africa. This practice is against the country's constitution (1996) which grants everyone the right to receive education in the official language or languages of their choice. The current Language-in Education Policy (1997) which is informed by the Constitution of the country in relation to the norms and standards published in terms of section 6(1) of the South African Schools Act of 1996 also promotes the development all the official languages, particularly the historically disadvantaged African languages. But the reality is that English is still the dominant language in education and other sectors of life. According to Heugh (2003) the current Language-in-Education Policy perpetuates inequality between English and Afrikaans on the one hand, and African languages on the other hand. In other words, the new democratic language policy has not succeeded in eradicating the patterns of language domination and inequality (Napier, 2011) associated with historical, political and socio-economic influences.

Regarding the choice of languages of instruction in South African schools, the government leaves that role to School Governing Bodies which represent parents who often opt for English, particularly in black schools. Due to the discriminatory government legislation of the past, including the Bantu Education Act which provided low quality education to African learners, many African-language speaking parents are suspicious of the use of mother tongue education in African languages as it is perceived as a means of denying African language speakers access to knowledge and social, economic and international advancement (Heugh, 2003; De Klerk, 2000).

According to Setati (2005, 2008) language has always been used as a political tool for subjugation of people on one side and conversely language has also provided a tool of resistance against subjugation and domination in South Africa. For instance, the spark that ignited the powder keg of student resistance in South Africa in 1976 was the compulsory use of Afrikaans as a language of instruction in all high school subjects in black schools. As a result, Afrikaans was perceived as a language of oppression and many black people developed negative attitudes towards it after the Soweto uprisings, while English became a symbol of liberation or empowerment (Alexander, 1989) and attained better status in almost all the formal sectors, including education. However, Afrikaans still enjoys a higher socio-economic status compared to all the official African languages. It is still recognized as a useful language in formal domains such as education and work or business although many black people still resent it as the language of racism and oppression.

English hegemony is a global concern. In many African countries, colonial languages (English, French, Portuguese, and others) are still used and promoted as languages of instruction. According to Mazrui (2002), Tanzania and South Africa in particular are countries that still support English in education despite their current progressive language policies which aim at developing African languages. In Tanzania Kiswahili is used as the language of instruction for seven years in primary education while in South Africa the African languages are used as languages of instruction for the first three years of primary education. The global view is that the European languages are "major economic languages" with linguistic capital value (Brock-Utne & Hopson, 2005, p. 13). The dominance of English over local African languages is one of the challenges facing many countries in the African continent which were under colonial rule (Tollefson & Tsui, 2004). Although medium of instruction policies of many African countries advocate multilingualism, and many African people speak more than one African language, it is ironical that multilingualism is seen from the European language perspective i.e. through proficiency in colonial languages such as English and French.

The influence of globalisation is another factor to consider with regard to the choice of language of instruction in many African schools. Global educational forces assume a monolingual approach to education which often leads to cultural and linguistic assimilation (Tollefson & Tsui, 2004). English is regarded as a global language and is used as the main language of instruction in many schools in Africa where there are many local languages. English hegemony has implications for teaching and learning, particularly in multilingual settings where there are mixed cultures and languages. South Africa joins many countries in the world in being influenced by global forces, striving to be competitive in the global market in terms of education, knowledge economy and economic development (Napier, 2011), and targeting mathematics and science education as a means of technological and economic development. South Africa's participation in international studies such as the Trends in International Mathematics and Science Study (TIMSS) (Napier, 2011; Reddy, 2006) and the Progress in International Reading Literacy Study (PIRLS) (Mullins, Martin, Kennedy, & Foy, 2006) though with poor achievement results, indicates South Africa's desire for global competitiveness. The low achievement scores obtained by South African learners in the (TIMSS) of 2003, particularly in black schools could be associated with their low proficiency levels in the English language in which the tests were administered.

Given that mathematics and science are regarded as key areas in scientific and economic development across the globe (Ogunniyi, 2005; Rogan and Grayson, 2003), the issue of the language of instruction in mathematics and science has received worldwide attention in education circles. Much research has been done particularly on the influence of and the importance of language in mathematics and science learning, including generally the role that language plays in the education of non-native speakers of English (Durkin & Shire, 1991; Hunting, 1988; Orr, 1987; Pimm, 1987; Stephens, Waywood, Clarke, & Izard, 1993; Clarkson, 2004; Setati, 2005; Makinde & Olabode, 2006).

In both developed and developing countries mathematics and science are regarded as priority areas for economic and technological advancement, and for improving people's lives and nation building (Wedikkarage, 2006; Ogunniyi, 2005; Rogan & Grayson, 2003). However, there are still challenges and inequalities in the education system due to the legacy of apartheid in South Africa. One of the challenges is the use of English as the main language of instruction for the majority of black learners to the exclusion of their home languages after Grade 3.

A study by Setati (2008) on teacher and learner preferences on the language of instruction indicated a preference for English by teachers because it is a "universal language" and provides access to knowledge because "textbooks are written in English, … [and] the question papers are in English." Learners on the other hand were divided on language preferences with some preferring English and others preferring their home language.

De Klerk's (2000) study that was conducted in a former white school the Eastern Cape Province of South Africa where isiXhosa is widely spoken, revealed that a small number (19%) of isiXhosa-speaking parents (middle class) showed negative attitudes towards the maintenance of isiXhosa in schools as they claimed that their children already knew how to speak isiXhosa, so there was no need to learn to read or write the language. In this study parents showed strong positive attitudes towards English as a medium of instruction for economic and academic or educational reasons, the availability of resources and other facilities, the low pupil-teacher ratio, and many other benefits that are not available in African or black schools in South Africa (De Klerk, 2000).

Iyamu and Ogiegbaen (2007) focused their study on teachers and parents' attitudes to the mother tongue as a language of instruction in Nigeria whilst a similar study was conducted by Ndamba (2008) on parents' and learners' attitudes towards the use of the mother tongue as the language of learning in Zimbabwean schools. Ndamba's (2008) study revealed that both parents and learners preferred English as the language of instruction. However, approximately 40% of Nigerian teachers in Iyamu and Ogiegbaen's (2007) study preferred English and 80% of parents preferred English as a medium of instruction in schools. In contrast to the findings of these studies, empirical evidence from international research indicates that learners who are taught in their mother tongue generally do better than learners who are taught in English in these subjects (Sentson, 1994; Langenhoven, 2005; Nomlomo, 2007; Mwinsheikhe, 2008).

Some writers state that there is reluctance and resistance to the use of African languages in mathematics and science teaching, ostensibly due to their lack of global status and the lack of appropriate terminology in the indigenous languages (Bunyi, 1997; Elugbe, 1990; Hameso, 1997; Prah, 2003). Clarkson (2004) challenged the dominance of western theories and curricula that assume that learners have mastery of the dominant language of instruction which is often not their home language. In the mathematics classrooms learners become exposed to a number of languages including the learners' language/s, the teacher's language/s, the official language of instruction, the language used in conversation (lingua franca) and the language used to teach mathematics (Clarkson, 2004; Mbekwa, 2008). Learners have to understand the languages involved in teaching and the content and language of mathematics (Halai, 2007) and these learners always experience difficulties when they learn through a foreign language. This indicates that the issue of language of instruction is a complex phenomenon in multilingual and multicultural settings and it has implications for pedagogical and learning strategies when a foreign language is used to teach mathematics.

This chapter focuses on teacher and learner perceptions on the use of the learners' home language (isiXhosa) in mathematics and science teaching. It is based on data collected as part of a project aiming at promoting the use of African languages in education in Tanzania and South Africa, the Language of Instruction in Tanzania and South Africa (LOITASA) research project which is described in the next section. It reports on South African research only and it considers the global influences on languages used in teaching and learning, particularly with regard to the role of mathematics and science education in economic development in South Africa. It seeks to address the following research questions:
- What do teachers and learners perceive to be the positive contribution of the use of the learners' home language in mathematics and science teaching and learning?
- What are the perceived challenges in the use of the learners' home language in the teaching and learning of mathematics and science?
- What are the implications of the use of the home language in mathematics and science education?

THE LANGUAGE OF INSTRUCTION IN TANZANIA AND SOUTH AFRICA (LOITASA) RESEARCH PROJECT

This chapter reports on the views of grade 4 teachers on the use of the learners' home language in mathematics and science teaching. It is based on a collaborative research project of three universities, namely, the University of Daar es Salaam in Tanzania, the University of Oslo in Norway and the University of the Western Cape in South Africa on the important issue of the language of instruction in schools. The project was established in 2003 "... to explore the use of African languages (Kiswahili and isiXhosa) as media of instruction in Tanzania (Kiswahili) and South Africa (isiXhosa)" (Nomlomo, 2007, p.2). The University of the Western Cape researched the use of isiXhosa, the dominant African language in the Western Cape, as a language of instruction in mathematics and science in primary schools, whilst the University of Dar es Salaam focused on the use of KiSwahili in secondary schools.

The project has been in its second phase since its inception in 2003. The first phase of the project which focused on science and geography ended in 2006. The second phase of the project, which commenced in 2008, substituted mathematics for geography. The project followed an experimental research design and focused on the teaching of mathematics and science through the medium of English and isiXhosa from Grade 4-6. This initiative was in response to the low numbers of learners, particulary from disadvantaged backgrounds, who pursue careers in the fields of mathematics and science in tertiary education.

RESEARCH METHOD AND FINDINGS

In the South African component of the study reported in this chapter, data were mainly collected by means of interviews from three grade four classes in three different primary schools. All these schools are located in a disadvantaged residential area of the Western Cape Province of South Africa. In the first phase of the research project two Grade four science teachers and ten learners were interviewed while the second phase focused on one Grade four mathematics teacher and five learners. In both cases the interviews were semi-structured and they focused on teachers' and learners' perceptions in relation to the research questions stated above.

All the teachers and learners involved in the study were mother tongue speakers of isiXhosa. The language of instruction for the schools involved in the study was isiXhosa from Grade 1-3 and a shift to English medium of instruction occured from Grade 4, but for the purpose of this study one class in each school was taught science and mathematics in isiXhosa. This arrangement was negotiated with the Western Cape Education Department (WCED), schools and parents at the start of the LOITASA research project which followed a longitudinal qualitative research design.

The data were audio-recorded and subsequently transcribed. Data analysis took the form of categorization of data from the transcripts according to emerging themes and subthemes corresponding to the research questions stated above.

Pedagogical and Learning Benefits

Teachers and learners generally displayed a positive disposition with respect to the use of the home language as a medium of instruction in school mathematics and science. Their positive attitudes can be construed as recognising the cognitive, pedagogical, the affective and socio-cultural benefits of teaching and learning through the home language. However, they also recognised the existence of structural and epistemic challenges.

Teacher Perceptions

The positive benefits of using the home language as a language of instruction, according to the teachers, manifest themselves in terms of active learner participation, better understanding of mathematical and science concepts, improved strategies of teaching and improved parental involvement. All the teachers expressed similar views with regard to the positive impact of isiXhosa on learners' class participation as one of the science teachers put it:

Thandi: Kuyabanceda kakhulu (ukusebenzisa isiXhosa)... iba yiklasi yonke ephendulayo ... bayalandela kakhulu ... Nabazali bayayinika inkxaso, ... bayayijonga le nto uyenzayo, ... batshintshile kunakuqala, ... babuye (abafundi) bethetha *more than* ubumxelele apha eklasini.

It helps them (learners) a lot (using isiXhosa) ... the whole class responds ... they understand very well. The parents give support, ... they look at what you are doing, they have changed than before, … they (learners) come back talking more than what you told them in class.

The mathematics teacher who was interviewed corroborated the science teachers' perception on the use of isiXhosa as a language of instruction. He expressed a positive disposition towards the LOITASA project because of its contribution in seeking to determine the best approach to the teaching of such a difficult subject as mathematics and also to facilitate conceptual and procedural understanding in mathematics. As he put it:

Sipho: Ndiyayixhasa le projekthi ngoba iyasincedisa thina singootitshala ukuze siphucule indlela abaqhuba ngayo abantwana kwimathematics. Ndiyaqwalasela ukuba abafundi bathabatha inxaxheba kakhulu kwingxoxo ngemathematics baze baphendule imibuzo ngcono xa besebenzisa ulwimi lwabo. Ndikwaqwalasela ukuba baqonda ngcono kwesi sifundo xa befunda ngolwimi lwabo.

I support the project because it seeks to assist us as teachers to improve the performance of learners in mathematics. I can see that learners participate more in discussion in mathematics and respond better to questions when they use their own language. I can observe also that learners understand the subject better when they learn it in their own language.

Learner Perceptions
Similarly learners perceived the use of isiXhosa as assisting them to understand subject content and to participate with confidence in mathematics and science lessons. Regarding academic achievement, learners not only performed better in mathematics and science but also showed confidence in terms of their competence in English. Despite the fact that they were taught mathematics and science through the medium of isiXhosa, they also performed better in English as a subject than some learners who were taught mainly through the medium of English as articulated by one learner below.

Vuyo: Siyabogqitha aba be-*English* ngo**ba siya-***understand*(a), sigqibe (umsebenzi) ngokukhawuleza.

We do better than the English learners because we understand better and finish (work) quickly.

The above comment is corroborated by studies which show that learners taught in their home language achieve better in other subjects as well (Nomlomo, 2007; Vuzo, 2007; Mwinsheikhe, 2009; De Klerk, 2000; Sentson, 1994). Learners also showed interest in learning English as a second language while retaining their home language (isiXhosa) as a medium of instruction. So they perceived the home language as a good foundation for learning English. Such responses reveal their intuitive awareness of additive bilingualism instead of subtractive bilingualism and the cognitive benefits of the home language as reflected in the following utterances:

> *Pumi*: Kufuneka *ilanguage* yakho uyifunde, … awunakufunda ezinye ii *"language"* ungayazi eyakho. Kufuneka uqale ngeyakho, ulandelise ezinye.

> You must learn your language … you cannot learn other languages if you don't know yours. You must start with your own (language), and thereafter learn others.

Affective Benefits

Teacher Perceptions
Both teachers and learners displayed positive attitudes towards the home language as a medium of instruction in school mathematics and science. For example teachers indicated feelings of comfort in the use of isiXhosa in teaching because they do not have to spend time doing explanations of concepts nor analyzing and simplifying questions for learners during assessment. This implies that the mother tongue is a useful tool for communication and conception. As one teacher put it:

> *Sipho*: Ndiziva kamnandi ndonwabile ngoba andichithi xesha lininzi ndicacisa. Iyandonwabisa ukubona abantwana bezihlalutyela ngokwabo imibuzo ye-*mathematics* beqonda intsingiselo yemibuzo. Loo nto indothulela umthwalo yenze kube mnandi ukufundisa.

> I feel good and happy because I do not have to spend a lot of time explaining. I feel happy because learners analyse mathematics questions on their own without my assistance and understand the essence of the questions. That makes things easier for me and makes teaching a pleasant experience.

Learner Perceptions
For learners, learning through the medium of the home language boosted their self-esteem and confidence in the classroom. These learners showed better confidence than their counterparts who learned through English. Some of their responses show the home language as having a positive influence on their socio-economic aspirations. They also showed pride in their language as a medium of instruction as can be gleaned from the following utterance by one learner:

> *Akhona*: Besifuna ukuthi gqi nathi ngesiXhosa kwiNatural Science nakwi mathematics … sibe zii-Black …. umntu wokuqala esiya phezulu, … siye kwi-space, singaziyekeli. Sifuna ukungenela i-competition, sifuna abanye abantwana, sibabonise ukuba sifunda kanjani ngesiXhosa.

> We wanted to come up with isiXhosa in Natural Science and mathematics … and become Blacks … the first black person going up, … going to space,

(and) don't underestimate our abilities. We want to enter for a competition, we want to show other children how we learn through the medium of isiXhosa.

The learners also showed enthusiasm and eagerness to continue with their home language as a medium of instruction beyond Grade 6. When asked how they felt about having to switch over to English as a medium of instruction in Grade 7 at the end of the project, learners responded that they wanted to go to higher educational levels with the home language as a medium of instruction. They aspired for life advancement through their own language (e.g. becoming astronauts, doctors, social workers, singers, etc.). The learners displayed positive self-concepts in terms of competing with other science learners internationally. They did not associate their home language with low standard jobs; instead they were positive about better opportunities in the economic environment. In addition, learners perceived their home language as a valuable resource to learn an additional language as articulated in the utterance below. This desire for an additional language is an indication of learners' awareness of the importance of additive bilingualism as previously stated and a perception of the need for language equality as stated in the South African Language-in-Education Policy (National Department of Education, 1997). The policy acknowledges the importance of protecting individuals' language rights while facilitating national and international communication through promotion of bi- or multilingualism.

Viwe: Siziva singayithandi (into yokuyeka ukufunda ngesiXhosa) kuba thina besifuna ukuqhubeka side siphume apha eZama, ngoba besifuna nathi ukuba siphumelele, sifunde zombini ezi-language ...

We don't like it (stopping from learning in our home language) because we want to continue until we leave Zama, because we want to be successful, to learn these two languages ...

ISIXHOSA AS A MEDIUM OF INSTRUCTION IN SCHOOL
MATHEMATICS AND SCIENCE

Challenges Experienced by Teachers

Teachers and learners reported that, whilst, in general, the benefits far outweigh the negatives in teaching and learning in isiXhosa, there are challenges that need to be overcome. The main challenges mentioned by the teachers and learners were linguistic and structural. The challenges experienced by teachers include the following: (i) specialized science and mathematics terminology, (ii) terminological ambiguities and (iii) linguistic variation in isiXhosa as a spoken language.

Specialized Scientific and Mathematical Terminology
In both mathematics and science education, one of the challenges is that there are no direct terminological equivalents in isiXhosa. In science, for example, terms such as photosynthesis, evaporation and others do not have isiXhosa equivalents. In this regard, Fischer, Weiss, Tshabe and Mdala (1985, p. 453) translate the term "photosynthesis" as: "*ukuguquka kwekhabhoni-diokside okwenziwa ngeklorofili nelanga ibe ziikharbohidrate/transformation of carbon dioxide by chlorophyll and the sun into carbohydrates*." Apart from the adoption of English terms such as chlorophyll, carbon dioxide and carbohydrates, one can see that the translation, though deficient, is a description of the process of photosynthesis. This is what Jokweni (2004) and Mbekwa (2008) refer to as a semasiological or meaning approach to translation which employs description as a translation device. As indicated above, the semasiological approach gives a complete description of photosynthesis instead of transliterating or borrowing and writing the term in isiXhosa as *ifotosinthesisi*.

Secondly, there are scientific terms which, when translated into isiXhosa, become unfamiliar in the everyday isiXhosa language use (e.g. "*inkqunto/actual thing*" for "*matter*"). Although translations of such words have relevant and appropriate meanings, they become inaccessible to learners as they do not hear them at all in their surroundings. Teachers confirmed the difficulty of using unfamiliar words which influenced them to make use of loan words from English.

Sipho: Ulwimi olusetyenzisiweyo luntsonkothile, luntsonkothile kakhulu … nalapha esiXhoseni akhona amagama endingawaziyo … Ndisebenzisa isiXhosa ngaphandle kwelo gama kuthi kube nzima ukulicacisa, … umzekelo "inkqunto" …. Ndibhenele esiNgesini but ndithethe isiXhosa.

The language used is complicated, very complicated … there are words I don't know even in isiXhosa … I use isiXhosa except for that particular word which is difficult to say in isiXhosa, perhaps it becomes difficult to explain it, … for example "inkqunto/matter" … I resort to saying it in English but explain it in Xhosa.

Likewise in mathematics, examples of terms which have no direct isiXhosa equivalents are terms like "place value; flow diagram; prime number" translated into isiXhosa as "*ixabiso-ndawo; umzobo wonxibelelwano-manani; inani elingenazahluli*." A literal English translation of the above isiXhosa translations of the mathematical terms would be: (place value; diagram of numerical correspondence; a number without divisor) respectively. Of these three mathematical terms, only one has a direct equivalent in isiXhosa viz. *place value*. The other two are isiXhosa descriptors of the mathematical terrms. These isiXhosa descriptors nevertheless capture the conceptual connotations of the English mathematical terms and hence facilitate conceptual understanding. It is therefore important that the translator should be someone who is a subject specialist and also a first language speaker of isiXhosa in order to capture the meaning and nuances of the scientific and mathematical terms.

The mathematics teacher who was interviewed indicated that the isiXhosa terms are not usually used in classroom mathematical discourse and hence are intimidating to learners. It is incumbent then for the teacher to help learners understand what these terms mean and hence also needs to give the English equivalents and diagrammatic representation for them where applicable. The teacher put it thus:

> *Sipho*: La magama [esiXhosa] awafane asetyenziswe eklasini yaye ngamagama angasetyenziswayo ekhaya nasekuhlaleni. Ngamagama angekhoyo kwisigama sabafundi. Ndiyavuma ukuba la magama asisiXhosa kodwa ayayifihla intsingiselo.

> These words [isiXhosa] are not frequently used in the classroom. They are also not part of everyday language at home and also not in use in day to day activities of the learners and thus do not form part of the learners' vocabulary. These terms are isiXhosa … yes but instead of facilitating understanding, they obscure meaning.

Terminological ambiguities in science and mathematics
Challenges relating to the science language include the absence of appropriate terms in isiXhosa, multiple meanings of certain isiXhosa terms and scientific symbols. For example, in cases where there are equivalent terms in isiXhosa, one may get the same translation or meaning for different terms, e.g. the two colours "*blue and green*," according to Fischer, Weiss, Tshabe, and Mdala (1985) have the same translation in isiXhosa i.e. "*luhlaza*." Likewise, the colours "*purple*" and "*violet*" have the same meaning "*mfusa*." It then depends on the translator to distinguish which colour is referred to when using the term "*luhlaza*."

Similarly these terminological ambiguities exist in mathematics, although no mention of this was made by the mathematics teacher. An example of such an ambiguity could be the term "*ixabiso*" which may refer to both price or cost and value in English. A similar observation by Halai (2007) showed that translation of Urdu terms into English was problematic in terms of capturing the mathematics discourse.

Dialectical Variation in isiXhosa
Dialectical variation in isiXhosa was another challenge in reading the translated text. Apart from urban and rural variants, isiXhosa has nine mutually intelligible dialects namely, isiGcaleka/isiNgqika, the standardized dialect, and the non-standardized dialects; isiMpondo, isiMpondomise, isiBaca, isiThembu, isiNtlangwini, isiHlubi, isiCele, isiXesibe (Nomlomo, 1993). One of the teachers who grew up in one Cape Town township found it difficult to understand certain terms used in the learner-support materials. Her concern relates to the perception that rural language variants are more difficult and richer than urban variants. One of the science teachers displayed an awareness of linguistic variation and suggested that translations should take into consideration the common dialect or variant

spoken in a particular area so that learners are not removed from the variant they use in their speech communities as she put it below:

Thembi: Ngaske xa ku"*translatwa*"i-English to isiXhosa ibe sisiXhosa esithethwa kuloo ngingqi ukwenzela ukuba abantwana kungafuneki ukuba batolikelwe isiXhosa …. (Umntu otolikayo) adibane notitshala, ohlala apha eKapa, othetha esi siXhosa salapha eKapa sisisebenzisayo ngoba isiXhosa asifani.

I wish that when translation is done from English to isiXhosa the language (isiXhosa) spoken in that particular area be used (sic) so that there will be no need to retranslate isiXhosa to learners … (The translator should) contact the teacher, who is speaking the Cape Town isiXhosa variant we use here because isiXhosa has different dialects.

In addition, the isiXhosa spoken in urban environments is dissimilar or anglicised as compared to the isiXhosa spoken in rural environments. To overcome linguistic and conceptual problems that learners are confronted with, the teacher proposed code switching, which implies the mixing of isiXhosa and English terms as an alternative teaching strategy.

Challenges Experienced by Learners

Whilst teachers experienced pedagogical and linguistic challenges in using isiXhosa as a medium of instruction, learners mentioned structural challenges as impacting on their learning. These structural challenges included lack of laboratories and libraries in their community. However, they did not refer to the lack of laboratories and libraries in their schools nor did they expand on their expectations on these challenges. Seemingly these learners would be satisfied with a general library serving some of the communities surrounding them. One informant articulated the frustration in this way:

Apha ku le ndawo sihlala kuyo akukho *library*. Mna ndirhalela ukuba sibe nazo izinto zoku *experimenta*.

There is no library where we stay. I wish we had tools for experimentation.

One can observe from the above utterance that learners' main challenge is infrastructural whilst those of teachers are educational and linguistc. The learners' perceptions could be attributed to their understanding and need to learn science through experimentation and mathematics from books and as far as they are concerned, these resources can only be found in laboratories and libraries.

IMPLICATIONS FOR TEACHING AND LEARNING

This study shows that both teachers and learners recognise the cognitive benefits of using the home language (isiXhosa) in the teaching and learning of mathematics and science. As shown in the discussion above, they have indicated that the use of isiXhosa facilitates active learner participation and better conceptual understanding of mathematics and science. This indicates the importance of language proficiency as facilitating conceptual understanding in mathematics and science This ties in with Cummin's (1979) notion of the Cognitive Academic Language Proficiency (CALP) which suggests that the home language is a good foundation for effective learning.

From this study it has become clear that it is feasible to use an African language as a medium of learning and teaching in school science and mathematics despite the general perception that African languages cannot be used in science and mathematics education because of their perceived lack of global status and appropriate terminology. Similar studies like the Six Year Primary School Project (SYPP) in Nigeria in the 1970s (Bamgbose, 2005), the LOITASA project (Qorro, Desai, & Brock-Utne, 2008) and a recent study in Ethiopia (Yohannes, 2009) have shown that it is possible to produce teaching and learning materials in local African languages.

Given that science and mathematics are priority areas in the South African education system, it is imperative that all learners have access to these subjects in order to participate in the economic and technological development of the country. Access to these subjects is possible if teaching and learning occur through a familiar language, namely, their home language as suggested by the teachers' and learners' responses. However, it is clear from the discussion above that there are challenges surrounding the teaching of science and mathematics through the meadium of isiXhosa. The pedagogical challenges can be addressed in various ways such as through teacher development programmes. These programmes could entail the use of appropriate teaching methods such as exemplification, which implies giving examples in cases where there is uncertainty and lack of clarity of scientific terms and diagrammatic representations to illustrate mathematical and scientific ideas and objects.

The linguistic challenges on the other hand may be addressed by making use of code switching and borrowing or use of loan words where isiXhosa terms are obscure in meaning or difficult to understand. Studies in code switching have shown that code switching is a useful linguistic and pedagogical resource in facilitating understanding in the classroom. (Mwinsheikhe, 2009; Setati, 2008; Nomlomo, 2007; Holmarsdottir, 2006). Consultation with subject teachers could also be useful during translation of teaching and learning material.

CONCLUSION

There is no doubt that English is a global or international language which all learners should have access to, but it should not be used as a tool to disempower or stop the use of home or local languages in education. English can be learned successfully as a subject as has occurred in many developed countries. Countries like Norway, the Netherlands, Japan, Iceland and many others have shown that people can learn through their home languages and learn English effectively as a foreign language. In the case of South Africa all learners should have adequate exposure to and support in their home languages and English. Such an exercise would facilitate additive bilingualism instead of subtractive bilingualism.

Many African countries, including South Africa, have the misconception that a language is learned better if it is used as a medium of instruction at schools, than when it is learned as a subject. This is despite the fact that most of the teaching in many classrooms occurs through code switching and mixing which involve the use of local languages. The unsystematic use of code switching, transliteration and assessment which are carried out in English as the instructional medium make the effectiveness of this practice questionable, particularly in black schools. Concerning the abstract and unfamiliar mathematics and science registers, code switching and translation pose a number of challenges in terms of conceptualizing the mathematical and science terms although the roles code switching and translation play as linguistic resources in teaching and learning cannot be disputed.

The discussion above has also shown that whilst teachers' views are not monolithic, the majority view is that the use of the home language facilitates teaching and learning. It also shows that the use of the home language is not unproblematic, considering the notions of linguistic ambiguities and variations, as well as the specialized languages of science and mathematics and the lack of resources. Hence it is incumbent upon policy makers, curriculum designers and teachers to take note of these problems and to devise appropriate means to address them. The first step to do this would be to take note of the teachers' proposals since teachers are at the forefront of the educational enterprise in science and mathematics. It is proposed that this study should be extended and empirical evidence be collected which would show the benefits of using the home languages of learners in their education.

REFERENCES

Alexander, N. (1989). *Language policy and national unity in South Africa/Azania.* Cape Town: Buchu Books.

Bamgbose, A. (2005). Mother tongue education: Lessons learnt from the Yoruba experience. In B. Brock-Utne & R. K. Hopson (Eds.), *Languages of instruction for emancipation: Focus on postcolonial contexts and considerations* (pp. 231-255). Dar es Salaam: Mkuki na Nyota Publishers.

Brock-Utne, B., & Hopson, R. K. (2005). Educational language contexts and issues in postcolonial Africa. In B. Brock-Utne & R. K. Hopson (Eds.), *Languages of instruction for emancipation: Focus on postcolonial contexts and considerations* (pp. 231-255). Dar es Salaam: Mkuki na Nyota Publishers.

Bunyi, G. (1997). Multilingualism and discourse in primary school Mathematics in Kenya. *Language, Culture and Curriculum, 10*(1), 52-65.

Clarkson, P. C. (2004). Teaching mathematics in multilingual classrooms: The global importance of contexts. In I. P. Cheong, I. J. Kyeleve, & O. Chukwu (Eds.), *Globalisation trends in science, mathematics and technical education.* Brunei Darussalam: Universiti Brunei Darussalam.

Cummins, J. (1979). Empirical and theoretical underpinnings of bilingual education. *Journal of Education, 163*(1), 16-29.

De Klerk, V. (2000). To be Xhosa or not to be Xhosa … That is the question. *Journal of Multilingual and Multicultural Development, 21*(3), 198-215.

Durkin, K., & Shire, B. (Eds.). (1991). *Language in mathematical education: Research and practice.* Milton Keynes, UK: Open University Press.

Elugbe, B. O. (1990). National language and national development. In E. N. Emenanjo (Ed.), *Multilingualism, minority languages and language policy in Nigeria.* Nigeria: Central Books Limited.

Fischer, A., Weiss, E., Tshabe, S., & Mdala, E. (1985). *English-Xhosa dictionary.* Cape Town: Oxford University Press.

Halai, A. (2007). Learning mathematics in English medium classrooms in Pakistan: Implications for policy and practice. *Bulletin of Education & Research, 29*(1), 1-16.

Hameso, S. Y. (1997). The language of education in Africa: The key issues. *Language, Culture and Curriculum, 10*(1), 1-13.

Heugh, K. (2003). Disabling and enabling: Implications of language policy trends in South Africa. In K. Heugh, *Language policy and democracy in South Africa.* Doctoral Dissertation. Sweden: University of Stockholm.

Holmarsdottir, H. B. (2006). *From policy to practice: A study of the implementation of the Language-in-Education Policy (LiEP) in three South African primary schools.* Unpublished Doctoral Thesis. Norway: University of Oslo.

Hunting, R. (Ed.). (1988). *Language issues in learning and teaching mathematics.* Melbourne: La Trobe University.

Iyamu, E. O. S., & Ogiegbaen, S. E. A. (2007). Parents and teachers' perception of mother tongue medium of instruction policy in Nigerian primary schools. *Language, Culture and Curriculum, 20*(2), 97-108.

Jokweni, M. (2004). Problems associated with the creation of isiXhosa terms for special subjects: The case of geography and science. In B. Brock-Utne, Z. Desai, & M. Qorro (Eds.), *Researching the language of instruction in Tanzania and South Africa* (pp. 169-176). Cape Town: African Minds.

Langenhoven, K, R. (2005). Can mother tongue instruction contribute to enhancing scientific literacy? A look at Grade 4 Natural Science classroom. In B. Brock-Utne, Z. Desai, & M. Qorro (Eds.), *LOITASA research in progress.* Dar-es-Salaam: KAD Associates.

Makinde, S. O., & Olabode, M. M. (2006). Effects of Yoruba and English media of instruction on students' achievement in biology in selected Lagos state secondary schools of Nigeria. Paper presented at the Language and Education in Africa Conference. University of Oslo: Norway.

Mazrui, A. M. (2002). The English language in African education: Dependency and decolonization. In J. W. Tollefson (Ed.), *Language policies in education – Critical issues* (pp. 267-282). London: Lawrence Erlbaum Associates Publishers.

Mbekwa, M. (2008). Translating mathematical texts for mother tongue teaching and learning of mathematics. A paper presented at the South African Comparative Higher Education Society (SACHES) Conference. Stellenbosch, 3 November 2009.

Mullis, I. V. S., Martin, M. O., Kennedy, A. M., & Foy, P. (2006). *IEA's progress in international reading literacy study in primary schools in 40 countries.* Chestnut Hill, MA: TIMSS & PIRLS International Study Center.

Mwinsheikhe, H. (2009). Spare no means: Battling with the English/Kiswahili dilemma in Tanzanian secondary school classrooms. In B. Brock-Utne & I. Skattum (Eds.), *Languages and education in Africa: A comparative and transdisciplinary analysis* (pp. 223-234). United Kingdom: Symposium Books.

Mwinsheikhe, H. (2008). Overcoming the language barrier: An in-depth study of the strategies used by Tanzania secondary science teachers and students in coping with the English-KiSwahili dilemma. In B. Brocke-Utne, Z. Desai, & M. Qorro (Eds.), *LOITASA: Reflecting on phase I and entering phase II* (pp. 123-142). Dar es Salaam: Vision Publishing.

Napier, D. B. (2011). Critical issues in language and education planning in twenty first century in South Africa. *US-China Education Review B, 1*, 58-76.

National Department of Education. (1996). *The South African schools act. Act no. 108 of 1996*. Cape Town: Government Printer.

National Department of Education. (1997). *Language-in-education policy*, 1-9.

Ndamba, G. T. (2008). Mother tongue usage in learning: An examination of language preferences in Zimbabwe. *The Journal of Pan African Studies, 2*(4), 171-188.

Nomlomo, V. S. (2007). *Science teaching and learning through the medium of English and isiXhosa: A comparative study at two primary schools in the Western Cape*. Unpublished Doctoral Thesis. Bellville: University of the Western Cape.

Nomlomo, V. S. (1993). *Language variation in the Xhosa speech community and its impact on children's education*. Unpublished M.Ed Thesis. Cape Town: University of Cape Town.

Ogunniyi, Meshach, B. (2005). Cultural perspectives on science and technology education. In A. A. Abdi & A. Cleghorn (Eds.), *Issues in African education: Sociological perspectives*. England: Palgrave Macmillan.

Orr, E. (1987). *Twice as less: Black English and the performance of black students in mathematics and science*. Norton: New York.

Pimm, D. (1987). *Speaking mathematically: Communication in mathematics classroom*. London: Routledge and Kegan Paul.

Prah, K. K. (2003). Going native: Language of instruction for education, development and African emancipation. In B. Brock-Utne, Z. Desai, & M. Qorro (Eds.), *Language of instruction in Tanzania and South Africa (LOITASA)*. Dar-es-Salaam: E & D Limited.

Qorro, M., Desai, Z., & Brock-Utne, B. (2008). Introduction. In M. Qorro, Z. Desai, & B. Brock-Utne (Eds.), *LOITASA: Reflecting on phase I and entering phase II*. Dar es Salaam: Vision Publishing Limited.

Republic of South Africa (RSA). (1996). *Constitution of the Republic of South Africa*. Pretoria: South Africa. Government Printer.

Reddy, V. (2006). *Mathematics and science achievement at South African schools in TIMSS 2003*. Human Sciences Research Council (HSRC) Report. Cape Town: HSRC Press.

Rogan, J. M., & Grayson, D. J. (2003). Towards a theory of curriculum implementation with particular reference to science education in developing countries. *International Journal of Science Education, 25*(10), 1171-1204.

Sentson, C. (1994). The effect of language of presentation on the pupils' performance in a mathematics test. *Language Matters*, 109-113.

Setati, M. (2005). Teaching mathematics in a multilingual classroom. *Journal for Research in Mathematics Education, 36*(5), 447-466.

Setati, M. (2008). Access to mathematics versus access to the language of power: The struggle in mathematics classrooms. *South African Journal of Education, 28*, 103-116.

Statistics South Africa. (2004). Census 2001: Primary Table. Retrieved from: http://www.statssa.gov.za.

Stephens, M., Waywood, A., Clarke, D., & Izard, J. (Eds.). (1993). *Communicating mathematics: Perspectives from classroom practice and current research*. Hawthorn, Victoria: Australian Council for Educational Research.

Tollefson, J. W., & Tsui, A. B. M. (2004). Medium of instruction in Slovenia: European integration and ethnolinguistic nationalism. In J. W. Tollefson & A. B. M. Tsui (Eds.), *Medium of instruction policies: Which agenda? Whose agenda?* New Jersey: Lawrence Erlbaum Associates.

Vuzo, M. (2005). Using English as a medium of instruction in Tanzanian schools: Problems and prospects. In B. Brock-Utne, Z. Desai, & M. Qorro (Eds.), *LOITASA research in progress*. Dar-es-Salaam: KAD Associates.

Wedikkarage, L. K. P. (2006). *English as a medium of instruction for Collegiate Level Science classes in Sri Lanka: Theory, policy and practice*. Doctoral Dissertation. Norway: University of Oslo.

Yohannes, M. A. G. (2009). Implications of the use of mother tongues versus languages of instruction for academic achievement in Ethiopia. In B. Brock-Utne & I. Skattum (Eds.), *Languages and education in Africa: A comparative and transdisciplinary analysis* (pp. 189-199). United Kingdom: Symposium Books.

Vuyokazi Nomlomo & Monde Mbekwa
University of the Western Cape
South Africa

149

PART IV

TEACHER IDENTITY, REFORM, DOMINATION AND TRANSFORMATION

BEATRICE AVALOS & DANAE DE LOS RÍOS

REFORM ENVIRONMENT AND TEACHER IDENTITY IN CHILE[1]

INTRODUCTION

In the last 20 years teachers around the world have been exposed to a wide range of transformations occurring in their education systems, which in turn have triggered challenges to their professional identities (Weber, 2007; Baker & Wiseman, 2005; van den Berg, 2002). School populations with complex demands have widened and now embrace a greater cultural and socio-economic diversity of pupils, rendering more difficult the work that teachers do (Esteve, 2006; Jacinto & Freytes Frei, 2007). Pressures to increase educational achievement in the light of standardised examinations, national and international (Day, 2002), as well as new forms of teaching based on technology are placing teachers under greater scrutiny and leading to re-definitions of their professional jurisdictions.

Since the beginning of the nineties Chile experienced a continuous wave of reforms, some closer to schools and classrooms and some that affect the system as a whole, such as major curriculum revamps and lengthening of the school day. Teachers have been part of these changes in various ways, but mostly as implementers of reforms decided with limited teacher participation. With the increased importance of standardised assessments' results, both national and international, as a measure of the effectiveness of reforms, teachers are targeted as solely responsible for low student results, and as such placed in the public limelight in political speeches and the media. As these processes occur, not much is known about how teachers perceive themselves in such reform and accountability environments, nor how they handle the new demands that the student population places upon them. The study that underlies this chapter is a recent attempt to learn about teachers in Chile, about how they view themselves and their work demands, and, in turn, about how they interpret their status in society. In what follows, we discuss results of this study from the perspective of teacher identity. Our purpose is to highlight teacher perceptions in particular educational policy environments marked by policy shifts and by requests for changes in the practices of teaching and dealings with students and other actors of the education system. To this end, we look first at changes occurring in the 1990s and 2000s in Chile, and then on the

---

[1] The research base of this paper was funded by the Iniciativa Científica Milenio, Project PO7S-21-F: "La Profesión Docente en Chile. Políticas, Prácticas y Proyecciones."

basis of a set of key constructs about teacher identity we present and discuss results from the study of primary and secondary teachers conducted in 2009.

THE EDUCATIONAL POLICY CONTEXT OF CHILE IN THE 1990S AND 2000S

As 17 years of military dictatorship in Chile came to an end in 1990, there was general agreement on the part of the new government that there had to be changes in the education system and its provisions, though it was acknowledged that this could only be done in the context of the existing law of education and without too much disruption to the school management structure inherited from the military government. Such structure is made up of a voucher type of public funding for two types of schools (municipal and public subsidised) and also includes around 9% of entirely private schools. Given these limitations, the focus of changes being undertaken by the Ministry of Education was then placed on the operation and teaching processes within schools through the development of major intervention programmes to improve equity and quality in the primary school (grades 1 to 8) as well as in secondary education (grades 9 to 12). These programmes encompassed several types of changes: a school curriculum review, free provision of teaching resources (textbooks and other materials), improvement of school buildings and gradual introduction of Information Communication Technology (ICT), beginning with the poorest and more remote municipal schools. A series of focused programmes aimed at vulnerable school populations were developed, covering first primary education (rural and urban poor) and later secondary schools, all of which involved new teaching strategies and the provision of ad hoc materials. During the entire decade of the nineties in the course of their implementation, these programmes were modified in the light of existing assess-ments of their effectiveness. Teachers were largely called upon to implement the teaching and management strategies associated with the changes, and a number of different types of professional activities were put in place to help them in this role.

However, by the end of the nineties there were some doubts about the effectiveness of such programmes, given the slow rate of improvement of learning results as measured by the national standardised assessment known as SIMCE (Education Quality Measurement System), a test which is administered by the Ministry of Education. Two key concepts floated around to justify the pursuit of new policies: incentives and structural reforms. Providing monetary incentives to well-performing schools might entice teachers in other schools to improve their performance and raise their students' scores. Sending teachers abroad to learn from other experiences might benefit the system and improve teaching and learning results. Changing the double-shift operation of schools to a longer one-shift school day would provide more time for learning, and therefore increase the chances of better school results. All these actions were tried, with the expectation that their efficacy would be evident through increased SIMCE results. However, while teachers appreciated the rewards offered when their schools fared well or the opportunity to travel abroad and learn from others, the beneficiaries of these opportunities constituted a small segment of the teacher population. The education system as a whole, especially the public sector, was still not performing as expected. Attention then turned more strongly to teacher accountability and demands for the establishment of a system of teacher performance evaluation.

The new century brought about an understanding between the Ministry of Education and the teachers' union to evaluate teacher performance (Avalos & Assael, 2006), based solely on performance in the classroom and not on pupil learning results. But, the new century also began to highlight evidence that SIMCE results favoured upper and middle class social groups who generally attended private subsidised and wholly private schools, while leaving behind the poorer sectors enrolled in municipal schools. It was recognised that the practice of granting an equal subsidy per pupil actually in attendance at schools had a detrimental effect on poorer schools that needed more money to assist all children to move ahead, and not just those who did not need extra support. To redress this inequality a law was passed to increase school subsidies for schools attending populations in need, which was tied to showing evidence of improvement (a form of the "No Child Left Behind" policy) and therefore with pressures on teachers to produce results or risk the closure of their schools.

The key role of SIMCE assessments was strengthened by deciding to test children every year in fourth grade, and by introducing a standards-based system to establish not just general scores, but also anchor points referred to what students know and are able to do in each one of the subject areas measured. Despite all these measures, current SIMCE results remain unsatisfactory in subjects such as mathematics and language arts, and Chilean students' performance in the PISA 2009 test while indicating improvement, is still below the participating countries' mean scores (OECD, 2010, http://www.oecd.org/dataoecd/54/12/46643496.pdf).

In this context of a system that has experimented with many improvement projects, that has changed the curriculum at least twice in two decades, that has offered incentives to teachers who improve school learning results, but that also until recently played down the effect of socio-economic differences on learning – teachers have been uncertain key players. This has been partly due to working conditions that require municipal or public school teachers to teach at least thirty chronological hours per week if they are employed full time (44 hours), excluding recess time, and a proportionally lower number of hours if they are employed for 30 hours (see Table 1). They may have classes as large as 45 students, especially in urban low socio-economic sectors, and compared to other professionals with similar background training, teachers earn 40% less (Valenzuela et al., 2010). On the other hand, teachers in private schools earn better salaries, have smaller classes and less teaching time than their counterparts in public subsidised and municipal schools. And their schools score highest on the SIMCE tests.

Thus, in the light of these complex developments in education in Chile and the fragile conditions in which large groups of teachers work, an obvious question is how this situation has affected their concept of the teaching profession and their own professional identity. Before answering this question, which is central to the chapter, we look at how the literature has dealt with issues related to teacher professional identity.

Table 1. Public school teachers' weekly workload according to terms of appointment.

Appointment (hours)	Recess (hours)	Classroom teaching periods (45 minutes)	Classroom teaching periods (60 minutes)	Non teaching activities (meetings, etc.)
44	3 hrs	43	32 hrs. 15 min.	8 hrs. 45 min.
30	2 hrs. 03 min	30	22 hrs. 15 min.	5 hrs. 27 min.
10	41 min.	10	7 hrs. 30 min.	1 hr. 49 min.

Source: Colegio de Profesores, www.colegiodeprofesores.cl

TEACHER IDENTITY CONSTRUCTION – KEY CONCEPTS

Teacher identity refers to how teachers define themselves in relation to their professional tasks and particularly in terms of educational and teaching relationships. From a social perspective, using Castells' words (1997, p. 6) identity may be defined as "a construction of meaning on the basis of a cultural attribute, or related set of cultural attributes, that is/are given priority over other sources of meaning." Teachers are entrusted by society with the task of educating children and young people, a sort of mission which generations of teachers have accepted and embodied as best as they can. And on the basis of this essential task they construct and reconstruct their identities over time, through giving meaning to their role and work in relation to the meanings others make about them (Beijard et al 2000). Teacher identity is therefore a co-construction involving one teacher and other significant agents, or teachers and the broader society to which they belong.

In considering how teachers identify themselves as professionals or how teachers define their responsibilities and work, the following key aspects stand out in the literature examined: (a) the meanings and definitions teachers give to their work and the degree of commitment or motivation that keeps them going; (b) the definition embodied in policies and reforms which affect teachers personally as well as in their work; (c) confidence in their ability to do the work, or the degree of self-efficacy feelings; and (d) the perception of differences between how teachers define their tasks and mission and how they perceive others and society as a whole value and respect their work.

Motivation and Commitment

Part of the initial preparation of teachers is centred on the importance of the tasks that will be entrusted to them. They are made aware to an extent of their future sphere of work and of the demands that will be placed upon them, as well as of the capabilities they will need to engage accordingly in this mission. At the stage of initial preparation, future teachers may see only a worthwhile task and feel theoretically motivated, depending on the degree to which they are faced with practical situations. As they begin to teach and progress through their career, their motivation and commitment may be strengthened or may be tested in critical situations (see Day et al., 2007). It is well known that new teachers are more likely to experience identity conflicts while entering the profession since they need to address new and demanding tasks. Instead, experienced teachers may experience identity conflicts as educational reforms request them to modify proven practices and expose their work and expertise to deep scrutiny or examination. Often reform initiatives seek to redefine professional practice, and as such, they represent a threat to the motivation and commitment that teachers have built over time.

Work Demands and Satisfaction

Teachers' identity formation is linked to educational tasks in the broad sense of the word and to teaching tasks in the smaller world of the classroom. It is also linked to the interactions and relationships with parents, colleagues and school authorities. Professional identity emerges from the knowledge and expertise accumulated through teaching and learning, and through integrating individual and collective experiences of what is at the core of the profession (Beijaard et al., 2004). The degree to which it is possible to carry out the demands of work as envisioned affects teachers' sense of responsibility and may call into question identity definitions. For example, if work is intensified through change demands, or there is limited time to do all that was planned, teachers may feel a growing sense of dissatisfaction and frustration with themselves as teachers. But also, they may feel empowered to defy the context and assert themselves as responsible professionals.

Self-efficacy

An important part of teacher identity has to do with capacity feelings or the sense that she or he is competent in the job. The degree to which a teacher feels personally efficacious is also the degree to which she or he becomes a conscious agent in educational contexts, with strength to alter and improve them (Brandt 1996 and Russsell 1996, cited in Day et al., 2007). A heightened sense of efficacy is of help when teachers are faced with demands to implement new methods as these are taken as challenges rather than burdens (van den Berg, 2002). A low sense of efficacy, in turn, will affect the mode of responding to new situations, including difficult or unmotivated students. Both self-efficacy and agency operate in interaction with the possibilities offered by social structures such as the school environment, or change demands produced extraneously. If these conditions clash with what teachers believe they can do or believe should be done, they may result in passive submission (lack of motivation) or in reasonable attempts to implement without leaving aside those practices already considered sound (Vandeyar, 2005)

Teachers in the Public Eye

Teacher identity is linked to the trust society places in them. Identity is shaped through traditions, social structures and collective norms that provide teachers with different levels of autonomy and jurisdiction. As with other professionals, the recognition of teachers' jurisdiction is a key element in how they view themselves and the degree to which they feel satisfied with their work. Yet the current status and recognition of teachers in many contexts appears to be in jeopardy. Partly this has to do with prevailing redefinitions of teachers' jurisdiction in terms of "consumers" or "clients" demanding results instead of children and young people demanding education (Hargreaves et al., 2007). It also has to do with the paradox involved in entrusting teachers with the responsibility of building a new social and economic order through education, while requiring them to correct its negative effects over the young generation through engaging in social protection tasks, which precisely are those least recognised in results-based pressure climates (Hargreaves, 2003).

THE STUDY

The basis of this chapter is a study of the teaching profession conducted in Chile. The study was broadly aimed at gaining understanding about teachers in primary and secondary schools, about their visions and interpretations of the profession, on how the reform environment of the 1990s and 2000s affected their working lives in the different school contexts to which they belong, and how they mediate between reform demands and their own convictions and experience. A key concept underlying the study is that of teacher identity. The broader study had three components: (a) a review of existing data bases on teachers in Chile, their working conditions and their salary structure; (b) a national representative survey of teachers; and (c) a set of six case studies of teachers in schools that were part of the national survey population, in five regions of the country. The study also gathered information from seven focus groups with teachers, in the city of Santiago, aimed at providing input to the design of the survey. For the purposes of this chapter, we draw from the analysis of the national survey and qualitative data gathered in focus group meetings and case study interviews.

The Population and Sample

The target population included 122,521 teachers in 5,026 schools in all except two of the 15 geographic regions of the country. Those excluded belong to isolated and sparsely populated geographical locations. Also excluded were small rural (less than 7 teachers) private schools. A stratified random multi-stage sample of all types of urban and rural schools and a non-proportional sample of teachers in these schools was selected. The achieved sample consisted of 1,929 teachers considered representative of the population with a 5 % margin of error. All these teachers had the required teaching qualifications for either primary or secondary teaching.

Selected teachers were delivered the survey questionnaires personally at their schools, which were also collected personally by field workers. The main characteristics of the sampled teachers are shown in Table 2.

Table 2. Description of the teachers studied

	N	%
Gender		
– Male	607	33.4
– Female	1213	66.6
Total responses	1820	94.3
Mean Age: 44 years		
Teaching experience		
– 0-3 years	213	11.4
– 4-10 years	463	24..9
– 11-24 years	645	34.6
– 25 or more years	542	29.1
Total responses	1863	96.7
Type of school		
– Municipal/Public	829	44.6
– Private subsidised	753	40.5
– All private	275	14.8
Total Responses	1857	96.3
School level		
– Primary	1219	66.4
– Secondary	618	33.6
Total	1837	95.2

Source: Teacher Survey

The Survey

The survey consisted of a questionnaire with 35 items that included information on personal and school teaching experience and workload. Teachers were asked questions about their work demands and their degree of satisfaction with these, the effect on their work lives of different reform initiatives, of school conditions, of pupils and of personal conditions such as health or family situations, as well as perceived effect on their teaching competency of initial and in-service teacher education and of experience. They were also asked about participation in reform actions and their perception of the effect of these reforms. Teacher identity perceptions were explored through questions related to reasons for choosing the teaching profession, degree of motivation, and degree of agreement with a set of statements describing a teachers' mission, and finally agreement/disagreement scales on the current status of the profession and degree of respect afforded by a list of stakeholders. The distribution of items and sub-items in each one of these areas is shown in Table 3. The survey was piloted among a group of 78 teachers representing the target population and the scale items were factor analysed to decide on the final form of the survey.

159

Table 3. Distribution of questionnaire topics

Categories	N° of items	N° of sub-items
Personal characteristics:		
– Age, gender, education and teaching qualifications	3	1
Socio-economic status:		
– Parents level of education, monthly home income, number of persons living at home	4	
Working conditions:		
– Type of school administration, school level	2	
– Total number of contract hours and weekly hours occupied in teaching-related activities (in and out of school)	2	
– School teaching experience (years, number of schools and length of teaching in school with higher contract hours)	3	
Satisfaction with working conditions		
– Feelings of stress	2	
– Time available for teaching-related activities	2	10
– Self-efficacy perceptions	1	4
Impact on teaching activities of four factors:	1	
– Educational policies		10
– School conditions		8
– Students		7
– Personal situations		5
Knowledge of and participation in framing, implementing and evaluating educational reforms	2	3
Impact of reforms and policies since 1990 on:		
– Teachers, school quality, school coverage and improvement, and teaching conditions.	1	7
Effect of initial teacher education, professional development and years of experience on the quality of teaching strategies and collegial interactions	1	14
Opportunity to interact with colleagues	1	6
Professional identity and motivation		
– Reasons for entering the profession	1	22
– Views on teachers' mission and main tasks	1	24
– Current and past degrees of motivation	2	
– Future plans (change of school, other responsibilities)	1	5
Status of the teaching profession		
– Traits describing the profession	1	19
– Place among other professions	1	21
– Respect afforded by other social groups to the teaching profession	1	14
– Changes in the status of the profession over time	1	6
– Actions that would improve the status of the profession	1	12
Total	35	198

On the basis of the response patterns to the questionnaire principal component analysis was used to produce a set of indices that would allow for a more fluid interpretation of the data gathered. For the purposes of this chapter the relevant resulting indices are presented in Table 4.

Table 4. Relevant indices

Themes	Indices and content
Motivation and commitment: reasons for entering the profession	Pedagogic commitment or vocation Former experience (family or school models) Work conditions Social role and status of the profession
Work demands and satisfaction	Degree of satisfaction with: time for lesson preparation, classroom management, teaching, professional activities, responses to Ministry of Education requests and demands. Impact of: policies affecting the school and teachers; school climate and conditions, student characteristics (background and motivation), personal situations.
Self-efficacy	Confidence in motivating students, being creative in class, improving student results, influencing learning of all/most students.
Teachers' in the public eye	Perceptions of professional status of teachers

The Focus Group Meetings

Seven meetings were held with 35 primary and secondary teachers from municipal, private subsidised and private schools. These teachers were not part of the surveyed group as the meetings were held prior to the survey with the purpose of exploring their views as input for developing the questionnaire. The groups were organised in terms of experience (teachers with less or more than five years experience) and socio-economic level of students (middle-low and high). Teachers were asked to comment on their teaching experiences (prior and/or current), how they perceived themselves in the coming years, what helped them to improve their practice, whether they had experienced changes or new reform projects in their schools, and how the perceived their students.

Case Studies

Eleven primary and secondary teachers were interviewed in six different schools that were part of the population surveyed. The schools represented all three different types of administration referred to earlier: municipal, private subsidised and private and were located in five regions of the country. Also interviewed were the principals of these schools. The teacher interviews centred on issues related to themselves as persons, their professional history, their current working conditions, their degree of satisfaction with their teaching responsibilities, as well as their professional development opportunities.

MAIN RESULTS

For the analysis of results we follow the key constructs used to assess issues related to teacher identity.

Motivation and Commitment

Teachers rated the degree to which a series of reasons had been important in their decision to become teachers. The highest degree of importance was given by all teachers to factors having to do with what we might call "pedagogic commitment" or "vocation." Such reasons included "self-fulfilment," "work with young people," "desire to share knowledge," "passion for education," "interest in subject-matter." and "teaching capacity." Most teachers were less inclined to have chosen teaching as a profession because of "satisfactory working conditions" or because of prior experience such as having had a model teacher in school or somebody in the family as a teacher. Teachers did not differ in these assessments by type of school in which they worked. However, teachers with more years of experience tended to rate "pedagogic commitment" as their main reason for entering the profession, compared to teachers with less experience. Clearly, the least important factors for all groups, but especially those with lesser experience were what we call working conditions (stable employment, flexible time-tables, holidays and salary). Likewise, the status of the teaching profession was not an important reason at all for half of the sample, and only somewhat important for another 23%.

> In eighth grade I took a test and I found that my vocation was to be a teacher. My family said that I would make no money, because our profession was not well paid, but I knew it. I took the test and my three first applications were for teaching careers. That was what I wanted. I knew the responsibility I was taking on. [*Municipal school teacher in focus group meeting*]

Another important factor was the ratings teachers gave to the degree of their current work motivation, and how this compared to the situation three years before. Teachers in municipal schools indicated a significantly lower degree of current as well as past motivation compared to teachers in private schools, but did not differ from those in private subsidised schools. In general, as teachers progressed in experience their degree of motivation decreased compared to teachers with less experience:

> I am tired, I have taught for 10 years, but this is a profession that wears you out professionally and emotionally. I have postponed my family at times

when I have to finish correcting papers and thus, I end up questioning myself about the gratifications of this profession. ... So sometimes I question myself I and how satisfied I am with the profession. [Case study *interview with teacher in a private subsidised school*]

Work Demands and Satisfaction

In line with the assumption that working conditions affect teacher identity, we asked a series of questions relating to teacher perception and degree of satisfaction with these conditions. We grouped the factors that might have an impact or be important either positively or negatively upon their work into the following four areas: educational policies, school conditions, pupils and personal situations.

Educational Policies and Reforms

Two types of policies were visible: those that directly affect the school and its functioning, and those that affect more closely the work that teachers do. Among the first kind of policies are the effects of lengthening the school day, curriculum changes and changes to the SIMCE test. Among the second kind of policies are those that impact teachers more directly such as teacher performance evaluation. Not all of these policies affect teachers in the same way, depending on the type of school in which they work. For example, lengthening of the school day has no particular effect on private schools, because they were already functioning with such a system. Teacher performance evaluation at present only targets teachers in municipal schools, placing constraints on their time, as they must prepare portfolios and videos for the process.

Table 5. Impact of policies on schools and teachers by type of school (Mean ratings: 1=not important; 2= little importance; 3=somewhat important; 4= important)

	Municipal		Private Subsidised		Private	
Effect of policies/reforms	Mean	S.E.	Mean	S.E.	Mean	S.E
– On the school as a whole	3.35**	0.03	3.44**	0.02	3.14	0.05
– On teachers' work	3.20**	0.04	3.29***	0.03	2.97	0.07

***Difference with private schools significant at P<0.001; ** Difference with private schools significant at P<0.01
Source: Teacher Questionnaire

As seen in Table 5, on the whole teachers in municipal schools and private subsidised schools rated the impact of policies affecting the school as a whole and their own work higher than did teachers in wholly private schools, and the differences were significant. This is not surprising as teachers in private schools are not affected much by public policies and reforms. In fact, the only public policy that affects schools and teachers in private schools, besides the national curriculum framework, is the system of school measurement (SIMCE) and the university entrance examination (PSU) as schools compete strongly against each other for a good place in the league:

> The school system is becoming more and more competitive. Students are coming to some schools because they have good results in standardized tests. In the end, there is a huge effort towards results, call it SIMCE or PSU. [*Private school teacher comment during focus group meeting*]

One of the issues surrounding teacher perceptions of reforms is the extent to which they felt considered when these were planned and implemented. Surveyed teachers were asked to refer to a reform that had affected them, and then asked what was their own role regarding that reform. Most teachers (71%) said they had no part at all in the planning of the reform; just over half (55%) of the teachers were involved in some way in its implementation in their schools and 43% had no part in any evaluation of its effect.

> Reforms have been quite selfish with teachers. Reforms do not take teachers into consideration. As far as I know, the reform has changed different subjects of the curriculum, but is not centered on teachers and how they can do a good work. It is hard to work with 45 pupils in the class. The reforms have not considered teachers' opinion. They have considered the view of experts, a PhD in curriculum or communication, but not the real actors: the teachers, who are in the classroom, and that is a huge weakness of the reforms. [*Case study interview with teacher in a public subsidised school*]

> I think one should talk about a before and an after in relation to the ESD (Extended School Day). There is an entirely new situation that starts with the education system itself ... and the world. Globalisation, issues arising from it, the Ministry. A Ministry that largely does not care about the problems, it slides over them, and as a colleague says: 'we have to put up'. Our current symbol, I think, is "to put up." Putting up with, rather than developing habits or teaching ... We suddenly have become policemen, referees, a bit of everything, in order to continue pushing on. [*Municipal school teacher in focus group*]

School Conditions

These refer primarily to school authorities and school climate, as well as to other teachers (their effectiveness, degree of commitment, changes of staff, and expectations). In general, most teachers rate issues relating to school managers and school climate as having a greater effect on their working conditions, than issues relating to other teachers. However, teachers in private subsidised and private schools rate these factors as having a greater impact than teachers in municipal schools, although differences between them are not significant. A possible explanation may be that head-teachers in municipal schools have less authority than they do in private schools, and therefore they offer less room for conflict.

Pupils

Here again there are two thematic areas: (a) the extent to which pupil socio-economic and cultural background impacts on teachers and teaching; and (b) the impact of pupil behaviour and degree of motivation. As shown in table 6 below teachers in municipal schools and private subsidised schools differ significantly from teachers in private schools in how they rate the importance of background factors. These teachers consider that socio-economic and cultural factors of pupils are important in relation to what they are able to do in the classroom. This accords with the fact that these types of schools, especially the municipal ones, get pupils from a lower socio-economic background.

Table 6. Impact of student factors on teachers classroom work (Mean ratings: 1=not important; 2= little importance; 3=somewhat important; 4= important)

	Municipal		Private Subsidised		Private	
Pupils conditions	Mean	S.E.	Mean	S.E.	Mean	S.E
Socio-economic and cultural background	3.67***	0.03	3.59**	0.03	3.49	0.03
Pupil behavioural factors	3.86*	0.01	3.84	0.32	3.80	0.02

*** P<0.001; **P<0.01
Source: Teacher questionnaire

Students' background factors are important to teachers depending on their years of experience. The following example illustrates, how a less experienced teacher analyses her relationship with different kinds of pupils, uncertain of how to deal with differences between groups of pupils.

It seems to me that students are used to being given everything fully digested. They have difficulty in drawing conclusions. For example, I was teaching science and needed to get them to think about the relationships between atmospheric pressure and height, and they had great difficulty in understanding this. It was difficult for them to provide examples, and I was struggling to prevent myself from providing the answers; because we are told that we have to let them think on their own. And one feels sort of anxious, as these children will become non-thinking adults. One is somewhat concerned. We have to continue trying because in fact they find it difficult to reason, to think analytically, even though they are in seventh grade. Now things might change, as I will be taking the sixth grade also for science, and I can already see they will be different. I know this because I taught them one lesson and saw that they participate differently, they are more active and they think. This might be a problem … I don't know. [*Municipal school young teacher in focus group*]

Compared to the effects of pupil background and cognitive characteristics, pupil behaviour is rated as a factor of greater importance by all three groups of teachers, although more so by teachers in municipal and private subsidised schools.

> Apathy has to do with the opportunities they have. Education used to be the only opportunity to improve. You either took it or lost it. My mother used to say that what a teacher said was the law and students should obey. Before, you needed to perform well. Nowadays, students perform poorly and they don't care, and parents condone these situations. Students' rights are overrated or misinterpreted. Students' rights are fine but students' obligations or responsibilities seem not to exist and that is quite problematic. [*Private subsidised school teacher in focus group*]

Personal Situations
Health problems, or unstable work-contracts, distance between location of schools and home are quite important factors for teachers in all types of schools, especially among teachers in municipal schools. A large proportion of teachers (65% to 70%) cited health problems and unstable work-contracts as their most important problems and did not differ significantly in this according to type of school in which they worked. But primary teachers were significantly more concerned about these problems as compared to secondary school teachers. Experiences of stress due to work demands were significantly more frequent among teachers in municipal schools compared to those in private subsidised and private schools.

Degree of Satisfaction
Time is a major factor in the surveyed teachers' lives that affects them. In general, municipal teachers are those least satisfied about time availability, especially time for planning, classroom management and classroom teaching. They differ significantly in this area from teachers in private subsidised and private schools.

> Teachers' work is heavy. One has a heavy workload. I don't know of any other type of employment in which employees take work back home. I think that this is a huge difference. I need to work at home, I need to plan, I need to prepare material, and grade exams at home. [*Private school teacher in focus group meeting*]

> Unlike other jobs, you need to work at home. Otherwise it is impossible because your contract does not include time to plan, to assess exams and homework. There just aren't enough hours. You come to school and you teach; you finish one class and then start another and then you have to prepare material for the next day or mark a test and you never stop. I have a sister, she is a nurse and I envy her because when she gets back home she has nothing more to do. I go home, I rest for a while, but then I need to go to the computer, prepare material, search in the Internet, I am always digging for material that may be useful for the school. [*Private subsidised school teacher in focus group meeting*]

Table 7. Teacher degree of satisfaction with available time (Mean ratings: 1=very dissatisfied; 2= dissatisfied; 3=satisfied; 4= very satisfied)

Time for:	Municipal		Private Subsidised		Private	
	Mean	S.E.	Mean	S.E.	Mean	S.E.
Lesson planning	2.11***	0.04	2.28	0.05.	2.45	0.04
Classroom management	2.93*	0.04	2.98	0.03	3.04	0.04
Classroom teaching	2.88*	0.03	2.97	0.03	2.99	0.04
Professional activities outside the classroom	2.69	0.03	2.73	0.03	2.74	0.05
Responding to external requests (i.e. Education Ministry)	2.70	0.04	2.78	0.04	2.76	0.06

*** P<0.001; *P<0.05
Source: Teacher questionnaire

Self-efficacy

Teachers were asked about their capacity to deal with a set of teaching demands. To what extent did they feel able to stimulate pupil interest in learning, be creative in their classrooms, improve pupil learning results and influence learning of all or almost all their pupils. Around 60% of all teachers surveyed felt satisfied that they were able to do these things. About a third felt very satisfied at being able to achieve such goals. There were no differences among the types of schools where they taught. Within this general level of satisfaction, teachers with less than 3 years of experience and between 11-24 years were somewhat less satisfied. Interviews with teachers in case studies and focus groups, however, show their expression of satisfaction is intermingled with their sense of mission or should we say, their "passion" for teaching.

I like to teach, I like to transmit my knowledge and I like it when students come back and say: "teacher, what you taught me was very useful." It pleases me when they come back and tell me: "I used to perform poorly in math at school but you taught me and I am very good at it." This is good for one's self-esteem and it very important." [*Case study private school teacher interview*]

I start from the notion that I love to be a teacher. I love to be a teacher. I love the classroom, and not the outside of it. Out of the classroom it's different. With parents it's like harder. During teacher meetings, I am a little shy, but in the classroom I am happy. Teaching is challenging and beautiful. I did my high school here. I worked in another school, but then I came back. I came back with more hours and a lower salary, but I feel that I belong to this place.

I came to the school to help, to make a difference, to be in the same classrooms. This is a huge challenge and every day I work to fulfill my goals as a teacher. [*Municipal school teacher in focus group meeting*]

In the light of this general satisfaction with their job as teachers, it is of interest to learn how they rated the contribution of initial teacher education, experience and professional development opportunities to their more specific sense of self-efficacy. Teachers clearly distinguished a differential impact of these factors on the development of specific teaching competences. Thus, over two thirds pointed to experience as their main source for developing the capacity to interact with colleagues, manage big classes and classroom routines, as well as handle discipline problems. Around half of all teachers considered their professional development opportunities as important in helping them to develop assessment skills, understand key concepts in the curriculum, use ICT, develop new teaching methods. But, teachers differed in their assessments depending on their years of experience. The following figures illustrate what are considered to be influential factors on teacher competency development as teachers grow in experience.

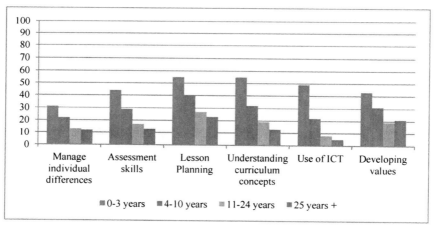

Source: Teacher questionnaire

Figure 1. Influence of initial teacher education on competency development by years of experience (%)

As seen in Figure 1, teacher education is clearly an important factor perceived by less experienced teachers to influence their teaching competence. After the first three years, professional development takes on a more prominent role as illustrated in Figure 2.

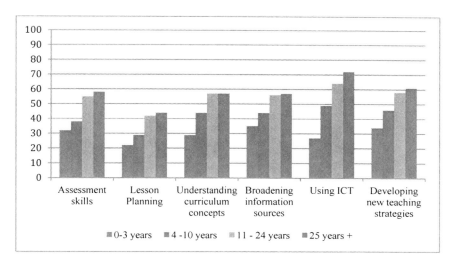

Source: Teacher questionnaire

Figure 2. Influence of professional development on competency by years of experience (%)

As teachers move on in their career, the experience gained is clearly viewed as the major factor explaining their self-efficacy in classroom management skills, especially handling of large classes, classroom routines, individual differences and pupil development (Figure 3).

Teachers in the Public Eye

In considering their profession, teachers are ambiguous about a series of characteristics that we group under the concept of social status. While they show personal commitment as teachers, they feel that others do not value their profession and that society generally holds teaching in low esteem. Teaching does not appear to be a particularly attractive profession. It is not well represented in the media and not sufficiently valued by government. Teachers have little autonomy and inadequate working conditions. As shown in Figure 4, teachers differ little by type of school regarding their lack or low degree of agreement that the profession exhibits a set of traits such as attractiveness, being socially valued or having good working conditions. Teachers in private schools are even more negative about the quality of working conditions and competence of the profession than are teachers in the other types of schools, even though objectively they have better working conditions and are generally considered to have a high degree of teaching competence, besides being appropriately qualified as are practically all teachers in Chile.

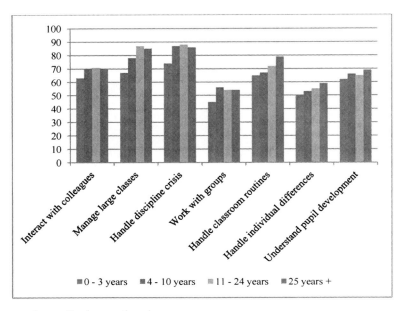

Source: Teacher questionnaire

Figure 3. Influence of experience on competence development by years of experience (%)

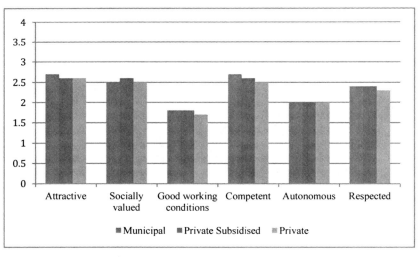

Source: Teacher questionnaire

Figure 4. Teacher degree of agreement on characteristics of the teaching profession by type of school: Mean ratings (1= disagree very much; 2= disagree; 3= agree; 4= agree very much)

With all these and other indicators referring to status of the teaching profession, we developed a "status" index. On that index, teachers in private schools showed the lowest degree of agreement about status of the teaching profession, and differed significantly in this from teachers in private subsidised and in municipal schools who were closer to agreeing on the status of the profession.

Asked about their view on the degree of respect shown to them as teachers by a set of social actors, teachers indicated that those closer to them (family, pupils, other colleagues) respect them more than those removed such as government authorities, union leaders, school administrators and other professionals. In fact only around 10% of all teachers felt they were well respected by government authorities. Figure 5 illustrates this perception showing some differences by type of school.

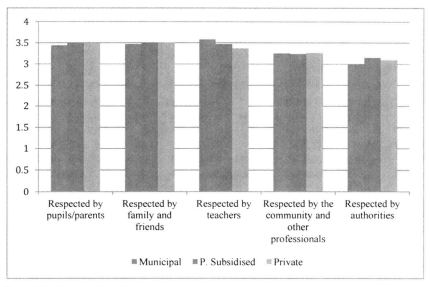

Source: Teacher questionnaire

Figure 5. Degree to which teachers consider that others respect them. Mean ratings (1=not at all; 2=little; 3=somewhat; 4=much)

Below are teacher voices from each type of school referring to how they feel others in Chile rate their work and their profession:

One is not recognized as a teacher. Teachers are at the lowest step of the ladder. In this society, you get paid according to the social status and that makes me a little sad. It has been said that this is an ideal job, especially for women. But it is not true, because you need to work a lot. It is not just a matter of money, because social recognition is more than money. [*Municipal teacher during focus group meeting*]

171

We have to do all sorts of things. We're like a circus. We have to do everything that is asked of us, and yet society continues to blame us. In some schools, some principals only pay attention to parents' complaints. Parents come to school to blame us, and school principals make us apologize. I am new here but I have heard and I know that some teachers are put under scrutiny because the notion is that the client is always right. Sometimes, school authorities say to us: "you need to talk to the parents and apologize." If you don't, you risk being fired at the end of the year. [*Case study interview with teacher in private subsidised school*]

Throughout the length of our career other professionals do not acknowledge us. We build understanding and knowledge in others, but those who construct buildings are valued more than a teacher who teaches people. Teaching is seen as the least prestigious profession. [*Case study interview with private school teacher*]

DISCUSSION AND CONCLUSIONS

The focus of the chapter has centred on the concept of teacher identity which we defined as a construction of meanings based both on the cultural attributions provided by society, as well as on teachers' own role definition and meanings about their work. In the first section of this article we highlighted four elements or fields which form part of this identity construction: the meanings and definitions that teachers give to their work and the intensity with which they feel committed to it (motivation and commitment); the overt or covert definitions embodied in the policies and reforms which affect teachers' personally as well as their work (work demands and satisfaction); the extent to which teachers in the light of their definitions of teaching describe their capacity (self-efficacy); and the extent to which there is a contrast between how teachers define their task and mission and how they believe society values and respects what they do (teachers in the public eye). These elements point to two major sources of identity construction: a personal one embodied in teachers' definitions and an external one embodied in policies, reforms, public messages and stakeholder perceptions (i.e. school authorities, parents, other teachers, etc.).

As we consider the evidence presented from the study we find that to a large extent teachers' identity in Chile is marked by the external elements represented specifically in the particularity of the three types of schools in which they teach. Municipal schools are largely schools for the poor; private subsidised schools support a mixed population (they may charge fees) and wholly private schools are for the elite in terms of power and income of the families who enrol their children in those schools. Municipal teachers are the only ones that are subject to performance evaluation, and have been the principal subjects of the improvement

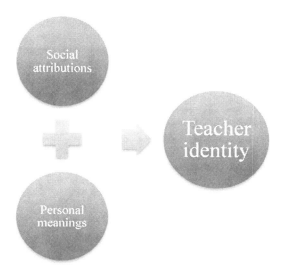

Figure 6. Sources of teacher identity

projects of the 1990s. Teachers in private subsidised schools work under very diverse owners and authorities. They do not profit from some of the contract benefits that the teachers' union secured for the public teacher corps, especially in relation to dismissals. Their work is more fragile compared to municipal teachers. Private school teachers enjoy better working conditions in terms of school environment, and are recruited among teachers who demonstrate high quality in their teaching skills. One might assume that given these differences, teachers would also differ in how they view their profession. And in some respects they do. For example, as we have seen, teachers in private schools do not suffer as much the effect public policies but consider more demanding the effects on their work of school related changes, or changes closer to their immediate environment. On the other hand, the three groups of teachers are joined in their perception that the teaching profession is not sufficiently valued by society and by important stakeholders such as government or removed community members. They value however the respect afforded to them by their pupils, colleagues, friends and family.

The evidence we have examined points to a certain 'disconnect' between the expectations and demands of the removed others (policy-makers, educational authorities) regarding their mission as teachers, and what teachers regard as important in their work. The overall dominance of the national school assessment system (SIMCE) determines in teachers' eyes a contradictory view of what is important in teaching. The repeated view of themselves is as educators who care for their pupils more than for the position of their schools in public rankings. The areas of conflict noted by van den Berg (2002) affecting teachers' identity construction are present both in the statements provided in the survey and in the views expressed during interviews and focus group meetings, which include their questioning of the legitimacy of work definitions provided by others. The distinction between these two sources of identity definition is most evident when teachers reflect on the quality of their working conditions, especially the scarcity of time, which is felt more harshly by teachers in the publicly funded system. Teachers realise that their task is a vast one, but feel the frustration of not being able to move ahead with it in the way they would like, because there simply is not enough time. And this affects an important component of their identity, which is to feel competent in their work. In stating that they believe others (public others) doubt their competence, the surveyed teachers also recognise that there is an element of truth in this, because the circumstances in which many work simply do not allow them to do a good job.

However, in most of the focal groups in which we worked, we found teachers that maintain a broad definition of their work and identity, even though they work under the same limitations as all their other colleagues:

I think everybody has many possibilities, and as a teacher this gives me hope. Hope that these kids will learn and will continue to learn whatever they need to develop freely and as individuals, without becoming a burden for the State or their parents. So when I have to complain to a class about the bad results of a test, I tell them, "this is your last chance." And the kids get on board and their school marks go up. And we have greater hopes, but not just for one of them, because we struggle for all of them, so they will improve their life chances. One has a certain degree of confidence that they will make it. I look at myself, where I come from. And there are many examples of people who struggle and move ahead. Opportunities exist, but we must show them and somehow provide them with these. It is tiring though. [*Young municipal school teacher in focus group*]

In conclusion, it would seem that together with the concerns that policy makers and education authorities in Chile may have about teacher quality and their effects on pupil results in schools, they should note in their actions, and decisions for change, that most teachers have forged a self-identity linked to broad education aims, and that demands for changes and reforms have to be built on these definitions. Not to do so, is to create conflict in their work lives, reduce their self-confidence or as occurs in well-documented circumstances, cause teachers passively or actively to resist the call for change however well-intentioned it may be. Because as Tenti Fanfani (2006, pp. 139-140) notes: "the key factor in the struggle for teacher professionalism is not the need for longer or better teacher preparation ... the issue is about who will control the development of the profession."

REFERENCES

Avalos, B., & Assael, J. (2006). Moving from resistance to agreement: The case of the Chilean teacher performance evaluation. *International Journal of Educational Research*, *45*(4-5), 231-324.

Baker, D. P., & Wiseman, A. W. (Eds.) (2005). *Global trends in educational policy.* International Perspectives on Education and Society, Vol. 6. Amsterdam: Elsevier.

Beijaard, D. P., Meijer, C., & Verloop, N. (2004). Reconsidering research on teacher professional identity. *Teaching and Teacher Education, 20*(2), 107-128.

Beijaard, D. P., Verloop, N., & Vermunt, J. D. (2000). Teachers' perceptions of professional identity: An exploratory study from a personal knowledge perspective. *Teaching and Teacher Education, 16,* 749-764.

Castells, M. (1997). *The power of identity.* Oxford: Blackwell Publishers.

Day, C. (2002). School reform and transitions in teacher professionalism and identity. *International Journal of Educational Research, 37,* 677-692.

Day, C., Sammons, P., Stobart, G., Kington, A., & Gu, Q. (2007). *Teachers matter: Connecting work, lives and effectiveness.* Maidenhead, England: Open University Press.

Esteve, J. M. (2006). Identidad y desafíos de la condición docente. In E. T. Fanfani (Ed.), *El oficio de docente. Vocación, trabajo y profesión en el siglo XXI.* Buenos Aires: Siglo Veintiuno Editores Argentina, S.A

Hargreaves, A. (2003). *Teaching in the knowledge society. Education in the age of insecurity.* Maidenhead/Berkshire/Philadelphia: Open University Press.

Hargreaves, L., Cunningham, M., Hansen, A., McIntyre, D., Oliver, C., & Peel, T. (2007). *The status of teachers and the teaching profession in England: Views from inside and outside the profession.* Final Report of the Teacher Status Project. Nottingham: Department for Education and Skills, UK.

Jacinto, C., & Freytes Frei, A. (2007). Coming and going: Educational policy and secondary school strategy in the context of poverty – Latin American case studies. In T. Townsend (Ed.), *International handbook of school effectiveness and improvement* (pp. 859-870). Dordrecht, The Netherlands: Springer.

OECD. (2010). Pisa 2009 Results Executive Summary: http://www.oecd.org/dataoecd/54/12/46643496.pdf. Retrieved 5 February 2012.

Tenti Fanfani, E. (2006). Profesionalización docente: consideraciones sociológicas. In E. Tenti Fanfani (Ed.), *El oficio de docente: Vocación, trabajo y profesión en el siglo XX.* Buenos Aires: Siglo Veintiuno Editores.

Valenzuela, J. P., Sevilla, A., Bellei, C., & de los Ríos, D. (2010). Remuneraciones de los docentes en Chile. Resolviendo una aparente paradoja. Document in www.nucleodocentes.uchile.cl, retrieved 26 December 2011.

van den Berg, R. (2002). Teachers' meanings regarding educational practice. *Review of Educational Research, 72*(4), 577-625.

Vandeyar, S. (2005). Conflicting demands: Assessment practices in three South African primary schools undergoing desegregation. *Curriculum Inquiry, 35*(4), 461-481.

Weber, E. (2007). Globalization, "glocal" development and teachers work: A research agenda. *Review of Educational Research, 77*(3), 279-309.

Beatrice Avalos
Centro de Investigación Avanzada en Educación
Universidad de Chile
Santiago, Chile

Danae de los Ríos
Universidad Diego Portales
Santiago, Chile

MICHALINOS ZEMBYLAS, CONSTADINA CHARALAMBOUS,
PANAYIOTA CHARALAMBOUS & PANAYIOTA KENDEOU

RESEARCHING AN INITIATIVE ON PEACEFUL COEXISTENCE IN GREEK-CYPRIOT SCHOOLS

A Mixed-Methods Study on Teachers' Perceptions and Emotions[1]

INTRODUCTION

In this chapter we examine the perceptions and emotions of Greek-Cypriot teachers regarding a recent governmental initiative that defined the development of "a culture of peaceful coexistence" between Greek-Cypriots and Turkish-Cypriots as a central educational objective of the 2008-2009 school year (Ministry of Education and Culture, 2008a, p. 1). This policy initiative sparked strong emotional reactions – both in the teacher community and in wider Greek-Cypriot society. The heated public debates that ensued revolved around the 'appropriateness' of such an objective in light of the island's forced *de facto* division and the past traumas of this conflict-ridden society (e.g. refugees, missing persons). In this chapter we provide an in-depth exploration of the intersection between tensions at the larger socio-political landscape and teachers' emotional readiness to deal with this initiative.

To do so, our research draws on the findings of two separate studies – one quantitative and one qualitative – conducted towards the end of the 2008-2009 school year. This research was underpinned by a conceptualization of teachers' emotions as constitutive components of teaching and educational change within contexts that are inevitably politicised (Zembylas, 2008), especially in the case of politically controversial issues (Clark, Hoggett, & Thompson, 2006; Goodwin, Jasper, & Poletta, 2001). In a world of unrelenting political and social change, understanding the emotional aspects of change is essential, if policy initiatives are to be more meaningful and successful.

RESEARCH CONTEXT

Before discussing our proposed conceptualization of emotions, we start with a brief overview of the ethnic conflict between the two rival sides in Cyprus – Greek Cypriots (the majority, around 80%) and Turkish Cypriots (the island's largest

---

[1] An extended version of this chapter is published as M. Zembylas et al. (2011). Promoting peaceful coexistence in conflict-ridden Cyprus: Teachers' difficulties and emotions towards a new policy initiative. *Teaching and Teacher Education*, 27(2), 332-341, February.

D.B. Napier & S. Majhanovich (eds.), Education, Dominance and Identity, 177–198.

minority, around 18%) – and the repercussions on current ideological landscapes in both society and education.

Cyprus emerged as an independent bi-communal state in 1960, following the Greek-Cypriot armed struggle against British colonial rule (1878-1960). Yet, independence was not enthusiastically welcomed since the anti-colonial rebellion, inspired by Greek nationalist irredentism, was undertaken for *enosis* or union with the Greek motherland (Mavratsas, 2004). Turkish Cypriots, also influenced by the rising Turkish nationalism, reacted negatively to the Greek-Cypriot ideal of *enosis* and they counterproposed *taksim*, or ethnic partition (Kizilyürek, 1993).

These ideological tensions have produced the intractable conflict in the politics of the region that came to be known as the 'Cyprus Issue:' first, between 1960-1974 the Turkish Cypriots were the main victims; then in 1974, after a failed military coup by the Greek junta to unify Cyprus and Greece, the Turkish invasion imposed the *de facto* partition of the island in two ethnically homogeneous parts and caused the forced displacement of Greek-Cypriot (about 200.000) and Turkish-Cypriot (45.000) populations to the south and north parts of Cyprus, respectively. After the declaration of the 'Turkish Republic of Northern Cyprus' in 1983 (considered legally invalid by the U.N. and recognized only by Turkey), there are in effect two rival states *in situ* (Constantinou & Papadakis, 2001) and they lack any sort of substantial contact.

This decades-long physical and cultural separation rendered the division in Cyprus almost complete – socially, emotionally, and politically – resulting in what Bryant (2004) described as 'ethnic estrangement.' Ethnic estrangement has also been reinforced by intensive processes of 'nation-building' after 1974 on both sides, which have heightened their respective 'Greekness' and 'Turkishness,' while constructing the other community as the 'ethnic-Other' and 'arch-enemy' of the collective Self.

In the spring of 2003 the permission granted by the Turkish-Cypriot side for unfettered access across the dividing 'Green Line' rekindled hopes for a final settlement before Cyprus' accession to the E.U in May of 2004. A few days before Cyprus' accession, a comprehensive U.N. proposal for re-unification on the basis of a bi-zonal bi-communal federation – known as the 'Annan Plan' – was put to simultaneous referenda on both sides, but it failed, with a 65% 'yes'-vote by the Turkish Cypriots but a 76% 'no'-vote by the Greek Cypriots. Today, despite on-going diplomatic efforts, the partition remains in place.

Importantly, ideological tension exists also *within* each community. In the case of the Greek-Cypriot community, research has recorded a long-standing conflict between two identity-discourses: the *Hellenocentric* discourse, which emphasizes the 'Greekness' of Greek Cypriots (traditionally supported by the political right) and the *Cypriocentric* discourse, which emphasizes 'Cypriotness' (mostly advanced by the political left) (Mavratsas, 2004; Papadakis, 2008; Spyrou, 2006). The left-wing party AKEL – now in power – has been the political power that, from early on after 1974, has led most 'rapprochement' efforts between the two communities, arguing for their shared 'Cypriotness.' Yet, until recently, the leftist pro-rapprochement ideology has been socially marginal, while Hellenocentrism has been the unmarked norm in Greek-Cypriot education (Charalambous, C., 2009; Papadakis, 2008). The dominance of Hellenocentrism was also sustained and reinforced by the importation of educational materials (e.g. textbooks) from Greece and the strong Greek-Cypriot reliance on the 'motherland' for educational policies and assistance, a practice still followed nowadays (Persianis, 2006).

With regards to the 'Cyprus Issue,' after 1974, the main educational objective has been what the Greek-Cypriot Ministry of Education and Culture calls 'I know, I don't forget and I struggle' [*Gnorizo, Den Xechno kai Agonizomai,* henceforth *Den Xechno*]. As a permanent objective at all levels of Greek-Cypriot public education, *Den Xechno* involves passing on information about the traumatic events around the Turkish invasion and teaching the geographical, social and cultural characteristics of the 'occupied territories' in the north. Yet, the cognitive part of the educational objective ('knowing' and 'remembering') is inseparable from the prescriptive part of 'struggling,' since knowledge and remembrance are seen as ways to help the younger (post-1974) generations to maintain the necessary 'militancy' for 'fighting' to claim these territories back (Charalambous, P., 2009).

After the permission of unfettered access between the two sides in 2003, the *Den Xechno* objective was somehow loosened in Greek-Cypriot education, yet things were more significantly changed after AKEL won the presidential elections in February of 2008. In August 2008, the new Minister of Education and Culture released a circular document to all primary and secondary schools (Ministry of Education and Culture, 2008a) announcing the introduction of a policy initiative to promote 'peaceful coexistence.' The new initiative set peaceful coexistence as the primary educational objective of the school year 2008-09, emphasizing that education "must cultivate those elements that unite us and characterize us as one people [...] [preparing] children and youth for peaceful coexistence and collaboration between Greek-Cypriots and Turkish-Cypriots" (Ministry of Education and Culture, 2008a, pp. 1-2). The circular concluded with the assertion that the values of peaceful coexistence should be diffused in all aspects of the curriculum and school life, and provided indicative suggestions for different types of activities (e.g. in-school actions, teaching practices, and out-of-school actions).

The yearly designation of certain educational objectives to be emphasized is a standard practice in Greek-Cypriot education and schools regularly respond with the organization of special events or relevant lesson-activities. Yet, the 2008 circular generated considerable debate and controversy, not only in schools but also in the media and press, the Parliament and in society more generally. Most reactions criticized the 'appropriateness' and 'timeliness' of an objective for peaceful coexistence, while a large part of Cyprus is still under Turkish occupation. As a matter of fact, a few months after the Minister's circular, the primary teachers' trade-union (POED) issued its own circular (February 4, 2009) stating its strong disagreement regarding the suggestion for visit-exchanges between Greek Cypriots and Turkish Cypriots, and announcing its refusal of any kind of institutional control of teachers' classroom practices (POED, 2009).

CONCEPTUAL FRAMEWORK AND PREVIOUS RESEARCH

Conceptualizing Emotions

Different understandings of emotions have produced conceptually and methodologically different approaches to the study of emotions in teaching and teachers (Chubbuck & Zembylas, 2008). While traditional approaches located emotions in the individual sphere, relying on sharp dichotomies (e.g. emotion–reason, individual-social) (Boler, 1999; Zembylas, 2005), more recent studies influenced by feminist and critical theories (e.g. Abu-Lughod & Lutz, 1990; Ahmed, 2004) have challenged this binary thinking as a remnant of patriarchal thought and historically consolidated power relations. Drawing on these perspectives, in this chapter we conceptualize emotions as transactional performances in the liminal space between the *individual* and the *social* in keeping with Leavitt (1996). In other words, we see emotions as neither strictly private, nor merely the effects or peripheral by-products of exterior social structures; instead, we reconceptualize emotions as a socioculturally constituted public space, which also functions as a constitutive force for (trans)forming individuals, social interactions and power relations. Our emphasis on the social, political and cultural contexts in which emotions are performed takes emotions to be socially and politically consequential. Thus, by focusing on the transaction between the individual psychic terrain and larger-scale social and political processes, our approach historicizes emotions but also acknowledges their ability to cause ruptures and discontinuities in power differentials (Zembylas, 2005; Boler, 1999).

Seen in this light, emotions in schools are viewed as both a private matter and a political space, and teachers are always engaged in political transactions when emotionally relating to school actors, structures and discourses. Therefore, we argue that a politicized analysis of emotions may help teachers reflect on the impact of various discourses on their perceived difficulties and emotions, particularly during policy reform efforts.

Teachers' Emotions and Peace Education Initiatives in Conflicting Societies

Reform initiatives around issues of peace and conflict create intense emotions both in schools and society (Bar-Tal, 2002, 2004; Zembylas & Ferreira, 2009). Teachers' affective repertoires around the conflict (e.g. issues of history, memory, and trauma) are in fact constitutive of the prevailing societal ethos that is hard to change (Zembylas, 2008). Therefore, in the case of politically controversial policy initiatives a richer understanding of the pivotal role of emotions in reproducing or disrupting existing perceptions appears even more imperative.

In other long-standing conflicts such as the Israeli-Palestinian conflict, and the conflicts in Northern Ireland and post-apartheid South Africa, emotions have proved vital in educational efforts to perpetuate or break the cycle of conflict (Bar-Tal, 2004; Murphy & Gallagher, 2009). As Murphy and Gallagher (2009) contended, in such cases teachers' support for peaceful coexistence should not be taken-for-granted. In fact, studies have shown that when a conflicting situation remains in limbo for decades, it is very likely that teachers – themselves educated in a conflict-based worldview – will be negatively predisposed towards such initiatives and meet them with emotional resistance (Bar-Tal, 2004; see also Napier, 2003, in the case of South Africa).

Yet, despite the evidence for the significance of emotions in peace-building, so far there has not been an explicit investigation of *how* teachers' perceptions and emotions are entangled with their perceptions of ideological and structural difficulties during peace education policy initiatives. Taking teachers' perceptions and emotions as inseparable from their ideological readiness to embrace peaceful coexistence (Bar-Tal, 2002), the present chapter addresses this bibliographic gap in the context of the ongoing 'Cyprus Issue.'

Education for Peaceful Coexistence

Despite the growing recognition of peace education as a way for promoting non-violence, coexistence and collaboration, the field has been long marginalized by mainstream education authorities (Synott, 2005) and early peace educational programmes have emerged as acts 2005) and early peace educational programmes have emerged as acts of resistance to dominant models of education (Salomon & Nevo, 2002). Especially in schools located in conflict-ridden areas, *education for coexistence* becomes imperative, Bar-Tal (2004) argued, if coexistence is understood as

> the conditions that serve as the fundamental prerequisites for the evolvement of advanced harmonious intergroup relations [...] the very recognition in the right of the other group to exist peacefully with its differences and to the acceptance of the other group as a legitimate and an equal partner with whom disagreements have to be resolved in non-violent ways. (ibid., p. 256)

Another terminological clarification is pertinent here: importantly, the literature defines 'peaceful coexistence' as closely related, but adequately distinct from the concept of 'reconciliation' (e.g. see Bar-Tal & Bennink, 2004; Kriesberg, 1998). Specifically, 'peaceful coexistence' is seen as the rudimentary level of positive relations (Kriesberg, 1998) that serves as a preparation for the more difficult and demanding task of 'reconciliation,' which involves deeper and longer psychological work that fundamentally transforms attitudes and emotions between the rival side (Bar-Tal & Bennink, 2004). When applied to the Greek-Cypriot case, the governmental initiative can be conceptualized as a step towards 'peaceful coexistence' rather than 'reconciliation.' Incidentally perhaps, the theoretical concept of peaceful coexistence coincides with the objective's lexical choice ('peaceful coexistence' [*eiriniki siniparksi*]).

RESEARCH DESIGN AND METHODOLOGY

Taking into account the above theoretical and historical contexts, we came up with two main questions that guided this research:

1. What are the main tendencies regarding Greek-Cypriot teachers' perceptions and emotions generally towards reconciliation and specifically towards the objective for peaceful coexistence?
2. What are the main challenges of Greek-Cypriot teachers when dealing with the prospect of peaceful coexistence and how does this affect their emotional readiness to implement the new objective?

To answer these questions, we employed quantitative methodology for the first and qualitative methodology for the second. The use of a survey questionnaire aimed to numerically chart the largely unknown terrain of teachers' dispositions towards the Ministry's initiative but also to help us design our main qualitative research. The qualitative phase involved a set of in-depth interviews with teachers that further explored some of the tendencies documented in the quantitative phase, focusing on complexities and interconnections between the reported difficulties and emotional resistances. Below we outline in more detail the methodological processes followed during our research.

The data collection of the quantitative phase took place in the beginning of spring 2009 and we recruited teachers working in Greek-Cypriot public education (n = 7500). Our cluster sample was randomly selected from the Ministry's catalogues of public schools (Ministry of Education and Culture, 2008b) and comprised of 1200 teachers (580 from primary and 620 secondary school teachers), from 90 participating schools in the Republic of Cyprus – 67 (out of a total 345) primary schools and 23 (out of a total 116) secondary schools. The school sampling was randomly stratified so that schools from all administrative districts of Cyprus were selected. Survey questionnaires were sent to all teachers working in each randomly selected school. With a response rate of 55%, our final sample consisted of 660 teachers; the school level (primary or secondary school), age level of teachers, and gender ratio demographics are presented in Tables 1 and 2.

Table 1. Demographic Information of the Sample

Variable	N	%
School Level		
Primary school teachers	281	43%
Secondary school teachers	374	56%
Gender		
Female	477	73%
Male	179	27%

Table 2. Age Groups of Teachers in the Sample

Age Group	Number of Teachers	%
Up to 36*	269	42
37-45	188	30.8
46-60	171	26.7

* Born after the Turkish invasion of 1974.

Our instrument was a self-reported anonymous structured questionnaire based on both information in the existing literature and on the language of the Ministry's circular (see Ministry of Education and Culture, 2008a). Face validity of the questionnaire was established by asking an educationist to evaluate the extent to which the items appeared to measure the target constructs. Reliability was evaluated post-data collection using Cronbach's alpha for the questionnaire parts 2-6. The analysis showed high internal consistency for these parts (α ranged from 82. to .93). The questionnaire consisted of the following eight parts:

Part 1) *general perceptions of reconciliation* (2 questions, 9 possible items)
Part 2) *perceptions of the feasibility of reconciliation* (9 items, 5-point Likert scale).
Part 3) *emotional readiness to promote reconciliation* (7 items, 5-point Likert scale)
Part 4) *perceptions of the new objective* (23 statements, 5-point Likert scale)
Part 5) *emotions about Turkish Cypriots* (9 items, 5-point Likert scale)
Part 6) *relations with Turkish Cypriots* (5 items, 5-point Likert scale)
Part 7) *personal experiences of the war* (8 closed-type questions)
Part 8) *demographic information* (gender, age, primary or secondary school)

With the exception of parts 1 and 8, all other parts included statements that assessed agreement on a 5-point Likert scale that ranged from 1=strong disagreement, to 5=strong agreement. In part 1, participants were asked to choose among 9 possible items those that best represented their perceptions of reconciliation, whereas in part 8 participants provided their demographic information. For the purposes of this chapter, we focus mainly on the findings of parts 1, 3 and 4 of this questionnaire (as shown in Table 3), with the intention of exploring:

(i)   perceptions of reconciliation in general (Part 1);
(ii)   emotions about reconciliation in Cyprus (Part 3);
(iii) perceptions of the new objective and its practical implementation (Part 4).

The data collection of the qualitative phase took place at the end of spring 2009 and involved semi-structured in-depth interviews with 40 primary and secondary school teachers – 20 teachers from each school level. To maximize variability in opinions, teachers were chosen from all districts in Cyprus through the 'snowballing' recruitment technique (Bernard, 2002, p. 185), namely the mobilization of the interviewers' social networks for accessing potential informants. To facilitate teachers to elaborate on their understandings, challenges and emotions about peaceful coexistence in Cyprus, we developed a topic guide, three areas of which corresponded to the three parts of the questionnaire used in the quantitative study:

(i)   perceptions of reconciliation in general (Part 1);

(ii)   emotions about reconciliation in Cyprus (Part 3);
(iii) perceptions of difficulties and emotions about the new objective and its implementation (Part 4).

Table 3. Questionnaire items for Parts 1, 3, and 4

Part 1: Perceptions About Reconciliation

General

1. to be able to negotiate with the other person, even if I am still angry with him/her
2. to be in a position to forget previous animosities and look to the future
3. to be in the position to forgive
4. to be in the position to financially compensate and be compensated for the damages incurred
5. reinstatement of human rights for all

Specifically in Cyprus

1. each community to forgive each other
2. to be in the position to financially compensate and be compensated for the damages incurred
3. to be in a position to forget previous animosities and look to the future
4. reinstatement of human rights for all.

Part 3: Emotional Readiness to Promote Reconciliation

1. I wish to promote the reconciliation of Greek and Turkish Cypriots in my school
2. I feel ready to promote the reconciliation of Greek and Turkish Cypriots in my school
3. Promoting reconciliation of Greek and Turkish Cypriots in school is possible
4. The existing curriculum is appropriate for promoting reconciliation
5. I need training regarding the promotion of reconciliation of Greek and Turkish Cypriots in my school
6. I need helpful materials to assist me in promoting reconciliation of Greek and Turkish Cypriots in my school
7. I prefer not to be involved in promoting the reconciliation of Greek and Turkish Cypriots through my work in school

Part 4: Perceptions of the Peaceful Co-Existence Objective

The cultivation of peaceful coexistence between G/C and T/C" in the context of education:

1. is important
2. demands the lapse of old conflicts between Greek and Turkish Cypriots
3. demands enhancing the instruction of the cultural habits and customs of Greek and Turkish Cypriots
4. demands that the Turkish language is taught to Greek Cypriots and the Greek language is taught to Turkish Cypriots
5. demands common educational activities between Greek and Turkish Cypriots
6. demands common cultural events between Greek and Turkish Cypriots
7. demands common political struggles between Greek and Turkish Cypriots
8. demands common social struggles between Greek and Turkish Cypriots
9. demands that the Greek Cypriots acknowledge the traumas they caused to Turkish Cypriots
10. demands that the Turkish Cypriots acknowledge the traumas they caused to Greek Cypriots
11. is important for the future political development of Cyprus

12. is an unfeasible educational objective
13. is an educational objective that is dangerous for the national identity of Greek Cypriot students
14. is an educational objective I disagree with
15. is an educational objective that may contribute to the resolution of our political problem
16. is an educational objective that evokes negative feelings in me
17. is an educational objective fraught with difficulties in its practical implementation
18. is an educational objective that will bring us closer to the Turkish Cypriots
19. is my duty, as an educator, to promote this educational objective
20. is an educational objective which will force educators to change their classroom practices
21. is an educational objective which will help educators accept students who are culturally different in the school
22. is an educational objective which will help students accept those students who are culturally different in the school
23. is an educational objective which can be promoted through the materials that have been provided by the Ministry of Education and Culture

Interviews were conducted in each participant's preferred location (usually their home or workplace) and lasted between 60-90 minutes. For the purposes of analysis all interviews were audio-recorded, carefully transcribed and, later, translated from Greek into English.

To analyze the quantitative data we computed the frequencies of the participants' responses concerning how they perceived reconciliation in general, and then specifically in the context of Cyprus. Also, we computed frequencies as well as means of the teachers' degree of agreement with statements about the emotional readiness to promote reconciliation between Greek- and Turkish-Cypriots via the educational system. Finally, we computed frequencies as well as means of teachers' degree of agreement with statements about the necessity and importance of the new educational objective on peaceful coexistence, the positive and negative potential impact of the new objective, and the feasibility of its practical implementation. Because we wanted to make comparisons between parts of the questionnaire with different item numbers, we computed means rather than sum scores. We computed all analyses of the quantitative data using SPSS (Field, 2000).

As to the interview data, our analysis involved thematic coding using the qualitative analysis software Nvivo 8 (Weitzman, 2000). The analysis was conducted collaboratively by two of the authors to ensure inter-coder reliability or auditability. Specifically, we proceeded in the following manner: first we separated the quotes focusing on teachers' difficulties in implementing the educational objective and the emotions triggered by these difficulties. Then, both coders performed a preliminary analysis of 5 interviews and came up with emerging themes, which were compared and grouped into code-families (for coding procedures see Richards, 2009). The coding scheme was further tested on another sub-set of 5 interviews and then finalized and applied to the whole body of interviews, with constant coordination between the coders. The main categories that accrued from the analysis are presented in the Findings section.

Before we discuss the findings, the following clarifications on our use of mixed methodology are prudent:

(i)   each phase was conducted using a different sample, although (a) both studies recruited participants from all main districts of the Republic of Cyprus, and (b) some of our interviewees happened to have previously completed our survey questionnaire.

(ii) the two studies were successive, not simultaneous: the quantitative survey intentionally preceded the qualitative interviews (with a two-month gap) in order to serve as our road map for the design of the in-depth interviews that followed.

(iii) finally, despite the striking correspondence between the topics addressed by the two phases, our aim was not to contrast or compare the two sets of findings; rather the first phase served to detect the main tendencies in the bigger picture (*what* teachers think/feel towards reconciliation and the new educational objective), while the second phase aimed to explore the reasons behind their perceptions and emotions (*why* they think/feel this way).

Despite these discrepancies between the two phases, we believe that their findings demonstrate a considerable degree of complementarity and expansion (see Johnson & Onwuegbuzie, 2004), with the qualitative study elaborating upon the important complexities behind the general tendencies that emerged in the quantitative study.

FINDINGS

Quantitative Phase

As outlined above, the first aim of the quantitative study was to explore Greek-Cypriot teachers' understandings of 'reconciliation,' both generally and specifically in the context of Cyprus. From the five general definitions we provided, shown in Table 3, Part 1 (General) two were the most predominant: 39.8% of teachers view reconciliation as *the reinstatement of human rights for all* and 35.2% view it as *forget previous animosities and look to the future.* When the question about reconciliation was transferred to the context of Cyprus (Table 3, Part 1, Specifically in Cyprus), the order of participants' preferences remained fairly consistent with their general views, yet with a considerable change in percentages: *the reinstatement of human rights was clearly more prevalent* (60%), while the option of *forget previous animosities and look to the future* decreased in popularity (24%). The fact that teachers tend to understand reconciliation in the Cyprus in terms of 'reinstatement of human rights' much more than 'forgetting' is an important finding that will be further discussed in our qualitative analysis.

The analysis of teachers' degree of agreement concerning their emotional readiness to promote reconciliation (7 statements) showed an overall medium level

186

of emotional readiness (M=2.9, SD=1.3). Specifically, the analysis showed low-to-medium levels of agreement with the *wish to promote the reconciliation of Greek and Turkish Cypriots in my school* (M=2.5, SD=1.2), coupled with medium-to-low preference for involvement *in promoting the reconciliation of Greek and Turkish Cypriots through my work in school* (M=2.4, SD=1.4). The same medium- to-low readiness and willingness was also reflected in their ambivalence as to whether *promoting reconciliation of Greek and Turkish Cypriots in school is possible* (M=2.8, SD=0.9). Furthermore, teachers' low agreement that *the existing curriculum is appropriate for promoting reconciliation* (M=1.9, SD=0.9) also heightened the feeling of insecurity and lack of readiness. Teachers' emotional difficulties were also related to their reported medium-to-high *need for training regarding the promotion of reconciliation of Greek and Turkish Cypriots in my school* (M=3.3, SD=1.4), and *need for helpful materials to assist me in promoting reconciliation of Greek and Turkish Cypriots in my school* (M=3.5, SD=1.3).

It is particularly important that when teachers were explicitly asked about their emotional readiness to promote reconciliation in their schools 55.4% indicated strong disagreement with 'feeling ready.' Two more questions constructed a strong negative consensus amongst Greek-Cypriot teachers: 75.9% of all respondents judged the existing curriculum inappropriate for promoting reconciliation, while a sizable 84.3% of teachers believed that they needed training in order to be able to promote reconciliation in their schools. The problems with teachers' emotional readiness were also evident in their responses on whether it is even possible to promote reconciliation with Turkish-Cypriots in Greek-Cypriot schools: although only 12% of teachers believed this to be impossible, only 23.7% firmly believed in the possibility of reconciliation, while a sizable percentage (64.3%) remained ambivalent about the issue.

Teachers' perceptions around the educational objective were assessed – through 23 statements – with respect to the following four categories:

1. demands and importance of the new objective (n=11; questions 1-11);
2. positive potential impact of the new objective (n=4; questions 15, 18, 20, 21);
3. negative potential impact of the new objective (n=5; questions 13, 14, 16, 19, 20);
4. feasibility of the practical implementation of the new objective (n=3; questions; 12, 17, 23).

The analysis showed a medium-to-high level of agreement with respect to the importance of the new objective (M=3.3, SD=0.9) and its potential positive impact (M=3.1, SD=1.1). The means of agreement with respect to the potential negative impact of the new educational objective (M=2.7, SD=1.1) and its practical implementation (M=2.6, SD=0.9) were lower, but still reflected a stance of being in the middle, neither positive nor negative.

Teachers' ambivalence with regards to the objective was also illustrated by the analysis of individual items:

- Statement (1) the cultivation of peaceful coexistence between Greek-Cypriots and Turkish-Cypriots in the context of education is important received some level of agreement by 93.4% of Greek-Cypriot teachers; only 6.6% of teachers strongly disagreed with this view.
- About one fifth of teachers (20.2%) described the objective as (12) an unfeasible educational objective, while a similar percentage (23.8%) stated that it (14) is an educational objective I disagree with
- Statement (15) the educational objective may contribute to the resolution of our political problem received some level of agreement by 85.2% of Greek-Cypriot teachers.
- Almost all teachers (97%) agreed to some extent that (17) the educational objective is fraught with difficulties in its practical implementation.
- Finally, only 16.8% of teachers agreed that (19) it is their duty, as an educator, to promote this educational objective.

Thus, the numerical analysis of the findings showed that despite the wide recognition of the objective's importance and potential positive impact, only a small percentage of participant teachers appear confident to implement it. On the contrary, the vast majority of Greek-Cypriot teachers still see important practical and ideological difficulties in the objective's implementation.

Qualitative Phase

The conceptualization of emotions as a social and political space, inseparable from wider material and ideological structures, was our point of departure for the qualitative phase. Our interview analysis focused on identifying teachers' reported difficulties in implementing the objective, exploring their emotional impact and locating them within larger social and political discourses in the Greek-Cypriot community. We argue that teachers' reported difficulties can be interpreted vis-à-vis the numerical tendencies (e.g. low readiness and little willingness to pursue the objective) and can provide insights into teachers' emotional reactions that can prove useful for future initiatives. Our analysis revealed the following main challenges:

(i)   Human rights violations
(ii)   The conflict's open traumas
(iii) The unsettled political problem
(iv)   The objective's negative political impact
(v)   The objective's 'leftist' political character
(vi)   The lack of institutional support

Human rights violations. Similar to the first item of the survey-questionnaire, at the beginning of the interviews teachers were invited to reflect upon the meaning of the word 'reconciliation.' Despite teachers' varied stances towards the issue, most teachers agreed on the word's semantic meaning as mostly 'living peacefully' and "respecting each other's rights." Nonetheless, when asked to talk specifically about the prospects of reconciliation between the Greek- and Turkish-Cypriots, several teachers seemed to admit (without being initially prompted) that what they described could not be realistically applied in Cyprus because of the Turkish violation of human rights:

> *Marina*: Reconciliation between Greek-Cypriot and Turkish-Cypriots means everything that applies all around the world, I mean free movement, everyone able to freely enjoy their properties. And then, once we have these, reconciliation will take place. [...]
> *Interviewer*: What feelings does the prospect of reconciliation between Greek Cypriots and Turkish Cypriots bring out in you? Your personal opinion.
> *Marina*: Personally, I believe that such a thing does not exist and will never exist.

This excerpt is representative of the way in which the restoration of human rights (e.g. free movement, property rights, Greek-Cypriot resettlement in the north, withdrawal of Turkish troops) was constructed as a precondition for any reconciliatory attempts, in both society and education. However, as evident in this example, teachers' understanding of human rights was most of the time limited to Greek-Cypriot rights, while Turkish-Cypriots' human rights as well as their political (collective) rights were either ignored or silenced. Consider the following excerpt:

> *Stelios*: They [Turkish Cypriots] are a minority and as such we can live together with them, with all their rights. In the same way there is the Armenian minority, in the same way other minorities exist. Basically in Cyprus there are the Greek Cypriots, who populated the island; the Turkish Cypriots who were a minority, a big minority; and other minorities. Under these conditions, I believe that we can coexist within this framework, I mean the Greek Cypriots to respect difference, the culture etc. of all minorities, also including the Turkish Cypriots.

These findings are strongly related to the public discourses that have prevailed in Greek-Cypriot society for decades, that is: first, the widespread perception that Turkish Cypriots are a minority in a predominantly Greek-Cypriot state, despite a political agreement by the two sides for a federal solution to the 'Cyprus Issue'; and, second, the basic political argument by the Greek-Cypriot side that Turkish occupiers consistently violate human rights and U.N. resolutions (see Constantinou & Papadakis, 2001). Thus, the ideological construction of Turkish Cypriots as a minority and of reconciliation as human rights restoration seemed to have contributed to the constitution of 'reconciliation' as something impossible, both in society and in education.

The conflict's open trauma. Beyond the issue of conceptualizing reconciliation, the history of violent conflict was the most frequently reported emotional challenge for implementing the new educational objective and half of the interviewees constructed it as "a major obstacle" to peaceful coexistence. In particular, six teachers pointed out the emotional delicacies involved in any educational attempt for peaceful coexistence between Greek Cypriots and Turkish Cypriots, complaining that these concerns were not taken into consideration by the policymakers who introduced the new objective. Excerpts from the interviews with two teachers are provided below.

> *Kostas*: The wounds from the [Turkish] invasion are still fresh. You cannot hastily push someone who is wounded and still carries the stigmata [of trauma] to reconcile with the other, and therefore, I don't think you can introduce such an educational objective.

> *Melina*: Ok, you [Ministry of Education and Culture] are my employer … But it [the new objective] caused us feelings of contempt for those in the Ministry who have no idea that I am obliged to teach refugee children, children that may have missing persons in their family, and I have to face this situation.

As seen in the excerpts above, many teachers constructed the material and emotional consequences of the war of 1974 as still tangible in Greek-Cypriot society today. Interestingly, 10 out of 40 interviewees used the metaphor of an *'open'* or *'bleeding' 'wound'* to refer to 1974, similarly to Kostas above. Arguably, this finding can be attributed to the numerous cultural technologies operating after 1974 within Greek-Cypriot society, including the state, media, and education (e.g. the *Den Xechno* objective), which have undertaken the task of reminding or 'teaching' the war traumas and, thus, establishing the patterns for collective remembering and forgetting (Christou, 2007). We interpret this as the reason why teachers perceive the past sufferings of some students' families (lost relatives, properties etc.) as rendering the objective's implementation inappropriate and even insensitive on their behalf.

Furthermore, some teachers expressed concerns that the new educational objective could actually produce the opposite results from those aspired. They feared that by bringing up these *"sensitive issues"* in the classroom they risked opening up past emotional traumas and awakening feelings of hatred amongst their students. As Charoulla said: *"If there are missing persons in a family and this topic is avoided, then bringing it up [in the classroom] may lead somewhere else, something that wouldn't help much the new objective."*

By perceiving the war narratives as still traumatic for themselves and their students, teachers justified their emotional 'blockage' when confronted with

190

teaching about peaceful coexistence and legitimated their abstinence and 'tabooing' of these painful issues.

The unsettled political problem. Difficulties arising from the still unresolved 'Cyprus Issue' were reported at both an ideological and a practical level. In particular, teachers who were negatively inclined towards the new objective considered its introduction 'untimely,' arguing that "a political settlement needs to be found first" before initiating any peaceful coexistence initiative. On a more practical level, teachers reported complications arising from the lack of common political ground between the two sides, but also amongst Greek-Cypriot political forces as to what is 'legitimate' to be said and done inside and outside the classroom. Consider the extract below.

> *Chrysoulla*: We don't have conditions of free communication. Shall I get my students and take them to the other side, after they show identity cards [at the checkpoints]? I cannot take this responsibility. [...] Or will Turkish Cypriots be allowed by their regime to come here? Under what status?

Beyond questions on what is 'say-able' and 'do-able' in the classroom, some teachers admitted that, due to the communities' prolonged physical separation, they felt awkward and emotionally insecure to talk about the Turkish-Cypriots in the classroom. As Myroula explained:

> I don't feel ready; to feel ready I would like to have more contact and more relations with Turkish-Cypriots, something that I don't have. [...] it feels strange to communicate this objective, since I don't know these people as individuals.

Other teachers described the prolonged ethnic separation and rivalry as imprinted in the discourses and objectives of the Greek-Cypriot education system itself. Joanna, for instance, pointed out the following:

> For years, we cultivated a negative attitude towards the Turkish Cypriots and the evil they caused us. It's very difficult for the teacher to try and develop positive feelings now. How can a teacher dismiss what children have been learning all these years?

The lack of a constitutional settlement of the conflict and its reported consequent difficulties can therefore explain the apparent lack of teachers' emotional and professional readiness that our survey pointed out. The social, political, and cultural realities created by the interminable negotiations to find a settlement to the 'Cyprus Issue' seem to perpetuate teachers' insecurities – both on an emotional and on a practical level.

The objective's negative political impact.   Eleven teachers saw the new educational objective as potentially damaging for both (a) the ongoing political negotiations, and (b) the Greek-Cypriot collective historical memory. Six interviewees used the word "danger" or "dangerous," explaining that the objective might give the erroneous impression that "everything is just fine," something that was feared it could exonerate the Turkish side in the political negotiations:

> *Chrysoula*: I believe that this objective gives the wrong impressions ... [...] to the students and generally to the foreign powers. It provides the Turkish side with arguments [to claim] that everything is just fine, the children communicate [between the two sides]. So, where is the problem? Why should the foreign powers help, if everything is just fine?

In other accounts the objective was constructed as yet *"another compromise"* or retreat on behalf of the Greek-Cypriots, since it was judged one-sided and not reciprocated by similar attempts by the Turkish Cypriots. The following extract is also illustrative:

> *Dimitris*: Since 1974, when the invasion took place, and onwards, we [Greek-Cypriots] constantly retreat. The Turks never retreated, so how could we cultivate a culture of peaceful coexistence? Peaceful coexistence means that we should approach the Turks and the Turks should approach us. We only approach them; they never do the same.

This outlook is in line with dominant views about who the 'victims' and 'perpetrators' are in the Cyprus conflict. These views have repeatedly constructed Greek Cypriots as the only victims, and the only proactive group constantly faced with the implacability of the Turkish side (Zembylas, 2008; Spyrou, 2006).

These social representations of the conflict seem to also give rise to a fear of 'forgetting' in teachers' talk. We saw earlier in the quantitative results that if we compare teachers' views on reconciliation in general and in particular for the Cyprus context, around 10% fewer teachers mentioned 'forgetting' when it came to the latter. This difference can be better understood, if one considers the importance attached in the interviews to Greek-Cypriot collective historical narratives. Several teachers expressed a fear that the objective might actually result in *"forgetting our history"* and ultimately lead to the falsification of Greek-Cypriot historical narrative and – by extension – to the elimination of Greek-Cypriot collective identity. Even positively inclined teachers underscored the need for ensuring that Greek Cypriots *"do not forget the past."*

The objective's 'leftist' political character.   Another important emotional and ideological obstacle that emerged in almost half (19/40) of the teachers' accounts was the view of the new objective as a 'leftist' pro-rapprochement initiative. The introduction of the objective soon after AKEL's political take-over was considered as a manifestation of leftist ideology. As explained in Section 2, the 'rapprochement' discourse has strong leftist connotations in Greek-Cypriot society and is, in no case, hegemonic within the Greek-Cypriot educational culture, something that resulted in the objective being met with considerable suspicion. For example, one respondent Niki remarked: "I think this was clearly a political decision. Rapprochement with Turkish Cypriots was always a leftist goal."

Seeing the objective as a political interference into the perceived neutrality of the educational realm led teachers to accuse the Ministry of *"propaganda"* and *"politicisation of schooling."* Teachers who disaffiliated from the idea of rapprochement especially felt that the objective was 'imposed' onto them and – in 19 instances – they employed the verbs *"coerce"* or *"impose"* to describe it. For example:

> *Kostas:* Any position on such an objective is political. No party or government has the right to impose on educators its political agenda. Education should cultivate commonly accepted values and ideas, not serve the politics of any government.

Furthermore, teachers raised concerns that supporting the new objective could be interpreted as a leftist political affiliation. Also, participants observed that the very attempt to cultivate peaceful coexistence made it hard – if not impossible – to stay neutral and avoid 'doing politics' in the classroom. Eliza wondered:

> How easy is it for a teacher to approach this issue objectively, without personal involvement, especially if someone has personal experiences? Or, what are the limits when approaching this objective?

The 'personal' and 'subjective' aspects to which Eliza referred are considered political and thus are contrary to the (supposedly) 'neutral' and 'objective' discourse of school knowledge. These findings demonstrate that the association of 'peaceful coexistence' with the 'rapprochement'-discourse functioned rather prohibitively for teachers who feared being ascribed to 'leftist' political affiliations.

The lack of institutional support. The last difficulty discussed here relates to educational rather than social and political structures: 33 (out of 40) teachers complained that the introduction of the new objective was not accompanied by the necessary institutional support (e.g. educational materials, training, guidance) – something that was also pointed out in our survey. The lack of institutional assistance was more frequently mentioned by teachers who appeared rather positively inclined towards the idea of peaceful coexistence. These teachers reported that they felt left 'on their own,' as the implementation relied merely on their personal initiatives. As a matter of fact many of them seemed to believe that the lack of necessary support contributed to the objective's 'unsuccessful' implementation. The following extract is a representative example:

> *Julia:* I would be willing [to implement the objective] if they organised first some training seminars, if they taught me something, a Turkish dance or whatever I am willing to show it. Or a song, if I had a CD and knew how to sing it, I am willing!

Furthermore, teachers reported that their only briefing was the circular itself, which did not address the practical difficulties of the objective's implementation and employed a vague and unclear wording that left them with many unanswered questions. Kyriaki, for example, was one amongst many teachers who complained that *"they just said 'reconciliation.' They did not explain to us the ways in which this thing can happen or how we are expected to talk about it to our students."* Thus, the overwhelming majority of the teachers, who like Julia, were willing to do something requested *"more specific instructions on how to implement the objective in practice"* (Melpo) and provision of appropriate materials from the Ministry.

On the other hand, teachers who were negatively inclined towards the new objective justified their refusal to engage in relevant practices on the lack of control mechanisms and encouragement by higher institutional actors (e.g. the Ministry, inspectors, head-teachers). Especially POED's (primary-school teachers' trade-union) announcement that rejected any institutional control on the objective's implementation was often used to legitimize teachers' denunciation of the objective, similarly to the extract below:

> *Stergios*: Our trade-union expressed similar [to mine] opinions, that's why it reacted against the objective. So I do not think that I do something extreme here by having this opinion [being very against the objective].

Given the social and political difficulties, the impact of these institutional structures on teachers' emotional readiness to implement the objective should not be underestimated. In fact, practical difficulties also have a political aspect, as they are not unrelated to the long-term dominance of the *'Den Xechno'* discourse in Greek-Cypriot educational culture, as evidence has shown in previous parts of this chapter.

DISCUSSION AND IMPLICATIONS

In this chapter we explored the significance of teachers' emotions in educational efforts for change, especially in cases where controversial political issues are involved. Focusing specifically on a new policy initiative for the cultivation of peaceful coexistence in Greek-Cypriot schools, we investigated teachers' difficulties in dealing with this controversial issue and examined the impact of these perceived difficulties on teachers' emotional readiness to implement the new policy initiative. The case of Cyprus proved a fascinating illustration of how, in contexts of unresolved political conflict, ideological battles are easily transformed into highly emotional ones, significantly complicating teachers' emotional engagement with relevant pedagogical processes.

Specifically, our quantitative findings revealed an emotional ambivalence towards the new educational objective: although most teachers recognized the importance of cultivating peaceful coexistence for both education and the conflict itself, the survey also documented a significant lack of readiness and willingness to implement the new objective, coupled with doubts regarding its feasibility within the Cypriot context. The analysis of quantitative data gave rise to two potential sources for teachers' emotional resistance, one ideological and one practical: (a) a strong tendency to define reconciliation within the Cypriot context in terms of human rights; and (b) a strong consensus (97%) as to the practical difficulties involved in the implementation of the objective.

In the qualitative phase of our project we were primarily concerned with explaining the teachers' emotional ambivalence that the quantitative phase revealed, through a careful look at the difficulties that teachers reported during in-depth interviews. Interestingly, the qualitative analysis confirmed that teachers' emotional resistance was triggered by both ideological and practical obstacles, similar to the findings reported from the questionnaires. Beginning with the ideological obstacles, our analysis illustrated the degree to which teachers perceived the objective as thoroughly political. Most difficulties reported related to the ideological complexities of the Cyprus Issue, either directly (e.g. open war traumas, interminable negotiations, ethnic rivalry and estrangement, lack of a 'legitimated' coexistence-discourse etc.) or indirectly, through a series of perceived ideological repercussions (e.g. the politicization of classroom discourse, fear of forgetting history, discourse of human rights violations, etc.). Practical obstacles mainly concerned the lack of institutional support and guidance for the implementation of the objective (e.g. lack of material and resources, training, instructions/advice, and curricula that were still grounded in the *Den Xechno* discourse) – issues that, of course, were not irrelevant to the Cypriot political scene.

The analysis of teachers' accounts showed the ways in which these difficulties produce a negative emotional climate that leaves teachers feeling 'coerced,' 'pushed,' 'not listened to,' and forced to 'give away' things they hold as emotionally precious. The sensitive, painful or even tabooed issues touched upon by the new educational objective rendered it 'inappropriate' and 'insensitive' in the eyes of participants and, in many cases, caused an emotional blockage hard to transcend. For these reasons, many teachers seem to reject the objective as politically biased and not representative of the dominant Greek-Cypriot societal ethos. By linking teachers' accounts to wider discourses and structures in the Greek-Cypriot society, our analysis showed the inseparability of emotional reactions from the broader socio-political context within which these were situated. Importantly, research on education for coexistence elsewhere (e.g. Abu-Nimer, 2004; Bar-Tal, 2000, 2004; Napier, 2003) also confirms that political ideas, ideological differences, and implementation problems are the most common emotional challenges in such initiatives.

Based on the literature and the data from both phases of our research, we suggest a number of recommendations of what to do to help teachers overcome emotional issues with an objective like the one under study. It seems that despite teachers' notable indications of positivity towards reconciliation *on a rhetorical level,* when it comes to implementation, the ideological, emotional and practical difficulties they face are disheartening and, often, insurmountable. Therefore, in order to utilize and build upon teachers' rhetorical commitment towards reconciliation, a great deal needs to be done at two levels: on a political level, teachers seem in need of a widely accepted 'official' discourse on these controversial issues; while on a psychological level, there is need for well-designed and consistently evaluated efforts that deal head on with tough emotional issues around the promotion of peaceful coexistence in schools.

On the political level, Bar Tal (2004) argued that large-scale policy attempts for coexistence should "begin formally only when the time is *ripe*. Without this ripeness, education for coexistence has a high risk of failure" (Bar-Tal, 2004, p. 266, added emphasis). In cases of on-going political confrontations, this ripeness could be pragmatically defined as achieving the lowest common denominator, which can unite the social body (teachers, political parties, NGOs) towards a broad program of action that takes into consideration political sensitivities, while it includes engagement with the other side. In other words, the 'ripeness' has to be gradually and carefully engineered in society and education – through policy measures and support mechanisms that include all interested parties in decision-making, even those who seem to wish the perpetuation of the status quo (Bar-Tal, 2000; Bekerman & Maoz, 2005).

In terms of the psychological level, emotional and organizational support should move to the direction of systematic and systemic initiatives (Abu-Nimer, 2004) that utilize teachers' negative perceptions and emotions in constructive ways, such as in teacher education workshops; curriculum development sessions, school leadership seminars, and action research projects. Radical and largely unplanned policy initiatives are unlikely to permeate into teachers and schools (Zembylas & Bekerman, 2008). These initiatives should adopt a holistic approach to curriculum development, school leadership and culture (Salomon & Nevo, 2002) and not refrain from dealing with the tough emotional issues. Instead, our research points to the need for a critically reflective approach to emotions, pedagogical practices and policy measures – an approach which questions established perceptions and emotions around peace and conflict (Zembylas, 2008). Although this is undoubtedly very challenging, the confrontation and critical engagement with 'difficult' emotional issues appears as the only way forward towards promoting education for coexistence in schools. Yet, it is always important to keep in mind that negative perceptions and emotions are learned over a long socialization process and a similar amount of time is needed for processing these difficult feelings, without ever a guarantee that any transformation will take place (Chubbuck & Zembylas, 2008). Nevertheless, as Bar-Tal (2004) asserted, education for coexistence can serve as a catalyst that slowly *encourages* change rather than instigates change.

REFERENCES

Abu-Lughod, L., & Lutz, C. A. (1990). Introduction: Emotion, discourse, and the politics of everyday life. In C. Lutz and L. Abu-Lughod (Eds.), *Language and the politics of emotion* (pp. 1-23). Cambridge: Cambridge University Press.

Abu-Nimer, M. (2004). Education for coexistence and Arab-Jewish encounters in Israel: Potential and challenges. *Journal of Social Issues, 60*(2), 405-422.

Ahmed, S. (2004). *The cultural politics of emotion.* Edinburgh: Edinburgh University Press.

Bar-Tal, D. (2000). *Shared beliefs in a society: Social psychological analysis*. Thousands Oaks, CA: Sage.

Bar-Tal, D. (2002). The elusive nature of peace education. In G. Salomon & B. Nevo (Eds.), *Peace education: The concept principles and practice around the world* (pp. 27-36). Mahwah, NJ: Lawrence Erlbaum.

Bar-Tal, D. (2004). Nature, rationale, and effectiveness of education for coexistence. *Journal of Social Issues, 60*(2), 253-271.

Bar-Tal, D., & Bennink, G. (2004). The nature of reconciliation as an outcome and as a process. In Y. Bar-Siman-Tov (Ed.), *From conflict resolution to reconciliation* (pp. 11-38). Oxford: Oxford University Press.

Bekerman, Z., & Maoz, I. (2005). Troubles with identity: Obstacles to coexistence education in conflict ridden societies. *Identity: An International Journal of Theory and Research, 5*(4), 341-357.

Bernard, R. (2002). *Research methods in anthropology: Qualitative and quantitative approaches*. New York: Altamira Press.

Bryant, R. (2004). *Imagining the modern: The cultures of nationalism in Cyprus*. London: I. B. Tauris.

Charalambous, C. (2009). *Learning the language of 'the Other': A linguistic ethnography of Turkish-language classes in a Greek-Cypriot school*. Unpublished PhD Thesis, King's College, London.

Charalambous, P. (2009). Classroom constructions of a 'militant ethos:' Social representations and textual ideologies in Greek-Cypriot literature education practices. Paper presented at the *Cyprus Colloquium: Discourse and Education in the Process of Reconciliation*. London: Metropolitan University.

Chubbuck, S., & Zembylas, M. (2008). The emotional ambivalence of socially just teaching: A case study of a novice urban schoolteacher. *American Educational Research Journal, 45*(2), 274-318.

Christou, M. (2007). The language of patriotism: Sacred history and dangerous memories. *British Journal of Sociology of Education, 28*(6), 709-722.

Clark, S., Hoggett, P., & Thompson, S. (2006). *Emotion, politics and society*. London: Palgrave.

Constantinou, C., & Papadakis, Y. (2001). The Cypriot state(s) in situ: Cross-ethnic contact and the discourse of recognition. *Global Society, 15*(2), 125-148.

Field, A. (2000). *Discovering statistics using SPSS* (2nd ed.). London: Sage.

Goodwin, J., Jasper, J., & Polletta, F. (Eds.). (2001). *Passionate politics: Emotions and social movements*. Chicago: University of Chicago Press.

Johnson, R. B., & Onwuegbuzie, A. J. (2004). Mixed-methods research: A research paradigm whose time has come. *Educational Researcher, 33*(7), 14-26.

Kizilyürek, N. (1993). *Cyprus beyond nation*. Nicosia, Cyprus: Cassoulides.

Kriesberg, L. (1998). Coexistence and the reconciliation of communal conflicts. In E. Weiner (Ed.), *The handbook of interethnic coexistence* (pp. 182-198). New York: Continuum.

Leavitt, J. (1996). Meaning and feeling in the anthropology of emotions. *American Ethnologist, 23*(3), 514-519.

Mavratsas, C. (2004). National identity and consciousness in everyday life: Towards a sociology of knowledge of Greek-Cypriot nationalism. *Nations and Nationalism, 5*(1), 91-104.

Ministry of Education and Culture. (2008a). *F:7.1.05.21, Objectives of the school year 2008-2009* [in Greek]. Nicosia: Ministry of Education and Culture of the Republic of Cyprus.

Ministry of Education and Culture. (2008b). *Annual report* [in Greek]. Nicosia: Arlo.

Murphy, K., & Gallagher, T. (2009). Reconstruction after violence: How teachers and schools can deal with the legacy of the past. *Perspectives in Education, 27*(2), 158-168.

Napier, D. B. (2003). Transformations in South Africa: Policies and practices from ministry to classroom. In: Anderson-Levitt, K. (Ed.), *Local meanings, global schooling: Anthropology and world culture theory* (pp. 51-74). New York: Palgrave McMillan.

Papadakis, Y. (2008). Narrative, memory and history education in divided Cyprus. *History & Memory, 20*(2), 128-148.

Persianis, P. (2006). *Comparative history of education in Cyprus (1800-2004)* [in Greek]. Athens: Gutenberg.

POED (Pangypria Organosi Ellinon Didaskalon). (2009). *Objectives under emphasis* [in Greek]. Nicosia: POED.

Richards, L. (2009). *Handling qualitative data: A practical guide* (2nd edition). London: Sage.

Salomon, G. & Nevo, B. (Eds.). (2002). *Peace education: The concepts, principles, and practices around the world*. Mahwah, NJ, Lawrence Erlbaum Associates.

Spyrou, S. (2006). Constructing "the Turk" as an enemy: The complexity of stereotypes in children's everyday worlds. *South European Society and Politics, 11*(1), 95-110.

Synott, J. (2005). Peace education as an educational paradigm: Review of a changing field using an old measure. *Journal of Peace Education, 2*(1), 3-16.

Weitzman, E. (2000). Software and qualitative research. In N. K. Denzin, & Y. S. Lincoln (Eds.), *Handbook of qualitative research* (2nd edition, pp. 803-820) Thousand Oaks, CA: Sage.

Zembylas, M. (2005). *Teaching with emotion: A postmodern enactment*. Greenwich, CT: Information Age Publishing.

Zembylas, M. (2008). *The politics of trauma in education*. New York: Palgrave, MacMillan.

Zembylas, M., & Bekerman, Z. (2008). Education and the dangerous memories of historical trauma: Narratives of pain, narratives of hope. *Curriculum Inquiry, 38*, 125-154.

Zembylas, M., & Ferreira, A. (2009). Identity formation and affective spaces in conflict ridden areas: Inventing heterotopic possibilities. *Journal of Peace Education, 6*(1), 1-18.

Michalinos Zembylas
Open University of Cyprus

Constadina Charalambous
European University Cyprus

Panayiota Charalambous
European University Cyprus

Panayiota Kendeou
Neapolis University Pafos

PART V

IDENTITY, DOMINATION AND REVOLUTION

NAGWA MEGAHED & STEPHEN LACK

WOMEN'S RIGHTS AND GENDER-EDUCATIONAL INEQUALITY IN EGYPT AND TUNISIA

From Colonialism to Contemporary Revolution

INTRODUCTION

After decades of submission and compliance, Tunisians and Egyptians succeeded in removing autocratic regimes that were once perceived as being unshakable. Their determination has inspired the region; revolts have been taken place in several Arab countries (Libya, Yemen, Bahrain, Oman, and Syria, among others). Clearly, the Middle East and North Africa region is living a momentous period of transition, calling for democracy. However, what kind of democracy is a question that remains unanswered. Will "democracy" be achieved through a theocratic, a civilian, or a military state? In this context, women and other vulnerable groups have also demanded their rights as equal citizens. It is well known that the pre-revolution regimes in Tunisia (since 1956) and Egypt (since 1952) embraced progressive secular ideas especially with regard to women's rights. Yet, according to a variety of international and regional reports, Arab countries, including Egypt and Tunisia, are in urgent need of gender-oriented educational reform in order to achieve gender equality.

The Arab Republic of Egypt today includes a territory of 1,001,450 square kilometers. Its population was estimated at 83 million in 2009 (World Bank, 2011d, p. 1) most of whom are Arabs with small minorities of Bedouins and Nubians. It is the largest country in North Africa with a projected population of more than 98.6 million by 2020 (UN, 2009, p. 193). Muslims constitute 90% of the population, although there have been critical cultural/political differences among Muslim groups (Ramadan, 1986; Ibrahim, 1987; Voll, 1994). Approximately 9% of the population is Coptic Christian and 1% is other Christian (World Factbook, 2012). There are also important cultural differences in rural/urban- and social class dimensions. The vast majority of Egyptians live along the banks and in the delta region of the Nile River; thus, while its overall population density is not very high (73 people per square kilometer), its large cities (particularly Cairo and Alexandria) are densely populated. The governorates surrounding these two cities are considered to be "urban," while the other 26 governorates (not including the Luxor region) are considered rural governorates (see CAPMS, 2006).

From 1996 to 2006, the percentage of the male proportion of the population increased to 51% and the average of family size declined to 4.18. The total fertility rate (children born per woman) decreased from 3.5 in 2000 to 3.1 in 2005 (Egypt State Information Service, 2012a, 2012b). Nonetheless, the adult literacy rate

D.B. Napier & S. Majhanovich (eds.), Education, Dominance and Identity, 201–222.

during the period 1997-2007 was much higher for men (74.6%) versus for women (57.8%) (UN, 2009). According to the World Bank (2011c), the gender-gap in enrollment rates for Egyptian secondary education was 4.8 in 2004 (in favour of males 87.5% versus females 81.9%), which consequently reduced the opportunities for female participation in post-secondary education. Although this gap decreased from 18.2 in 1990 (when it was 77.6% for males and 59.4% for females), the rate of gender reform in Egypt has been painfully slow (World Bank, 2011c).

The Republic of Tunisia, with a population of approximately 10,374,000 and encompassing an area of 162,155 square kilometers is significantly smaller than Egypt. However, Tunisia has been a leader in the region in terms of gender equality and reform since the 1990s to the present. Tunisia's population is 98% Muslim, with small Christian and Jewish minorities. Furthermore, the male to female ratio in Tunisia is almost 50/50 (Tunisia National Institute of Statistics, 2011). Tunisia gained independence from French rule in 1956. Since that time the Republic of Tunisia has actively promoted equality for Tunisian citizens, regardless of gender or faith. Therefore it is unsurprising that Tunisia had a gross secondary enrollment gender gap of −4.7 in 2003 (males 75.8% and females 80.5%), which improved to −5.5 in 2008, with 89.4% for males and 94.4% for females (World Bank, 2011c). To sum up, the gender gap in Egypt is in favor of males while in Tunisia it is in favor of females thus the minus quantities in Tunisia show improvement for female gross secondary enrollment rate which is higher than that of males.

Both Egypt and Tunisia are Muslim-majority societies with heavy political involvement with the Middle East. In this chapter we examine the issue of gender and education in these two countries in relation to their ties with the Middle East and North Africa region. Depending on national and international documents and reports as well as available literature and statistical data, we compare the past and current status of women and gender inequality in education in Egypt and Tunisia. We begin with a historical overview of colonial legacy, education, and the status of women in Arab countries in general--and in Egypt and Tunisia in particular--which highlights the influence of colonialism on gender and education in this region. This is contextualized in the interplay of cultural, ideological forces that have continued to shape the discourse of gender equality and women's rights in Arab Muslim-majority societies, including a) "Islamic" teachings and local traditions concerning women's roles in a given society, b) Western, European colonial perceptions of women's rights, and c) current international policy for women's rights and its national responses. We follow with an examination of gender inequality in terms of female participation in pre-university and higher education as well as employment opportunities for women in Egypt and Tunisia.

COLONIAL LEGACY, EDUCATION, AND THE STATUS OF WOMEN

After the defeat of the Ottoman Empire in the First World War the period of colonization of the Arab world began, mainly by France, Britain, and Italy. The French colonized and "protected" Algeria, Tunisia, Morocco, Lebanon and Syria.

The British occupied Egypt, Jordan, Palestine and Iraq; whereas the Italians occupied Libya. While Algeria was a settler colony, Morocco and Tunisia were protectorates, where, de facto European colonial rule prevailed.

Although under colonial rule, schools in the Middle East and North Africa region (MENA) were largely restricted to European settlers, their families, and those nationals necessary to the administration, large numbers of religious intuitions existed throughout this region and remained largely intact. Therefore, as the MENA countries gained independence, the existing structure of religious institutions combined with the colonial educational system provided a framework from which the modern educational systems arose (World Bank, 2008). According to the World Bank (2008), integration of the old and new systems was the key challenge of early reformers in the 1950s and 60s.

The colonial powers had constructed a secular legal system replacing the religious/Islamic laws (Shari'a) (Daun & Arjmand, 2002). They "gradually increased their control over education in the region. This control took the form of imposing French and English as the languages of instruction at all levels" (Benhamida, 1990, p. 295). For example, during the occupation in Egypt the British sought to Anglicize the language of instruction and the corps of teachers in the government schools in Egypt (Ali, 1995; Reid, 1974, 1977). Lord Cromer, who was British Consul-General in Egypt from 1883 to1907, promoted the learning of English (vs. French and Arabic), and brought in teachers from England (Erlich, 1989, pp. 24-25). According to Williamson (1987, p. 82) there was a slow shift:

> English gradually came to replace French as the principal foreign language but the devaluation of Arabic was seen by nationalists as another indignity inflicted on them by the British, and this sense of indignity was clearly reinforced by authoritarian teaching methods, a lack of contact between English teachers and their pupils and the way in which the British cut themselves off socially from the Egyptians they governed.

The situation was not much different in other Arab countries, but the Anglo-French plan backfired. It inspired, activated and articulated the struggle for independence around Arab nationalism. According to Akrawi and El-Koussy (1971, p. 181),

> Arab nationalism … began as a movement for liberating the Arabs from Ottoman rule, [and] continued after the First World War to free the countries from the four Western powers (France, Great Britain, Italy and Spain), and then had to face the rise of the State of Israel, which poses a continuing problem. But the struggle for independence was only one aspect of Arab nationalism. It has tried for a hundred years to revive the Arab culture, to create an Arab consciousness and some form of Arab national unity, and to renovate the whole social and economic fabric of Arab life, which has been torn apart by centuries of invasion, foreign rule and neglect.

In terms of the status of women, the colonial influence varied and national responses took different forms. However, a better understanding of women's status prior to, during, and after colonialism in Arab Muslim-majority countries requires a discussion of three different cultural and ideological forces that have severely shaped the on-going discourse of women's rights and gender equality. These forces have been influenced by three factors. One is "Islamic" teachings and local traditions concerning women's roles in a given society; another is a Western, European Colonial perception of women's rights; and the third one is reform policies of national governments in response to international/Western pressure versus local cultural traditions/norms. These factors are discussed next.

WOMEN'S RIGHTS AND SOCIAL PRACTICE: ISLAMIC/LOCAL TRADITIONS VERSUS EUROPEAN COLONIAL PERCEPTION

As Christina, Mehran, and Mir (1999, p. 355) explained, "any discourse about female education in the Middle East must take into consideration the fact that the teachings of Islam, combined with indigenous customs and tradition, play a crucial role in determining the status of women and their education in the region." However, this should also be placed in the socioeconomic political context and dynamics. According to Golley (2004, p. 522), "religion cannot and should not be seen independently of the socioeconomic and political context within which it unfolds. Like any other human activity ... it is subject to change, at least in its function." As Douglass and Shaikh (2004, p.5) explained,

> Muslims and non-Muslims alike frequently use the adjective, Islamic, to elevate cultural expressions to the position of normative or consummate institutions or practices .... [P]ublic commentators often fail to make any distinction between that which pertains directly to Islam and its doctrines, and actions its adherents perform in the cultural or social realm.

Thus, the distinction between what is purely Islamic and what are considered entirely cultural and social practices/actions of Muslims will always be debated among Muslims and non-Muslims. This is especially the case, taking into consideration that cultural traditions and social norms in Muslim-majority societies combine the values and principles associated with Islam but also adapt and integrate the indigenous habits and customs of people (Muslims and non-Muslims) in a given society (Megahed, 2010a).

For example, there are different interpretations of Islamic law whether women have the right to be educated to a high level, to possess and dispose of property, to undertake a trade or profession, and to vote and to serve as government officials (AWIR and MEPC, 1998; Ali & Ali, 2006). From this perspective, although these "civil rights" were to have been granted to women by Islam more than 1,400 years ago, some Islamic communities and societies do not implement all or most of them. It is argued, especially by those active in Muslim feminist movements, "that many extant Islamic practices derive from patriarchal interpretations of the Qur'an in male-dominated societies where the prevailing norms influenced men's largely biased interpretations of the holy book" (Ramazi, 1995; see also Bennoune, 1995; El-Saadawi, 1995). For example, the majority of Muslim women wear the hijab, some by personal choice in countries such as Egypt, Morocco, Tunisia, Lebanon,

Syria, Iraq, and others. But in Saudi Arabia, law prescribes wearing of the hijab. Muslim women differ regarding whether they are covering their heads (and other parts of their bodies) because of personal choice; duty to God; or coercion/oppression by family members, religious leaders, and/or government officials.

The West commonly perceives women in the Muslim-majority countries to be the victims of oppression, hidden behind the veil and secluded from the world. Gender segregation and hijab (head cover) stand as the most visible "Islamic" practices that are viewed by some as contradicting Judeo-Christian or "Western" ideas of liberty and modernization. However, Golley (2004) argued that gender segregation was common in ancient Judaic, Greek, and Byzantine cultures. He further explained that in the pre-Islamic world, the veil served to differentiate between 'respectable' women and 'available' women, and was worn by upper-class women until the early 20th century (Golley, 2004, p. 525). In fact, today the veil is as much a political symbol as a religious one.

The hijab has come to dominate the discussion of women's status in the Middle East; whether in academia, the media, or politics the hijab is ever-present. Such a case helped create a visible pattern, as if the region as a whole is suffering from an identity crisis, as nations seek to find a balance between accepting and rejecting a certain conception of modernization and the Western ideology behind it. Clearly, many women throughout the Arab world have turned to the veil as a symbol of political protest, an affirmation of their religious (Islamic) identity, and a rejection of Western culture. Meanwhile it is true that for many other Muslim women the veil is a symbol of religious piety and for some others it is a combination of both submission to God's will and resistance of Western culture.

Furthermore, Mule and Barthel (1992) argued that in a traditional gender separated society, the veil offers women the ability to move freely in the public sphere that has traditionally been the domain of males, such as the workplace and the classroom. However, Mule and Barthel (1992) also contended that the influx of Western culture and ideologies has presented Arab society with new challenges. Traditional gender roles conflict with the image of the modern Western woman. The hijab is a visible distinction of "Islamic" culture when compared to the unveiled women of the West. Such a case is not new but in fact rooted in the colonial past.

In Algeria, for example, according to Marshall and Stokes (1981), French colonial powers attempted to undermine traditional culture and social structure. In order to completely dismantle the existing political structure and remove the traditional political elite, French nationals dominated government administration at every level. Furthermore, France consistently undertook measures to suppress Algerian indigenous and religious culture. Operating under the belief that women's liberation coincided with modernization, French efforts focused heavily on women's liberation and equality.

Traditions and institutions under direct threat from colonial powers tended to become the most important symbols of resistance. As a result, there was a backlash against all things European, including the emancipation and equality of women

(Marshall & Stokes, 1981). A 2004 World Bank report, Gender and Development in the Middle East and North Africa: Women in the Public Sphere, explained that popular resistance movements associated gender-related reforms, introduced top-down, with the reigning socio-political elite that had allied itself with the French. Thus, gender-focused reform became associated with the Western conception of modernization and was often a central point of Algerian government opposition (World Bank, 2004).

Tunisia, however, as a protectorate, remained politically autonomous and French interference was rather limited. The government remained, at least theoretically, in Tunisian hands. The transition into independence was much smoother in Tunisia as a result. Marshall and Stokes (1981) explained that this resulted in the Tunisian government's ability to confront and break down long standing traditions. Since gaining independence from France in 1956 Tunisia aggressively reformed the status of women and the traditional family structure. Furthermore, the traditional cultural constraints on women associated with ethnic norms and/or conservative interpretations of Islamic teachings were removed or undermined. According to the International Women's Rights Action Watch (2002),

> Tunisia is often viewed as one of the most progressive Islamic states. While the Constitution stipulates that the president must be Muslim and the state religion is Islam, the government has also taken steps to secularize the country and move society away from Islamic fundamentalism .... As a part of a secularization effort, which began under the presidency of Habib Bourguiba (1956-1987), the Tunisian government banned all political groups formed on a religious basis; one of the groups banned as a result of the law included the Movement for Islamic Tendency (which was later renamed Al-Nahda).

In 1957, Tunisia became the first and only Muslim state to abolish polygamy. The Tunisian government grounded the decision in *Shari'a* (Islamic Law) that states a man must treat all his wives equally. The Tunisian government claimed this was humanly impossible. Furthermore, Tunisia's Personal Status Code enacted in 1956, in addition to the 1986 abolition of the *hijab* (veil or head cover) and the abortion legislation of 1973 are arguably the most extensive but certainly the most controversial in the region. According to Valentine Moghadam (1993 cited in Makar, 1996), "Tunisia's Personal Status Code of 1956 is unique in the Muslim World as it applies a modernistic interpretation of Islamic law and a daring interpretation of the traditional laws in a feminist way."' Currently, the wearing of *hijab* is forbidden in government offices. In addition, Tunisia's current abortion law which dates from 1973, authorizes the performance of abortions during the first three months of pregnancy (International Women's Rights Action Watch, 2002).

Women actively participated side-by-side with men in the Jasmine revolution of 17 December 2010 to 14 January 2011. In post-revolution Tunisia, the Independent High Authority for the Election adopted a rule that requires parties to alternate men-and-women candidates in order to ensure gender equality in the election process (Medien, 2011). According to Dickinson (2011),

206

[H]alf the candidates were women … In all, more than 4,000 female politicians ran for office. And when the results were tallied, 24 per cent of the seats went to women. It was far from an equal share … but it was also far better than the international average; a mere 17 per cent of seats in the U.S. Congress are held by women.

The once-banned movement, which became the moderate Islamist, *Al-Nahda* party won the majority of seats in the Tunisia's newly elected constituent assembly. *Al-Nahada* partnered with the two runners-up in the election – the liberal Congress for the Republic Party and the left-of-centre *Ettakatol* Party. On November 2011, the three parties formed the interim government and Moncef Marzouki became the interim president (*Al-Ahram Weekly*, 2011; *Aljazeera*, 2011; *Guardian*, 2011). In post-revolution Tunisia, concerns have been raised regarding women's gained rights which caused debate and division in public opinion. For example, Ayadi (2011) reported that

The niqab … [face veil and full cover] surfaced in Tunisia after the Revolution, and has been the cause of heated debate within Tunisian society. Women wearing the full veil are presently a common sight in all cities of the country, and this has divided public opinion. On the one hand, many reject the phenomenon as a negation of women's emancipation, claiming it has nothing to do with Tunisian tradition, while others say that wearing the niqab is a manifestation of freedom of the individual in post-Revolution Tunisia.

In Egypt, with its semi-independence from the British in 1922, the state had a large number of educated professionals. Salmoni (2003) stated that, much like their Turkish counterparts, post-independence Egyptian officials viewed education as an ideological tool in the nationalist movement. This perception was further promoted after the 1953 revolution. Throughout history, reform movements have sought to garner the support of women through policies of gender reform. Egypt was no different. During the 1930s, men and women alike celebrated the public presence and participation of "unveiled women" (Salmoni 2003). However, Salmoni explained that by the late 1930s through the 1940s, educational gender equality began to decline with the reaffirmation of traditional female domestic roles. From the 1950s through the 1970s according to the World Bank (2004) many of the newly independent governments sponsored gender equality and women's liberation in efforts to forge new national identities.

Whereas Algeria rejected all things European, Egypt maintained a stable political elite who modeled their nation after the modern European societies with which they had become so familiar. Egyptian writers and politicians, such as Abiidir Hakim (cited in Salmoni, 2003), viewed the education and equality of women as a necessity. The maternal role of women ensured that women were responsible for the shaping and nurturing of future generations. Therefore, an educated and moral woman was necessary in the production of cultured young men dedicated to the nationalist cause.

Perceptions of women's roles and rights have changed over times in Egypt due to the political and socioeconomic transformations shifting the country from a socialist- to a capitalist-oriented society and due to the reemergence of radical and non-radical Muslim fundamentalist groups. For example, during the 1970s the Sadat government sought to address Egypt's pressing economic problems by encouraging Western European and North American investment. At the same time, Sadat empowered once again a group known as the Muslim Brotherhood, which dates back to 1928. The Muslim Brotherhood rapidly gained influence, particularly among university students, as a political force opposing the Nasserists' socialism advocates. Different Islamic groups grew out of the Muslim brotherhood many of which have since been opposing legal and social reforms especially those directed to women's rights. In Egypt and as Guenena and Wassef (1999, pp. 6-7) explained,

> Throughout almost three-quarters of a century, the Muslim Brothers stood at different junctures in relation to the government .... While national liberation and political independence were causes that inevitably brought the association and the state together, any attempt by the state at social or legal reform was met with opposition, especially if it fell within the realm of [Islamic law] Shari'a.

Al-Ali (2002) illustrated a clear example of the Government of Egypt's efforts in undermining the influence of conservative Islamist opposition to civil rights for Egyptian women. The Islamists opposed the reform of the Personal Status Law initiated by the president's wife Jehan Al-Sadat. Nonetheless, the proposed law, which granted women legal rights in matters such as marriage, divorce, and custody was implemented in 1979 as Law No. 44 by presidential decree. Law No. 44 represented a leap forward in Egypt's personal status laws. Significantly, Law No. 44, following the Hanafi view of Islamic jurisprudence, giving the wife a right to divorce if she was not informed of a subsequent marriage or if it harmed her, though court approval was not necessary for husbands to enter polygamous marriages. By right, a wife could seek a legal separation if continued married life caused her unbearable harm" (Brandt and Kaplan, 1995, p. 112). In the same year, another law that introduced changes to women's representation in parliament was also implemented. According to Al-Ali (2002, p. 8) "[these] reforms spearheaded a two-pronged strategy of undermining the strength and legitimacy of Islamists and demarcating the state's social agenda from that of the Islamists as a form of internal and international mobilization against them."

During the 1980s and under the Mubarak regime, due to strong opposition from the Islamists, women lost some of their gained rights when the 1979 Law was amended or rather repealed by the 1985 Law (Al-Ali, 2002; see also Brandt & Kaplan, 1995). Currently and according to the Egypt State Information Service, several legal reforms were undertaken. For example, a Republican decree was issued by means of which the first female judge was appointed in January 2003. Moreover, amendments were made to the Egyptian nationality law in order to give Egyptian nationality without pre-conditions to children born to Egyptian women married to foreigners (*Al-Ahram Weekly*, 2003; Ministry of Justice, 2005). Furthermore, "in 2005 Egypt granted women expanded divorce rights. But efforts to change the law to allow women to travel without the permission of a husband or father were dropped by the government for fear that they were too radical to pass" (Kimani, 2008).

In terms of education, Brandt and Kaplan (1995) clarified that Islamists have not produced a backlash against female education due to the fact that Islam stresses education including religious education for both men and women. From Brandt and Kaplan's perspective (1996, p. 105) "[m]any of the Islamist groups in Egypt and elsewhere, while confronting the government, rely upon educated, activist women as part of their movement."

However in practice, contradictions between the Egyptian government and Islamist ideologies concerning women's rights have penetrated school settings. Many confrontations occurred between the 1990s through to 2010, in relation to school girls and the hijab (head cover, veil) or the niqab (face veil and the head-to-toe garment). For example, in the mid-1990s, "The government linked accounts of school girls forced to wear veils by conservative teachers and school personnel to a broader Islamic campaign. In response, it issued a prohibition against veils in school without a written request by a child's parents. ... Courts rejected the veil prohibition. Earlier, they had rejected a government ban on wearing the 'niqab' ... in school" (Brandt & Kaplan, 1995 p. 106). As a renewal of its prohibition against the veil in school, the Egyptian Ministry of Education issued Ministerial decree 6/2006, restating the need of a request by a child's parents to wear the hijab in school (Almasry Alyoum, 2006). Furthermore, in October 2009 the Egyptian Minister of Education, Yousry Algamal, announced the activation of the Ministerial decree of 1995 which banned both female teachers and students from wearing the niqab inside classrooms. This time, the decree was supported by the Egyptian Administrative Court in January 2010; the court decision was issued in response to a petition filed by 50 female students who protested against the ban (Moheet, 2009; *Shorouk News*, 2010). Clearly, the wearing of hijab and niqab was discouraged and not welcome during Mubarak's regime. However, it has been and still is encouraged and celebrated socially and widely practiced among Egyptian women in schools, universities and other public spheres.

Egyptian women actively participated in the 25th January to 14th February 2011 revolution and they were in the frontlines of protests in Tahrir square. Yet, in the post-revolutionary Egypt, "female representation in the newly-formed Egyptian cabinet is limited to just one woman ... women have been excluded from the government [but also] from the constitutional drafting committee" (*Equality Now*, 2011). Fears emerged that women's rights in Egypt are "slipping away" (*Equality Now*, 2011). Similar to Tunisia, in the parliamentary election of Egypt the Muslim Brotherhood group gained its first political recognition when the group established the "Freedom and Justice" party, the party that won the majority of seats in the parliament.

INTERNATIONAL POLICY FOR WOMEN'S RIGHTS AND NATIONAL RESPONSES

International support for gender-educational equality has existed for some time. Of special interest in this section is the General Assembly of the UN Convention on the Elimination of all forms of Discrimination Against Women (CEDAW) in December of 1979. The CEDAW represented a conscious effort on behalf of the international community to recognize and eliminate gender inequalities. However, the convention met with limited success in the Middle East and North Africa. "Egypt ... entered reservations with respect to Article 2, articulating the commitment to eradicate discrimination; Article 9, delineating equal citizenship rights; and Article 16, containing provisions for the elimination of discrimination in marriage and the family" (Brandt & Kaplan, 1995, p. 118).

Egypt's reservations to the CEDAW provisions were explained by the assumption that Islamic law had already "liberated [women] from any form of discrimination." However, Article 16 was the only provision for which Egypt expressly stated that a reservation was necessary to comply with the *Shari'a* (Brandt & Kaplan, 1995, p. 118).

Egypt remains one of the most secular societies within the MENA region. However, and as explained earlier, conservative movements have had an impact on female status and practices for decades. For example, according to Cook (2001), although the right to free basic education has been granted to all Egyptians by the constitution, the resurgence of fundamentalist Islamic beliefs has had a profound effect on women in education. Many women, including those who choose to attend post-secondary education and the university, opt to wear the veil. Yet, education has increased the average age of marriages, as an early marriage is no longer feasible. In Egyptian society, marriage is the optimum goal for women. Thus, for an unmarried young woman pursuing her education, the *hijab* offers an escape from the disgrace or shame often faced by unmarried women. For example, a young Egyptian woman who attended university felt that the veil offered her the freedom to pursue her education without facing shame or criticism. Before taking the veil she was uncomfortable talking to men outside the classroom from fear of public opinion, however after taking the veil she felt greater security, and took comfort from the fact that no one was going to accuse her of immorality (Mule & Barthel, 1992).

Similarly, and despite Tunisia's progressive stance on women's rights and gender issues, the state held reservations toward the Articles 9, 15, and 16 of the 1979 Convention on the Elimination of All Forms of Discrimination against Women (CEDAW) (see Brandt and Kaplan, 1995, International Women's Rights Action Watch, 2002). In particular, Article 15 stated "States Parties shall accord to women, in civil matters, a legal capacity identical to that of men and the same opportunities to exercise that capacity. In particular, they shall give women equal rights to conclude contracts and to administer property and treat them equally in all stages of procedure in courts and tribunals" (UN, 1979).

Tunisia was reluctant to enact any legislation that might conflict with the Tunisian constitution. According to the Tunisian government, Tunisia's reservations were only a temporary measure until the Articles of the convention could be fully integrated into the constitution. Brandt and Kaplan (1995) explained that the Convention did not contradict or conflict with the Tunisian constitution; therefore, Tunisia's reservations were based upon political and religious concerns regarding the sovereignty of the state. It is worth mentioning, that although Tunisia has legally abolished all forms of gender discrimination through the nation's progressive legislation, the International Women's Rights Action Watch (2002) reported that as of 1991, 70% of illiterate Tunisian women were unaware of their legal rights.

In addition, women's educational rights have also received global attention. For more than two decades the international "Education for All" (EFA) movement has emphasized equality and quality of education. In 1990, the World Conference on Education for All in Jomtien, Thailand, sought to provide a new direction in education by creating flexible and inclusive educational systems, in addition to achieving education for all by the year 2000 (UNESCO, 1990). However, slow progress was made; thus, the Dakar Framework for Action was outlined at the World Education Forum of 2000 held in Senegal. The Dakar Framework reaffirmed the commitments of EFA and with a focus on female education, pledged to provide quality education for all by 2015. Furthermore, EFA sought to eliminate gender disparities in primary and secondary education by 2005 and achieve gender equality in education by 2015 (UNESCO, 2000, p. 8). It called for a new direction in education, with special focus on cultural diversity, problem solving and the interdependence of the global world. As reported by UNICEF (2007, p.14),

> Tunisia first began its literacy programme in the 1960s, with the aim of reducing the illiteracy rate, which in 1956 was estimated to be 84.7 percent (96 percent for females). The Government of Tunisia intensified its efforts following the Dakar Education for All Forum in 2000 by turning the literacy programme into an adult education programme that imparts literacy skills and practical childcare skills.

In its Post-Beijing National Plan of Action 1997-2001, the Ministry of Women and Family Affairs in Tunisia stated that "the major victims of illiteracy are women, and a national plan has been set up to combat illiteracy entirely among women between the ages of 15 and 45 by the year 2006 ... the goal is to lower the women's illiteracy rate from its 1992 figure of 30% to 17.3% in 1997" (Republic of Tunisia, 1997).

Though the Tunisian Education Act of July 2002 declared the provision of free education to all citizens, "regardless of gender, social origin, skin colour or religion" (Tunisian Education Act 23, July 2002), illiteracy rates continued to be higher for girls than boys in urban and rural areas in all age categories (International Women's Rights Action Watch, 2002).

Gender gaps in adult literacy (aged 15 and above) are still present in the region; it is estimated during the period 2000-2004 that only 60% of women are literate versus 80 per cent for men in Algeria, Iraq, Morocco, Saudi Arabia, Sudan and Tunisia (UNICEF, 2007, p. 14). In Egypt, the adult literacy rate during the period 1997-2007 was much higher for males (74.6%) versus females (57.8%) (UN, 2009). In addition, although illiteracy rates decreased over the years from 2003 through 2005, a higher percentage among females aged 15 and older persisted, as shown in Table 1.

Table 1. Illiteracy rates (+15) during the period 2003-2005 in Egypt

Year (as at 1ˢᵗ January each year)	Males	Females
2003	22.0	47.0
2004	20.4	45.8
2005	18.3	43.8

Source: Central Agency for Public Mobilization and Statistics (CAPMS), cited in Egypt State Information Service, 2012c.

To further examine gender inequality, in the following section we focus on female participation in pre-university and higher education.

GENDER-EDUCATIONAL INEQUALITY: FEMALE PARTICIPATION IN PRE-UNIVERSITY AND HIGHER EDUCATION

Education has been highly valued in North African Arab countries. Alexandria in Egypt was home to the world's largest and most extensive library, set up in the 3ʳᵈ century. Ancient Egyptians constructed monuments of such mathematical precision that remain awe-inspiring even in today's world; the construction techniques continue to baffle modern science. With the introduction of Islam in the 7ᵗʰ century AD, the educational traditions of the ancient world thrived. The Arab world gave the world Algebra, the concept of zero, and the decimal system. As medieval Europe slipped into intellectual stagnation, the Arab world, including North Africa, kept alight the flame of knowledge. Arab scholars preserved the classical knowledge of Ancient Greece, Persia, and India. Islamic schools (*Madrasa*) were open to men, women, rich, and poor. Daniel (2003) reported that teachers in the classical Arab world included women, highly valued for their poetry and skill in medicine.

As the Ottoman Empire crumbled and European powers became more involved in the region, educational quality began to decline. At a meeting of Arab education ministers in January of 2003, John Daniel (2003) reminded the assembled education ministers from around the Arab world of the historical position of education in Arab culture. He quoted the Prophet Mohammed who said that, "It is the duty of every Muslim man and woman to seek education."

The *Arab Knowledge Report 2009*, released by the United Nations' Development Programme, clearly acknowledged that the: "Inequality between men and women is longstanding and rooted in history. Ending discrimination means upsetting many delicate balances that have become immutable principles" and that, "political and cultural pressures and social constraints form multiple and complex restrictions … contradictory to those of justice, equality, and freedom" (*Arab Knowledge Report*, 2009, p. 49).

Although progress has been made, North African countries still lag behind the rest of the world in educational standards. Recently, however, educational reform movements have gained momentum in the MENA region. With the support of national and international agencies and non-governmental organizations, governments in the region have begun to take action in order to improve educational quality, enrollment rates, literacy rates, and gender equality.

The demographic profile of Arab countries is such that 35% of the Arab population in 2010 was under the age of 14. While this figure has declined from 38.1%, the Arab world remains home to one of the largest populations of school-aged youth in the world. Falling under the regional average, approximately 23.4% of Tunisians are under the age of 14. However, an estimated 32.8% of Egyptians are under the age of 14 (Population and Development, 2011, p.14). Due the large population of school-aged youth the provision of universal access to education in the MENA region as a whole is a unique challenge.

Development initiatives, such as Education for All (EFA), the Millennium Development Goals, and more recently Education for Sustainable Development are aimed at improving educational access, quality and gender equity in the region (UNESCO, 1990, 2009; UN, 2007). The *Arab Knowledge Report, 2009* stated that the high illiteracy rate of women combined with low enrollment rates especially in higher education was found to be the most glaring example of gender inequality in the Arab world. The report acknowledged the need for a dynamic approach for gender-oriented educational reform.

Arab educational ministers met in Beirut, in 2003 to discuss the current state of education in the Arab world. John Daniel (2003) outlined the current status of education in the region. Daniel highlighted the lack of knowledge, educational freedom, and female involvement. Furthermore, Daniel described current Education for All (EFA) initiatives, not as development, but as an effort to recover the great educational traditions of the Arab world. High female illiteracy rates and the lack of female participation in public life were major weaknesses in the educational development of MENA. Daniel proclaimed that, "In order to lift injustice education must have quality" (Daniel, 2003).

According to the Global Gender Gap Report 2009, countries in the MENA region continue to lag behind global averages in education statistics. On the *Global Gender Gap Index 2009 rankings* Tunisia is ranked 109th, while Egypt is 126th (Hausmann et al., 2009, p. 9). Not only have both Egypt and Tunisia failed to improve, they have actually moved down in the rankings. However, they are not alone; the MENA region as a whole ranks last on the global index, having closed approximately 58% of its gender gap (see Figure 1). This compares to around 65% in Sub-Saharan Africa and Asia; 67% in Latin America and Eastern Europe; and over 70% in Oceania, Western Europe and North America (Hausmann et al., 2009, p. 17).

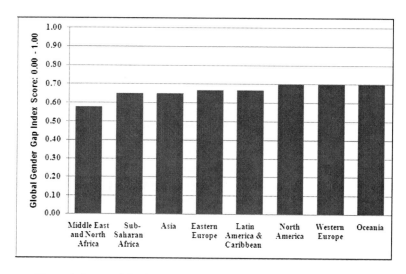

Figure 1. Regional Performance on the Global Gender Gap Index 2009.
Source: Hausmann et al. (2009, p. 17)

Tertiary gross enrollment rates (GER), are slightly better. The MENA region turned in a regional GER of 25.6; while not outstanding, the numbers are consistent with the global average. The World Bank (2004) contended that while the MENA region has experienced rapid educational development, extremely low levels of enrollment and educational standards during the 1960s and 1970s continue to play a role in the poor statistical performance of the region (World Bank, 2004).

Although literacy rates remain mediocre at 77.7% in Tunisia and unemployment rates remain high at 14.2% (World Bank, 2011c), the Tunisian government remains committed to the universal provision of access to education. The Tunisian Education Act (2002) made education a national priority, in addition to guaranteeing educational access to all. As of the 2008-2009 school year, 2.01 million students are enrolled at pre-university level. That accounts for 97.7% of the eligible population, with 98% of females enrolled compared to 97.4% of males (Tunisian National Institute of Statistics, 2011).

In post-secondary and university education, there are clear signs that the number of Tunisian women entering post-secondary education is rising (International Women's Rights Action Watch 2002). In the 2009-2010 academic year, more than half of all university students were women, representing 60.1% (see Table 2). However, despite gender equality in Tunisian higher education, school administrations still tend to be male-dominated (Brandt & Kaplan, 1995).

In Egypt, the government has perceived education as being the most important mechanism for women's empowerment in Egypt (Egypt State Information Service, 2012b). In 2006-2007, the total number of students enrolled in pre-university education was 17 million, which accounts for 90.2% of the school-age population.

The female enrolment rate reached 90.3%, slightly higher than that of males at 90% (MOE, 2007, p. 31).

At the tertiary level, as of 2010 and in addition to the longstanding Al Azhar University, there were 18 public universities of which 12 are located in the Cairo, Alexandria, and Delta regions (in the north of Egypt) while only six universities are in the Upper Egypt regions (in the south). In addition, private higher education sector included 19 universities plus 151 middle and higher specialized institutes (MOHE, 2011). The total number of enrolled students in university and higher education reached around 2.5 million undergraduate students and about 215, 000 postgraduate students in 2009–2010; among these, female students represented only 46% (MOHE, 2009; SPU MOHE, 2010, p. 30). In recognition of gender inequality in higher education, the Strategic Planning Unit (SPU) at the Ministry of Higher Education in Egypt stated in its 2010 country report that "while there was a slight increase in women's enrolment in Higher Education between 2002/2003 and 2005/2006 (from 45% to 46%), this percentage still needs further improvement" (p. 32). The SPU 2010 report further explained that women's enrollment in higher education is influenced mostly by the unequal distribution of higher education institutions across governorates/provinces. Thus, it is not surprising to find the lowest female enrollment rates exist in the Upper Egypt governorates which are not only the poorest in the country but considered socially and culturally to be more conservative and protective toward women (Megahed, 2010b). Table 2 provides a comparison between Egypt and Tunisia in terms of female enrolment in pre-university and tertiary education as well as the total number of universities and higher education institutions.

Table 2. Pre-university and tertiary education in Egypt and Tunisia

Pre-university education	Egypt (2006–2007)	Tunisia (2008–2009)
total number of students	17 (million)	2.01 (million)
total enrolment rate	90.2 %	97.7 %
male enrolment rate	90 %	97.4 %
female enrolment rate	90.3 %	98.5 %
Tertiary education	Egypt (2009-2010)	Tunisia (2009-2010)
total number of students	2.5 (million)	357,472 (thousand)
percentage of female students	46 %	60.1 %
number of public universities	18*	13*
number of private universities	19	–
number of public and private post-secondary institutions	151	193

* Plus Al-Azhar University in Egypt and the General Direction of Technological Studies in Tunisia. Sources: MOE, 2007; MOHE, 2009; SPU MOHE, 2010; MOHE, 2011; Tunisian National Institute of Statistics, 2011; MHESR, 2009-2010.

According to the World Bank (World Bank, 2011c), Egypt and Tunisia report similar GERs in post-secondary education. In 2008, the GER for higher education in Tunisia was 30.8, while the nation boasted a gender gap of –7.3%. The GER for Egypt was almost 30 in 2008-2009 and the gender gap in higher education was 7% in the same year (MOHE, 2008-2009). However, according to the World Bank, despite the "historic" speed with which Egypt narrowed the gender gap, it still lags behind in terms of gender equity (World Bank, 2007).

Both Egypt and Tunisia continue to improve gender equality in education. Access to primary/basic education in both countries is nearly universal. However, disparities remain, and it remains clear that full gender equality in higher education has yet to be reached. Many women continue to enroll in traditionally female areas of study such as humanities, education and nursing. For example, in 2009, the World Bank reported an 80% gender gap in the field of mathematics. The enrollment of women in the engineering and technology fields nationwide in Egypt is approximately 32.5% of the total. These statistics are alarmingly low since women enrolled in science and mathematics have increased job opportunities, due to growth in the field of technology (El-Sayed et al., 2009; Megahed, 2010b; SPU MOHE, 2010).

Despite growing enrollment rates in higher education, unemployment rates remain high in both Egypt and Tunisia but also in the region as a whole. The unemployment rate for females is much higher than for males. In addition, the gap between female and male unemployment rates (17% versus 10%) is much wider in the MENA region than in other world regions (World Bank, 2009, p. 6). In Egypt 19.2% for females versus 5.9% for males were unemployed in 2008. In Tunisia, the most recent data available show that in 2005 female and male unemployment rates reached 17.3% and 13.1%, respectively (World Bank, 2011a, b).

It is worth mentioning that the unemployment rate is much higher in the 15-24 age group. In 2006-2007, over 20% of young men and 30% of young women in the Middle East and North Africa were unemployed; whereas the world average was 12.5% for young women and 12.2% for young men. As reported by the World Bank (2009, p. 6) the highest unemployment rates, where again the unemployment among young women are significantly higher than those of men, are found in Jordan (48% versus 24%), Egypt (40% versus 21%) and Syria (39% versus 21%). High youth unemployment rates, among many other factors, were identified as a main cause for the recent revolts in several Arab countries. It is not surprising, then, that young men and young women have taken the lead in these revolts. Thus, genuine democracy and social justice including gender equality thus, can no longer be neglected as basic human rights in the MENA region.

CONCLUSION

North African countries are associated with the Arab culture of the Middle East, not only due to a shared language and religion but also due to their common struggle for independence and revival of "Islamic" teachings and Arab heritage. Our examination of gender inequality and the status of women in Egypt and Tunisia is thus contextualized in the interplay between three cultural and ideological forces that have continued to shape the discourse of gender equality and women's rights in Arab Muslim-majority societies. We have examined women's rights and social practice in the context of "Islamic" teachings and local traditions versus Western, European colonial perceptions. In addition, we discussed national governments' gender-oriented reform policies in response to international pressure.

The case studies of Egypt and Tunisia demonstrate similarities and differences between the two countries' respective reform policies towards gender equality but also highlight the confrontation between conservative and progressive ideologies which occurred in each country with the implementation of their respective gender-related reform policies. The colonial legacy and Western perceptions of Muslim women – perceived as victims of oppression, hidden behind the veil and secluded from the world – have reinforced the opposition to gender-related reform policies in order to preserve religious (Islamic) identity in the two countries. Tunisia has aggressively reformed the status of women and family law while Egypt has improved women's social status and legal rights more cautiously.

Unlike other Arab countries, Tunisia was a protectorate, with limited French interference. Thus, opposition to its gender-related reform was less associated with the Western, colonial perception of modernization. Nonetheless, in order to implement its reform agenda, the Tunisian government banned all groups formed on a religious basis and promoted "a modernistic interpretation" of Islamic law. By contrast, Egypt has experienced opposition to its gender-related reforms from different Islamic groups. Although some legal reforms were undertaken, confrontation between fundamentalists and the government has continued into the present and it has also penetrated school settings.

Considering the dual role of education as an agent of change and/or perpetuation, female education in the Arab region has been supported by fundamentalist groups, national governments and the international community. Egypt and Tunisia have achieved universal access to basic education and have dramatically reduced the gender gap in secondary education. However, disparities remain in which gender equality in higher education has yet to be reached, especially in Egypt.

Egypt and Tunisia, like other developing countries, have pursued educational policies geared towards increasing access to education, and, having achieved success, they have shifted their focus to improving the quality of education. However, to date, high female illiteracy rates, lack of freedom and democracy, socio-economic disparities and high unemployment rates especially among women continue to constitute major challenges for the educational and socio-economic development of the Middle East and North Africa region. One might argue that the recent uprisings were thus inevitable.

With the beginning of 2011, uprisings began in Tunisia and Egypt. Arab voices, of men and women, were heard around the world. Post-revolution, the once-banned Islamic groups gained political recognition, formed parties, and won the parliamentary election. Public opinion is divided and debate has taken place in Tunisia, Egypt and the region. The concern has been, are women's rights "slipping away!" In their transition towards democracy, Egypt, Tunisia and other Arab countries need to promote genuine gender-oriented educational reforms. In the meantime, different religious and non-religious interest groups need to give up their conflict over power at the expense of women's rights and shift their efforts towards promoting freedom and equity for all.

REFERENCES

Akrawi, M., & El-Koussy, A. (1971). Recent trends in Arab education. *International Review of Education, 17*(2), 181-197.

Al-Ahram Weekly. (2003, February 13-19). Tahani El-Gabali: No winding pathways for Egypt's first woman judge. Accessed 17 February 2012 from http://weekly.ahram.org.eg/2003/625/profile.htm.

Al-Ahram Weekly. (2011, November 3-9). On Tunisia's election results. Accessed 10 January 2012 from http://weekly.ahram.org.eg/2011/1071/re4.htm.

Al-Ali, N. (2002). The women's movement in Egypt, with selected references to Turkey. United National Research Institute for Social Development, Civil Society and Social Movements Programme, Paper Number 5, April 2002. Accessed 2 February 2010 from http://www.unrisd.org/unrisd/ website/document.nsf/0/9969203536f64607c1256c08004bb140/$FILE/alali.pdf.

Ali, M., & Ali, A. (2006). Women's liberation through Islam. The Institute of Islamic Information and Education (III&E). Accessed 3 March 2011 from http://www.huda.tv/articles/women-in-islam/189-womens-liberation-through-islam .

Ali, S. (1995). *Dawour Al-Táleem Al-Misryi fi Al-Kefah Al-Watani (The Role of Egyptian Education in the National Struggle -During British Colonialism).* Cairo, Egypt: El-Hayaah El-Misria El-ámaa Lelketab [in Arabic].

Aljazeera News. (2011, November 14). Final Tunisian election results announced: Moderate Islamist Ennahda party officially declared winner of country's landmark post-Arab Spring vote. Accessed 10 January 2012 from http://www.aljazeera.com/news/africa/2011/11/20111114171420907168.html.

Almasry Alyoum. (2006, November 22). The Ministry of Education prohibits students from wearing the niqab and renews the conditions of wearing hijab. Accessed on 14 June 2011 from http://www.almasry-alyoum.com/article2.aspx?ArticleID=38177&IssueID=495 [in Arabic].

Arab Knowledge Report. (2009). Towards productive intercommunication for knowledge. Mohamed bin Rashed Al Maktoum Foundation and the UN Development Programme. Accessed on 2 January 2010 from http://www.mbrfoundation.ae/English/Documents/AKR-2009-En/AKR-English.pdf.

AWIR (Arab World and Islamic Resources) and (MEPC) Middle East Policy Council. (1998). *The Arab world studies notebook.* California: A Joint Publication of: AWIR and Middle East Policy Council.

Ayadi, H. (2011, October 25). Niqab divides Tunisian society. Accessed 11 January 2012 from http://www.latunisievote.org/en/society/item/373-niqab-divides-tunisian-society.

Benhamida, K. (1990). The Arab states. In W. Halls (Ed.), *Comparative education: Contemporary issues and trends* (pp. 291-317). Paris/London: UNESCO/Jessica Kingsley.

Bennoune, K. (1995). Islamic fundamentalism represses women. In D. Bender & B. Leone (Eds.), *Islam: Opposing viewpoints* (pp. 64-71). San Diego, CA: Greenhaven Press.

Brandt, M., & Kaplan, J. A. (1995). The tension between women's rights and religious rights: Reservations to CEDAW by Egypt, Bangladesh and Tunisia. *Journal of Law and Religion, 12*(1), 105-142.

CAPMS (Central Agency for Public Mobilization and Statistics). (2006, July). *The statistical year book.* Arab Republic of Egypt.

Christina, R., Mehran, G., & Mir, S. (1999). Education in the Middle East: Challenging and opportunities. In R. Arnove & C. Torrers (Eds.), *Comparative education: The dialectic of the global and local* (pp. 345-370). Lanham/Boulder/New York/ Oxford: Rowman & Littlefield Publishers.

Cook, B. (2001). Islam and Egyptian higher education: Student attitudes. *Comparative Education Review, 45*(3), 379-411.

Daniel, J. (2003, January 19-23). *Education for all in the Arab world: Past, present and future.* Meeting of Arab Education Ministers on Education for All, Beirut, Lebanon. Accessed on 14 November 2011 from http://portal.unesco.org/education/en/ev.php-URL_ID=28052&URL_DO =DO_TOPIC&URL_SECTION=201.html.

Daun, H., & Arjmand, R. (2002). Arab countries: Oil boom, religious revival, and non-reform. In H. Daun (Ed.), *Educational restructuring in the context of globalization and national policy* (pp. 205-225). New York: Routledge Falmer.

Dickinson, E. (2011, November 2). Tunisian's women demand equal rights. *The Interdependent,* A publication of UNA-USA. Accessed 11 January 2012 from http://www.theinterdependent.com/ 111102/tunisias-women-demand-equal-rights.

Douglass, S. L., & Shaikh, M. A. (2004). Defining Islamic education: differentiation and applications. *Current Issues in Comparative Education, 7*(1), 5-18.

Egypt State Information Service. (2012a). Population. Accessed 17 February 2012 from http://www.sis.gov.eg/En/Story.aspx?sid=9.

Egypt State Information Service. (2012b). Woman and health. Accessed 17 February 2012 from http://www.us.sis.gov.eg/En/Story.aspx?sid=2263.

Egypt State Information Service. (2012c). Women in education. Accessed 17 February 2012 from http://www.sis.gov.eg/En/Story.aspx?sid=2264.

El-Sayed, K., Hosy, H., Mohsen, M., & Gadalla, A. (2009, April 19). Women in physics in Egypt: The status and needs of female physics students. In *Third IUPAP International Conference on Women in Physics* (pp. 111-112). American Institute of Physics, Conference Proceedings, Vol. 1119.

El-Saadawi, N. (1995). Women should reject Islamic gender roles: An interview by Gorge Lerner. In D. Bender & B. Leone (Eds.), *Islam: Opposing viewpoints* (pp. 80-88). San Diego, CA: Greenhaven Press.

Erlich, H. (1989). *Students and university in 20th century Egyptian politics.* Totowa, NJ: Frank Cass & Co.

Equality Now. (2011, July 23). Women's rights slipping away in the aftermath of the Egyptian revolution. Accessed 13 January 201 from http://www.equalitynow.org/press_release/ womens_rights_slipping_away_in_the_aftermath_of_the_egyptian_revolution.

Golley, N. (2004). Is feminism relevant to Arab women? *Third World Quarterly, 25*(3), 521-536.

Guardian. (2011, November 22). Tunisia's election winners form interim government after uprising. Accessed 11 January 2012 from http://www.guardian.co.uk/world/2011/nov/22/tunisia-election-winners-ennahda-ettakatol.

Guenena, N., & Wassef, N. (1999). *Unfulfilled promises: Women's rights.* Population Council, West Asia and North Africa Regional Office, Cairo: Egypt

Hausmann, R., Tyson, L., & Zahidi, S. (2009). *The global gender gap report 2009.* Geneva, Switzerland: World Economic Forum.

Ibrahim, I. (1987). Religion and politics under Nasser and Sadat, 1952–1981. In B. Stowasser (Ed.), *The Islamic impulse* (pp. 121-134). London: Croom Helm.

International Women's Rights Action Watch. (June 2002). *IWRAW to CEDAW country report: Tunisia.* Independent information for the twenty-seventh session of the Committee on the Elimination of Discrimination Against Women (CEDAW). Accessed 2 February 2010 from http://www1.umn.edu/ humanrts/iwraw/publications/countries/tunisia.htm.

Kimani, M. (2008). Women in North Africa secure more rights despite hurdles, notable legal, political and social progress. *Africa Renewal, 22*(2). Accessed 3 February 2010 from http://www.un.org/ ecosocdev/geninfo/afrec/vol22no2/222-women-secure-more-righs.html.

Makar, N. (1996, November). New voices for women in the Middle East. Paper presented at the Middle East Librarians Association Annual Meeting, Providence, Rhode Island. Accessed 3 February 2010 from http://www.mela.us/MELANotes/MELANotes6566/makar65.html.

Marshall, S., & Stokes, R. (1981). Tradition and the veil: Female status in Tunisia and Algeria. *The Journal of Modern African Studies, 19*(4), 625-646.

Medien, A. (2011, 13 August). Today, post-revolutionary Tunisia celebrates Women's Day. Accessed 11 January 2012 from http://www.tunisia-live.net/2011/08/13/today-post-revolutionary-tunisia-celebrates-womens-day/.

Megahed, N. (2010a). Cultural overview of Islam and education. In Z. Yong et al. (Eds.), *Handbook of Asian education: A cultural perspective* (pp. 319-326). United States: Routledge.

Megahed, N. (2010b). *Access to the university and women's participation in higher education in Egypt.* The Middle East Institute Web-based Volumes on Higher Education in the Middle East, Empowering Underserved and Vulnerable Populations 2010 (Vol. 2). Accessed on 20 March 2011 from http://www.mei.edu/LinkClick.aspx?fileticket=vBOcNODJbGg%3d&tabid=541.

MHESR (Ministry of Higher Education and Scientific Research). (2009-2010). Features of higher education and scientific research. Republic of Tunisia: Office of Studies, Planning and Programming. Accessed 17 February 2012 from http://www.mes.tn/anglais/donnees_de_base/leaflet_09-10.pdf.

Ministry of Justice. (2005, July 26). A summary of the laws of Egypt. Accessed 17 February 2012 from http://www.reunite.org/edit/files/Islamic%20Resource/EGYPT%20text.pdf.

MOE (Ministry of Education). (2007). *National strategic plan for pre-university education reform in Egypt 2007/08-2011/12.* Arab Republic of Egypt.

MOHE (Ministry of Higher Education). (2008-2009). Statistics-sectors. Accessed 25 December 2011. http://mhe-spu.org/new/admin/uploads/statistics/sectors%202008-2009.pdf [in Arabic].

MOHE (Ministry of Higher Education). (2009, October). *Higher education in Egypt: Facts and numbers.* Accessed 21 December 2011 from http://mhe-spu.org/new/docs.php?id=157 [in Arabic].

MOHE (Ministry of Higher Education). (2011). *News letter.* Accessed 11 January 2012. http://www.egy-mhe.gov.eg/english/periodical2011.pdf [in Arabic].

Moghadam, M. (1993). *Modernizing Women: Gender and social change in the Middle East.* Boulder, London: L. Rienner.

Moheet. (2009, October 13). Egypt: the Ministry of Education announces activating the decree on banning the niqab in schools. Accessed 14 June 2011 from http://www.moheet.com/show_news.aspx?nid=308525&pg=2 [in Arabic].

Mule, P., & Barthel, D. (1992). The return to the veil: Individual autonomy vs. social esteem. *Sociological Forum, 7*(2), 323-332.

Population and Development: The demographic profile of the Arab countries. Accessed 20 March 2011 from http://www.escwa.un.org/popin/publications/new/DemographicprofileArabCountries.pdf.

Ramadan, A. (1986). *Egypt during Sadat's era: Opinions on politics and history.* Cairo, Egypt: Maktabet Madbooly [in Arabic].

Ramazi, N. (1995). Islamic government need not repress women. In D. Bender & B. Leone (Eds.), *Islam: Ppposing viewpoints* (pp. 72-79). San Diego: Greenhaven Press.

Reid, D. (1974). The rise of professions and professional organization in modern Egypt. *Comparative Studies in Society and History, 16*(1), 24-57.

Reid, D. (1977, July). Educational and career choices of Egyptian students, 1882-1922. *International Journal of Middle East Studies, 8*(3), 349-378.

Republic of Tunisia. (1997). The Ministry of Women and Family Affairs, Post-Beijing National Plan of Action 1997-2001, Accessed on 20 March 2011 from http://flamme.org/documents/tunisia.html.

Salmoni, B. (2003). Women in the nationalist-educational prism: Turkish and Egyptian pedagogues and their gendered agenda, 1920-1952. *History of Education Quarterly, 43*(4), 483-516.

Shorouk News. (2010). The administrative court confirms the ban of wearing the niqab in Egyptian universities. Accessed 14 June 2011 from http://www.shorouknews.com/ ContentData.aspx?id=168446 [in Arabic].

SPU MOHE (Strategic Planning Unit Ministry of Higher Education). (2010). *Higher education in Egypt: Country background report.* Arab Republic of Egypt.

Tunisian Education Act. (2002, 23 July). Accessed on 25 June 2011 from http://www.anglais.edunet.tn/offic_docs/edu_act_2002.pdf.

Tunisian National Institute of Statistics. Statistical Information: Demographic and Social Data. Accessed on 25 June 2011 from http://www.ins.nat.tn/en/donnee_demografiques0.php?code_theme =0201.

UN (United Nations). (1979). Division of the Advancement of Women, the Department of Economic and Social Affairs. Convention on the elimination of all forms of discrimination against women: Full text of the convention in English. Accessed 11 January 2012 from http://www.un.org/womenwatch/daw/cedaw/text/econvention.htm#article15.

UN (United Nations). (2007). Millennium Development Goals. Accessed 12 January 2012 from http://www.un.org/millenniumgoals/.

UN (United Nations) (2009). *Human development report. Overcoming barriers: Human mobility and development.* UN Development Programme. Accessed on 25 June 2011 at http://hdr.undp.org/en/media/HDR_2009_EN_Complete.pdf.

UNESCO. (1990). *World declaration on Education For All.* Accessed on 5 December 2009 from http://www.unesco.org/education/efa/ed_for_all/background/jomtien_declaration.shtml.

UNESCO. (2000). *The Dakar framework for action.* World Education Forum. Accessed on 20 March 2011 from http://unesdoc.unesco.org/images/0012/001211/121147e.pdf.

UNESCO. (2009). *Bonn Declaration.* World Conference on Education for Sustainable Development. Accessed on 5 December 2009 from http://www.esd-world-conference-2009.org/fileadmin/download/ESD2009_BonnDeclaration080409.pdf.

UNICEF. (2007). The state of the world's children 2007: Middle East and North Africa edition – Women and children: The double dividend of gender equality. Accessed 20 March 2011 from http://www.unicef.org/sowc07/docs/sowc07_mena.pdf.

Voll, J. (1994). *Islam: Continuity and change in the modern world,* 2nd ed. New York: Syracuse University Press.

Williamson, B. (1987). *Education and social change in Egypt and Turkey: A study in historical sociology.* London: Macmillan.

World Bank. (2004). *Gender and development in the Middle East and North Africa: Women in the public sphere.* MENA Development Report. Washington, D.C.: World Bank Publishing.

World Bank. (2007). *Arab Republic of Egypt: Improving quality, equality, and efficiency in the education sector, fostering a competent generation of youth.* Report No. 42863-EG. Human Development Department: Middle East and North Africa Region.

World Bank. (2008). *The road not travelled: education reform in the Middle East and Africa.* MENA Development Report. Washington, D.C.: World Bank Publishing.

World Bank. (2009). The status and progress of women in the Middle East and North Africa. World Bank Middle East and North Africa Social and Economic Development Group. Accessed 20 March 2011 from http://siteresources.worldbank.org/INTMENA/Resources/MENA_Gender_Compendium-2009-1.pdf.

World Bank. (2011a). Data indicators: Female unemployment. Accessed 20 March 2011 at http://data.worldbank.org/indicator/SL.UEM.TOTL.FE.ZS?page=1&display=default.

World Bank. (2011b). Data indicators: male unemployment. Accessed 20 March 2011. http://data.worldbank.org/indicator/SL.UEM.TOTL.MA.ZS/countries?display=default

World Bank. (2011c). Edstats – country profile. Accessed 14 June 2011 at http://web.worldbank.org/WBSITE/EXTERNAL/TOPICS/EXTEDUCATION/EXTDATASTATISTICS/EXTEDSTATS/0,,contentMDK:21605891~menuPK:3409559~pagePK:64168445~piPK:64168309~theSitePK:3232764,00.html.

World Bank. (2011d). Egypt, Arab Rep. at a glance. Accessed 15 December 2011 from http://devdata.worldbank.org/AAG/egy_aag.pdf.

221

World Factbook. (2012). Accessed 10 January 2012, from https://www.cia.gov/library/publications/the-world-factbook/geos/eg.html.

Nagwa Megahed
Ain Shams University

Stephen Lack
American University in Cairo

AMIR SABZEVAR QAHFAROKHI, ABBAS MADANDAR ARANI &
LIDA KAKIA

THE IMPACT OF EDUCATIONAL SYSTEMS
ON POLITICAL VIOLENCE IN THE
MIDDLE-EAST REGION

INTRODUCTION

When the Shah of Iran was overthrown by The Islamic revolution in 1979, we were adolescents closely following political events. Taking part in demonstrations which was frowned upon by teachers was a form of giving vent to our emotions. But we would call off classes and flood into the streets with great jubilation. Teachers could not or did not want to stop us and at the same time we were the happiest pupils ever on Earth. Upon the victory of The Islamic revolution, one of the first things we learned was that in Islam, politics and religion are equal to each other and that they are two sides of the same coin. The outbreak of war between Iran and Iraq coincided with two periods of our educational lives, that is, high school and university. Furthermore, different political events were clear indications that politics affects not only our religion but also every aspect of our lives. After 25 years, when we watch the videos dating from the time of the revolution, we are nostalgic yet excited and wish we could be young again and that once more we could write slogans on the walls of classes and schools.

Watching the videos of the Iran-Iraq war, we reminisce about the students and pupils who used to sit at the same desk with us and all the fun we had together. But some of them were killed in the war against Saddam Hussein. The second author of this chapter remembers a time when people had to leave the city of Isfahan due to Iraqi missile attacks (known as the War of Cities) , but he and a friend had to stay to complete a term project and submit it on time. In this war, thousands of Iranian pupils and students were wounded or disabled, or suffered severe physical and mental injuries, and nearly 4,000 of them were killed. Our youthful days are behind us and we are now in our early 40s; when we look back, we realize that our being alive borders on the miraculous or resembles a Hollywood action movie. Revolution, demonstrations, political divisions, closure and re-opening of universities, war, education, marriage and work have all come to pass. Now, we have a clearer understanding why in the Middle East, no student can avoid political issues and their consequences. One can easily see, via mass media, the active presence of students in recent and current political issues of Turkey, Iran, Iraq, Lebanon, Palestine, Egypt, and other countries in the region.

In this chapter, we reflect on the issues and the interrelationships among education, religion and political violence in the Middle East region. We offer a

D.B. Napier & S. Majhanovich (eds.), Education, Dominance and Identity, 223–235.

personal perspective on commonly held misconceptions about the links between political violence and Islamic education; we discuss the complexities of forms of Islamic and secular education in the region that are often misunderstood by outsiders to the region; and we consider some realities about other factors that contribute to political violence, based on our survey of pertinent literature and drawing on our experiential knowledge from living in Iran. We also argue that there is an important potential role for comparative education in eliminating misconceptions about education, religion, and political developments in the region, and in promoting equitable access to education.

POLITICAL VIOLENCE IN THE MIDDLE EAST

Before we discuss the general characteristics of political violence in the region, it is important to define 'the Middle East.' It should be noted that the definition of the term Middle East is not set in granite, as the region is not an area of the world that is designed exactly. It is sometimes referred to as the Near East or Southwest Asia; in India the region is known as Western Asia. What the area is called sometimes depends on one's position on the globe. Even then, not everyone agrees on which countries should be included within a geographic domain. The issue is confusing not only due to the region's location but also due to culture and ethnicity (Riphenburg, 2011; World Atlas, 2011; World Bank, 2011). If the Middle East is defined solely as the Arab states and Israel, Iran would be excluded. If it is thought to include Israel and the predominantly Muslim states in the area, then the North African states of Algeria, Libya, Morocco, and Tunisia, plus Afghanistan, Pakistan, Azerbaijan, Kyrgyzstan Kazakhstan, Turkmenistan, Tajikistan, Uzbekistan, the Sudan, and Turkey, would also have to be included. We take this latter area as the Middle East region. However, apart from terminological differences, the first issue which comes to mind regarding political violence in the region is the concern of governments over their domestic and foreign security. This has compelled countries in the region to be regular purchasers of western arms.

The estimates of the Stockholm International Peace Research Institute show that military expenditure of Middle East countries has increased from $40 billion dollars in 1988 to more that $60 billion in 2006 (SIPRI, 2007). In an international comparison it was also revealed that the world region with the highest relative military spending increase in 2005 was the Middle East, mostly influenced by a massive increase in Saudi Arabia's defense budget. Total military spending in the Middle East would be substantially higher if the military expenditure of Iraq and Qatar were not excluded owing to lack of consistent data (Stålenheim, Fruchart, Omitoogun, & Perdomo, 2006).

In spite of the fact that in the past decades countries in the region have been regular buyers of arms and weapons, the social and political conditions in recent years have revealed that political conflicts have changed from international levels (national and among states) to intra-national levels within countries as social, political, and religious conflicts. The natural consequence of this is the involvement of ordinary people in political violence which leads to the emergence of a phenomenon called "Terrorism and suicide bombing." Lack of democracy, totalitarian governments, and continuation of conflicts have caused people – particularly women, teenagers and children – to be in danger and to suffer severe physical and mental problems. There are no exact statistics as to how many young people have been injured or killed due to political tensions. Nevertheless, according to reports from the UN (2007a), an estimated 177 children have been killed in the contemporary conflict in Lebanon to date. According to UNICEF (2010), one third of the approximately 3,000 injured and 45 per cent of the 800,000 internally displaced people in Lebanon are believed to be children. The Special Representative took this opportunity to remind all parties that the Security Council, in resolution 1612, adopted in 2005, expressed its determination to ensure respect for international norms and standards for the protection of children affected by armed conflict. Security Council resolution 1539 prohibited serious violations against children during times of war including killing, maiming, denial of humanitarian access and attacks on schools and hospitals.

In another report by this office, the number of children killed in Lebanon in the recent hostilities was noted as approximately 400. In the Palestinian Territories, 124 were killed in 2006 and today, almost 400 are still in detention. In addition, 8 children were killed or injured on the Israeli side. Researchers point out that many children in the conflict areas need psycho-social care (UN, 2007b). On the other hand, women and children are being used as puppets in the hands of politicians to act as terrorists for killing other women and children. This phenomenon dates back to the 1940s as Smith (2005) described:

Nearly all national movements seeking independence have been accused of terrorism. This is clear in the depiction of nationalist resistance by English or French colonial regimes after World War II, but it is also manifested in Jewish celebrations of Zionist resistance to the British after World War II. I should refer to the 1966 book by Geula Cohen titled Woman of Violence: Memoirs of a Young Terrorist, 1943-1948, a memoir which celebrated terrorism specifically as justified violence for the sake of freedom. David Ben-Gurion, first prime minister of Israel, wrote a laudatory preface calling the book "a proud memorial to the daring fighters who offered their lives for the cause of Jewish redemption." (www.nps.edu)

The above-mentioned historical reminder shows that in this respect, the region leads other parts of the world in terrorist groups. However, the processes of globalization, development of mass media, TV and the Internet in particular, have opened the public's eyes to these violent movements more than ever. Studies show that in most cases both the terrorists and the victims were women, children and teenagers (El Sarraj & Butler, 2002; Gordon, 2002; Radu, 2003; Zedalis, 2004; Mitchell, 2007). In fact, the suicide bomber terrorist phenomenon is a growing element in the international terrorists' arsenal, but it remains a weapon with a religious background. It was, and is everywhere, a weapon of the relatively educated. For instance, Tamil Hindu women were able to mix well at Buddhist electoral meetings in Sri Lanka; Palestinian high school and university students

QAHFAROKHI ET AL.

posed as Israelis on occasions; and it was Western-educated Islamists who trained to murder thousands in America on the terrorist attack of September 11, hundreds in Bali, many in Casablanca and Riyadh (Radu, 2003).

Moreover, some studies emphasize that terrorism is a product of poor, desperate, naïve, single young men from third world counties, vulnerable to brainwashing and recruitment into terror. In fact, most of the terrorists came from moderately religious upper middle class families; a large number were expatriats living in other countries, they had high levels of education, 73% were married and most had children. The majority had no criminal background, and were generally in normal mental health (Sageman, 2005). Meanwhile, researchers, especially those working in the field of comparative education have drawn attention to formal and informal educational systems as institutions that can work toward the spread of political violence in the Middle East. The belief is that in the Middle East region, families, parties, governments and religious communities by making use of formal education (state-run schools) and informal education (religious schools and textbooks) urge and prepare young people to take part in and promote political violence (Volkan, 1995; Castle, 2005; Darwish, 2005; Teach Kids Peace, 2005; Tohid, 2005).

FORMAL EDUCATIONAL SYSTEM

For a better understanding of the position of Islamic education, we should take a deeper look at the functions of formal education in the region. Statistical evidence and international studies show that as far as formal education is concerned students are limited to reading only one book in every school subject. From a quality standpoint, those students whose studies are confined to limited sources and books, do not achieve much success in their schooling. The results from international exams in the past two decades show that Middle Eastern students had the lowest academic competencies (Glass, 2008; World Bank, 2008). According to UNESCO in 2005, Middle Eastern students took second place in repeating a grade in both primary and secondary schools (Huebler, 2005).

The report of the World Bank indicated the low quality of the educational system and its minimal impact on economical growth of the region. This study also showed that Yemen, Morocco and Iraq have the lowest rates of educational access, efficiency and quality among the countries in the region. Egypt, Iran, Lebanon and Palestine have an average standard. Jordan and Kuwait enjoy better conditions compared to other countries in the region. Generally speaking, from an educational quality point of view, countries in the Middle East are at a very low level by global standards.

This shows that the formal education systems have not been successful in presenting effective teaching and learning methods to children and teenagers. The question is how it would be possible for schools which are not successful in training students in math and science to undertake teaching complicated social, political and religious concepts. Is there really not any different understanding and attitude between the young and older generations in the region? Is formal education in any way able to inculcate all the religious, social and cultural values into the young generation (Renaerts, 1999; Alagheband, 2005; Sepehri & Arani, 2007).

It must be admitted that most of the educational subjects that students learn and go through in the region's schools are devoid of any practical effect on their social lives or in creating crises in political issues. As a result, most of the information about the tendency of teenagers toward political violence is related to the disputes between Palestinian and Israelis which is a unique situation. This very condition cannot be generalized to children and youth of other countries in the region (Darwish, 2005; Teach Kids Peace, 2005). Moreover, the notion that whatever is taught to children at schools contains political impressions from religious concepts is a misunderstanding. One common misunderstanding is the term "Jihad." What is commonly referred to as jihad consists of fighting against things Muslims should avoid including a wide spectrum of bad behaviors at both individual and collective levels. All around the Middle East in most of the schools , teachers do their best to teach youngsters that the teachings of Islam are peaceful and based on the premise that Islam is a religion of mercy , kindness and pity, and this is in itself a kind of jihad incumbent on every Muslim (Zakir & Rajan, 2006) .

Nowadays new developments in political scenes are in progress. The awakening of Arab nations has spread to almost all the Middle East and has overthrown a number of dictators. However, we can observe that these revolutions were not propagated by well-educated youth; these uprisings were spurred by the needs and demands of poorly educated youth, whose knowledge and skills do not meet the demands of a rapidly advancing world (Adams & Winthrop, 2011). On the other hand, it must be admitted that educational systems in the Middle East, except for those in Turkey and Israel, are highly traditional and conservative, and are strictly controlled by governments. Without any exception, all the governments in the region disagree with the engagement of educational systems in political issues especially terrorist activities. Most of governments in the region expect principals, teachers and pupils to remain loyal to their own political regime. For instance, authoritarian Arab governments have long used education as a tool to ensure public loyalty to the regime. This loyalty is transmitted through civic education at schools, thus reflecting the state's non-democratic ideology and laws. Instruction in humanities and social sciences continues to drill obedience and submission to the regime rather than encourage freedom of thought (Faour, 2011). Teaching in most Middle East states continues to be overwhelmingly didactic and teacher-directed rather than student-centered, and is adverse to environments that foster critical thinking, creativity, and problem-solving capacities.

INFORMAL EDUCATIONAL SYSTEM

In dealing with a scattering of political violence and in line with discovering the likely causes of this violence in the region, the role and function of the religious system has drawn the attention of researchers. The researchers' acceptance of the idea that most political violence in the region stems from religious foundations, should not prevent them from investigating other variables such as political, economical, cultural, and social systems which have an effect on the creation and development of violence. It must be pointed out that in recent years all groups involved in political violence have tried to use religious symbols to accuse their opponents of abusing religion. In light of this and with regard to the religious background of most of the population in the region, the role of Islam in transferring concepts based on confirmation or denial of political violence to youth, has been the center of attention (Mojab, 1998; Guven, 2005; Jackson, 2007) .

The general belief is that violent groups make use of the educational system as leverage for conveying their own ideas. They also try to brainwash teenagers and provoke them to take part in political crises. In this regard, the role of Islamic schools has received close attention, more than any other factor. One of the authors of this chapter has already tried to show the relationship between political systems and educational systems through separating the role of formal and informal education in different countries in the region (Arani, 2003), in an attempt to take a closer look at the role of Islamic schools as one of the most significant educational means in the Middle East region.

The first aspect that should be pointed out is that the presence of religion in education has a long history in all Muslim countries, designed in different forms to meet students' needs. It must also be mentioned that use of the term "Islamic schools" is not accurate because it encompasses a wide variety of schools. For example, the terms "Maktab" (Traditional school), "Islamic school," and "Hoze Elmiye" should be differentiated from each other. What is commonly referred to as "Maktab," is a type of school very common in some Muslim countries such as Indonesia, Pakistan and Afghanistan mainly focused on teaching women and children, especially girls, basics such as Islamic customs, and reading and writing in Arabic. The learner and the teacher have no common ground as far as politics is concerned and as a result, seeing children reading the Quran and performing religious rituals has nothing to do with radical religious teachings (Ling & Fui, 2007; Srimulyani, 2007).

Applying the term "Islamic" to these traditional schools results in misunderstandings about the social conditions of countries in the region and it contributes to the development of a phenomenon called "Islam phobia" in the world (Buang & Ismail, 2007; Meer, 2007). Therefore, in dealing with the functions of "Maktab" two points should be kept in mind. Firstly, in most Islamic countries these schools are no longer in demand and they are being closed. Influential factors in the closure of traditional schools include the development of state-run schools, high enrollment in modern schools, classification of students based on age groups, better learning and teaching methods, and lower costs of modern schools. Secondly, the experience in some countries reveals that in critical situations where state-run schools cannot discharge their duties or when families cannot enroll their children in modern schools due to financial difficulties, these traditional schools can fill a gap. Indonesia's experience with girl's education, and the war in Afghanistan with the closing of schools by the Taliban, are good examples to show different ways traditional schools have helped young people (Karlsson & Mansory, 2003; Jones, 2007).

The second term "Islamic schools" brings something special to mind; namely, if "Islamic schools" are compared to "non-Islamic schools" such as Christian, Jewish, Hindu or secular schools, based on the religious population of countries in the Middle East region, then most of the schools are Islamic. The formal education system has to inform children and teenagers of religious ideas according to the beliefs of the majority. Turkey is an example of such a system, one of much interest to researchers. The experience in this country reveals two major points. First, by establishing a non-Islamic educational and social system, the secular government realized that the young generation suffers from social and cultural degradation. As a result and as a reaction to this phenomenon, from the late 1940s Islamic teachings were introduced into the curriculum of fourth and fifth grade pupils. Surprisingly, this was generalized to first and second grades of lower secondary schools by the military government in 1980 (Salmoni, 2000). Most researchers neglect to mention that in Turkey, it was the secular and military state which for the first time introduced religious education into school books (Guven, 2005), and second, it was the secular state that paved the way for religion to be included in schools. Also, this secular state provided religious individuals and groups with a suitable economic and social atmosphere which eventually resulted in Ardughan becoming Premier of Turkey. Iran during the rule of the Shah is another example. At that time, some of the textbook writers, of religion and social sciences in particular, were critics of the Shah. After the revolution, these people took on important political positions including even the Prime Minister. The experience in Iran, Turkey, and even Algeria is very important. In these countries we have seen that those who were against a government based on Islam, later accepted Islam as the inspirational source for educational policies. This, in turn, has caused political Islam to develop through the educational system and to spread to all walks of life (Salmoni, 2000).

The third term "Hoze Elmiye" can be taken to mean what western media refer to as the general term "Islamic Madrase or school" (Bernholz, 2004; Wiktorowicz, 2005; Ling & Fui, 2007; Thobani, 2007; Venkatraman, 2007; Fair & Shepherd, 2008). In fact, the students in Islamic schools are teenagers (girls over 9 and boys over 12-13). So far there has been no survey on the gender and age distribution of pupils in these countries but direct observations and personal experiences of the authors of this chapter in countries such as Iran, India and Pakistan show that there are very few Elmiye schools for women, and that such schools are comprised mostly of teenagers and adults. It should be pointed out that the number of such schools is not proportional to the number of young people in these countries. The number of people attending Hoze Elmiye compared to Madrase and formal schools is very low. Also, there are fewer such schools compared to other types of schools.

Therefore, overemphasizing the role of these schools is not realistic. In fact, in the unlikely case that we accept the role and impact of these schools in the Middle East crises, the idea that this influence is all the same for all countries should be avoided. The following table shows the role of Islamic schools and their order of influence in countries in the region.

Table 1. Position of Islamic schools in terms of their role in political violence in the Middle East countries

Low influence	Medium influence	High influence
Iran/Turkey/ Syria/Lebanon Azerbaijan Turkmenistan	Kuwait/United Arab Emirates/ Bahrain / Qatar/ Palestine/Jordan/ Yemen	Iraq/Egypt/ Saudi Arabia/ Pakistan & Afghanistan

In fact, the above table indicates that religious schools in most of the countries in the region are not hotbeds of terrorism but that they only engage in training clergymen. Such schools do not develop politics and politicians and therefore, what is claimed by the media is an exaggeration of the function of these schools (Kadi, 2006). In addition, we draw attention to the difference between Islamic Education and Muslim Education as emphasized by some scholars (Buang & Ismail, 2007).

The relationships shown in Table 1 are not firm or based on hard data, rather, we suggest them based on our interpretation of the literature cited and on our personal perspectives and experiential knowledge. Therefore, the content of Muslim education in some countries might be radical and supportive of violence. In general, this is due to some mullahs' personal misunderstandings and misinterpretations of Islam and Quranic verses. But, Islamic education *per se* vigorously denies violence and strongly stresses the relationship and dialogue among different religions (Huda, 2007).

A further implication of the above table is that the role of Islamic schools in promoting political violence is evident in governments which have been long-time allies of Western powers. There are clear indications that Saudi Arabia is the main supporter of the Taliban that makes use of Islamic schools in Pakistan and Afghanistan. At present, the country is also establishing religious schools which have led to the radical religion of Wahabism (see Millard, 2004, for the role of these schools in Indonesia and Singapore).

In addition and in reality, in most cases there is no logical relation between religious schools and terrorist attacks. Many people proposed a hypothesis and then looked for evidence to prove it. Careful examination of the background of the bombers in London, New York and Washington throws serious doubts over such claims. None of the young men involved appears to have received a substantial religious education, to have graduated from the theology departments of Islamic universities, or even to have attended a separate faith school (Ghannoushi, 2005). In a nutshell, we argue first that the term Islamic Schools is ambiguous and cannot be applied to all schools in Muslim countries. Secondly, we argue that most education provided in Islamic schools in the Middle East region is merely religious and not political. Thirdly, the role of Islamic schools in political violence is not equally the same among countries in the region.

ROLE OF COMPARATIVE EDUCATION

Many years ago, Sir Michael Sadler commented on England's educational system that "education is in no way a product of what is learned at schools" (quoted in Higginson, 1980, p. 11). According to Sadler, what is understood as teaching and learning in England is a plethora of effects connected to someone's life experiences including ties to family and, church, daily contact with contemporaries, love toward parents and country. Nowadays a comparativist realizes with great surprise that what Sadler said is true for most Middle East countries. In fact, like most parents in other parts of the world, parents in the Middle East simply want better education for their children, and would consider an Islamic school if they could be certain that it would result in opportunities to enter the labor market afterwards (Renaerts, 1999).

Parents hope an Islamic school will serve two goals: a stronger self-identity and better educational standards (Dwyer & Meyer, 1996). On the other hand, comparativists have found that in most countries of the Middle East region, teachers of religion often find themselves facing a real challenge with teenagers. They try to teach them some principles relating to the application of religious law and schools of law. In the final years of secondary school, ethical issues are raised. With regard to new issues facing mankind, such as contraception, euthanasia, and organ donation, Islam does not usually provide a set answer, but calls for reaction, research and interpretation based on the main texts and treaties of the different schools of law (Renaerts, 1999). Despite parents' desire to provide their children with an appropriate educational atmosphere devoid of any violence, it must be admitted that most formal and informal educational systems have so far been unable to adjust to the requirements of the 21st century and to make necessary changes. Thomas (2002) argued that Asian educators need to deliver a form of civics education that provides opportunities for learners and teachers to discuss the role of participation in decision-making affecting social issues. In particular, Jackson (2003) averred that they need "to employ methods that take account of the debates about culture, nationality, ethnicity and religion and, crucially, that engage students by connecting with their personal experience and concerns" (p. 19).

It must be regretfully stated that international organizations such as UNESCO have not been able to play a vital role in solving the problems of educational systems in the region. These organizations have been pushed to the margins and they lack any active and essential contact with educational and political decision – making centers (Sepehri & Arani, 2007). Furthermore, it cannot be ignored that in some countries in the region, governments do not have a positive attitude toward these organizations and do not approve of their assistance and involvement in their internal affairs. In this situation, the establishment of national foundations of comparative education could be of great help and could also bridge the gap between political/educational systems and the above-mentioned organizations. Surprisingly enough, only Turkey has such a foundation in the region. The role of comparative education associations is to remind everyone both nationally and regionally that the responsibility of comparative education is to emphasize peace, international understanding and common ground that exists among cultures.

CONCLUSION

We have tried to distinguish between formal and informal educational systems in the Middle East region. We believe that different factors can result in the emergence of political violence, among which education systems might well have the least influence. We have tried to show that in most countries of the Middle East, formal educational systems have not even been able to properly teach students non-ideological subjects such as mathematics and science. Therefore, the strength of the formal system of education in transferring the opinions of politicians to young people should not be overestimated. On the other hand, in considering the role of Islamic education, in regional conflicts, more care should be taken and various religious schools should be differentiated. Applying the term "Islamic schools" to all of the schools can result in misunderstanding of the functions and role of these schools. Once more we emphasize that formal education, to a very limited extent, and informal education through some Islamic schools, to a small extent, are responsible for and contribute to violence. Therefore, in order better to understand the reasons for political violence, it would be better to focus more on political and economic issues and less on the role of educational systems. Despite the emphasis that educators put on educational systems in the Middle East, it must be admitted that society, in general, and politicians, in particular, do not place much value on them.

Yet, we cannot deny the emergence and expansion of political violence in the region. It is evident that in countries like Iran, Syria, Iraq, Lebanon, and Palestine, youth are being used as tools for the development of violence. In this context, politicians focus on both formal and informal educational systems. They try to transfer their ideas to the youth through curriculum and extra-curricular activities. Education remains a key arena for societal conflict and change, as does religion, but we have attempted to demonstrate that the larger realities are more complex than is often acknowledged, and that countries in the Middle East currently undergoing radical social and political transformation offer contemporary illustrations of multiple forces at work. Our experiences of our earlier lives and education in Iran prompted us to reflect on the historical shifts as well as on the enduring issues in education, society, politics, and political upheaval.

REFERENCES

Adams, A., & Winthrop, R. (2011). The role of education in the Arab World revolutions. Brookings Institution, Retrieved on 10 June 2011 from http://www.brookings.edu/opinions/2011/0610_arab_world_education_winthrop.aspx.

Alagheband, M. (2005). Religiousness of youths. A report of Dr. Nikpay's speech at Iranian Sociology Association. *Faslno* (an Iranian e-journal). Retrieved on 10 July 2007 from http://www.fasleno.com/archives/000456.php.

Arani, A. M. (2003). Review of book: Comparative education: Continuing traditions, new challenges and new paradigms. *Peabody Journal of Education, 79*(4), 138-150.

Bernholz, P. (2004). Supreme values as the basis for terror European. *Journal of Political Economy, 20,* 317-333.

Buang, S., & Ismail, M. (2007). The life and future of Muslim education. *Asia Pacific Journal of Education, 27*(1), 1-9.

Castle, S. (2005). Girl next door who became a suicide bomber. *The Independent,* 2 December, Retrieved 18 March 2008 from http://www.newsindependent.co.uk/europe/.

Darwish, N. (2005). How I was raised for Jihad. *Teach Kids Peace,* March. Retrieved 8 January 2008 from http:// www.hyscience.com/archives/2005/04/how_i_was_raise.php.

Dwyer, C., & Meyer, A. (1996) The establishment of Islamic schools: A controversial phenomenon in three European countries. In W. A. R. Shadid, & P. S. Van Koningsveld (Eds.), *Muslims in the margin: Political responses to the presence of Islam in Western Europe.* Kampen: Kok Pharos.

El Sarraj, E., & Butler, L. (2002). Suicide bombers: Dignity, despair, and the need for hope: An interview with Eyad El Sarraj. *Journal of Palestine Studies, 31*(4), 71-76.

Fair, C. C., & Shepherd, B. (2008). Who supports terrorism? Evidence from fourteen Muslim countries. *Studies in Conflict & Terrorism, 29*(1), 51-74.

Faour, M. (2011). Will the Arab Spring lead to a revolution in education? *Middle East Foreign Policy,* Retrieved 31 October 2011 from: http://mideast.foreignpolicy.com/posts/2011/10/31/will_the_arab_spring_lead_to_a_revolution_in_education.

Ghannoushi, S. (2005). Where does terrorism start? Retrieved 11 February 2008 from http://www.martinfrost.ws/htmlfiles/terrorism_start.html.

Glass, A. (2008). Arab world failing children, February 5. Retrieved 9 February 2008 from http://www.Arabianbusiness.com/510404-arab-education-quality-disappointing.

Gordon, H. (2002). The suicide bomber: Is it a psychiatric phenomenon? *Psychiatric Bulletin, 26,* 285-287. Retrieved 11 July 2007 from http://pb.rcpsych.org/cgi/reprint/26/8/285.

Guven, I. (2005). The impact of political Islam on education: The revitalization of Islamic education in the Turkish educational setting. *International Journal of Educational Development, 25,* 193-208.

Higginson, J.H. (1980). *Selections from Michael Sadler.* Liverpool: Dejall& Meyorre, 11.

Huda, Q. (2007). *Iran trip report: The dialogue of Islam and peacemaking in Iran.* The United States Institute of Peace, Retrieved 18 December 2007 from http://www.commongroundnews.org/article.php?id=22316&lan=en&sid=1&sp=0.

Huebler, F. (2005). Primary school enrollment 2002/03, May 22, Retrieved 8 January 2008 from http://huebler.blogspot.com/2005/05/school-life-expectancy.html= links.

Jackson, E. (2007) Crafting a new democracy: Civic education in Indonesian Islamic universities. *Asia Pacific Journal of Education, 27*(1), 41-54.

Jackson, R. (2003). Citizenship, religious and cultural diversity and education. In R. Jackson (Ed.), *International perspectives on citizenship, education and religious diversity.* London: Rutledge Falmer.

Jones, A. M. E. (2007). Muslim and Western influences on school curriculum in post-war Afghanistan. *Asia Pacific Journal of Education, 27*(1), 27-40.

Kadi, W. (2006). Education in Islam – Myths and truths. *Comparative Education Review, 50*(3), 311-324.

Karlsson, P., & Mansory, A. (2003). *Islamic and modern education in Afghanistan – Conflictual or complementary.* Paper presented at the Development Studies Research Conference, January, Lund University, Sweden.

Ling, O. G., & Fui, C. M. (2007). They play soccer too! – Madrasah education in multicultural Singapore. *Asia Pacific Journal of Education, 27*(1), 73-84.

Meer, N. (2007). Muslim schools in Britain: Challenging mobilizations or logical developments? *Asia Pacific Journal of Education, 27*(1), 55-71.

Millard, M. (2004) Interview Yaacob Ibrahim: Economic success helps maintain Harmony, Retrieved 10 July 2007 from http://www.qantara.de/webcom/show_article.php/_c-476/_nr216/i.html?PHPSESSID=a0a703e59942f14dde609744 c02172dd.

Mitchell, C. (2007, February 13). The inner world of female suicide bombers. *CBN News*. Retrieved 15 February 2007 from http://www.cbn.com/cbnnews/index.aspx.

Mojab, S. (1998). The State, university, and the construction of civil society in the Middle East. *Futures, 30*(7), 657-667.

Radu, M. (2003, October 21). E-Notes: Radical Islam and suicide bombers. Retrieved 10 July 2007 from http://www.fpri.org/enotes/20031021.americawar.radu.islamsuicidebombers.html.

Renaerts, M. (1999). Processes of homogenization in the Muslim educational world in Brussels. *International Journal of Educational Research, 31*, 283-294.

Riphenburg, C. J. (2011). Middle East Definition. Retrieved 7 July 2007 from http://www.cod.edu/middle/maps/defined.htm+middle+east+definition&ct=clnk.

Sageman, M. (2005, February 22). Terrorism and Islamic extremism in the Middle East: Perspectives and possibilities, emerging terror networks. Conference Report. Center for Contemporary Conflict, Alexandria, VA. Retrieved 18 February 2008 from http://www.ccc.nps.navy.mil/events/recent/terrorismandislamicextremismFebo.

Salmoni, B. (2000). Islam in Turkish pedagogic attitudes and education materials, 1923-1950. *The Turkish Studies Association Bulletin, 242*, 23-61.

Sepehri, M., & Arani, M. A. (2007). *The role of educational systems in international crises: A reappraisal of Middle East countries.* Paper presented at XIII World Congress of Comparative Education Societies, Sarajevo, 3-7 September.

Smith, C. (2005, February 22). Terrorism and Islamic extremism in the Middle East: Perspectives and possibilities, Israel and the occupied territories. Conference Report. Center for Contemporary Conflict, Alexandria, VA. Retrieved 18 February 2008 from http://www.nps.edu/Academics/SIGS/ccc/conferences/recent/terrorismandislamicextremismFeb05.html.

Srimulyani, E. (2007). Muslim women and education in Indonesia: The Pondok Pesantren experience. *Asia Pacific Journal of Education, 27*(1), 85-99.

Stålenheim, P., Fruchart, D., Omitoogun, W., & Perdomo, C. (2006). Military expenditure. *SIPRI Yearbook*. Oxford: Oxford University Press.

Stockholm International Peace Research Institute. (2007). *Military expenditure in Middle East, 1988-2006.* Retrieved 18 February 2008 from www.sipri.org/contents/milap/milex/mex_regions.html.

Teach Kids Peace. (2005, March). Teenage human bombs. Retrieved 8 January 2008 from http://www.teachkidspeace.org/section.php2id=1,

Thobani, S. (2007). The dilemma of Islam as school knowledge in Muslim education. *Asia Pacific Journal of Education, 27*(1), 11-25.

Thomas, E. (2002). Values and citizenship: Cross-cultural challenges for school and society in the Asian Pacific Rim. In M. Schweisfurth, L. Davies, & C. Harber (Eds.), *Learning democracy and citizenship: International experiences* (pp. 241-254). Oxford: Symposium Books.

Tohid, O. (2005, June 17). Who are the suicide bombers? Pakistan's answer. *The Christian Science Monitor*. Retrieved 1 January 2008 from http://www.csmonitor.com/2005/0617/p07s01-wome.html.

UNICEF. (2010). Humanitarian action report. Retrieved 20 February 2010 from www.unicef.org/.../UNICEF_Humanitarian_Action_Report_2010-Summary_Report_WEB_EN.pdf.

United Nations. (2007a). Middle-East Crisis – How many children will die before the parties agree to stop hostilities? Office of the Special Representative of the Secretary-General for Children and Armed Conflict. Retrieved 18 February 2008 from http://www.un.org/children/conflict/pr/pressreleases2007.html.

United Nations. (2007b, April 19). Middle East: Peace must come to the Middle East for the sake of the children. Office of the Special Representative of the Secretary-General for Children and Armed Conflict. Retrieved 18 February 2008 from http://www.un.org/children/conflict/pr/pressreleases2007.html.

Venkatraman, A. (2007). Religious basis for Islamic terrorism: The Quran and its interpretations. *Studies in Conflict & Terrorism, 30*(3), 229-248.

Volkan, V. D. (1995). Suicide bombers. Retrieved 18 February 2008 from http://www.healthsystem.virginia.edu/ internet/csmhi/suicide-bomber-psychology.pdf.

Wiktorowicz, Q. (2005). A genealogy of radical Islam. *Studies in Conflict & Terrorism, 28*(2), 75-97.

World Atlas. (2011). Modern definition of the Middle East. Retrieved 20 February 2010 from http://www.worldatlas.com/webimage/countrys/me.htm.

World Bank. (2008, February 13). World Bank report calls for educational system reform. Retrieved 15 February 2008 from http://www.ZAWYA.com/Story.cfm/siDZAWYA20080213065952/SecIndustries/pagE.

World Bank. (2011) MENA. Retrieved 16 January 2011 from http://web.worldbank.org/WBSITE/EXTERNAL/COUNTRIES/MENAEXT/0,,menuPK:247619~pagePK:146748~piPK:146812~theSitePK:256299,00.html.

Zakir, H., & Rajan, T. (2006, 27 January). Frank dialogue on understanding Islam. *The Straits Times*, H6.

Zedalis, D. D. (2004). Female suicide bombers. *The Strategic Studies Institute Newsletter*. Retrieved 15 February 2007 from http://www.strategicstudiesinstitute.army.mil/pdffiles/PUB408.pdf.

Amir Sabzevar Qahfarokhi
Islamic Azad University, Shahrekord Branch
Iran

Abbas Madandar Arani
 Lorestan University
Iran

Lida Kakia
Ministry of Education
Iran

LIST OF CONTRIBUTORS

Abbas Madandar Arani is an Assistant Professor at the Department of Education, Lorestan University, Iran. His research and teaching interests in the field of comparative education include: education reform and restructuring in the context of globalization and internationalization, gender, class, religion and schooling, multiculturalism, feminist and postcolonial studies in education, Muslim education, education in Iran & the Middle East countries, Educational management & leadership. He currently works with the Ministry of Education investigating Private schools and their challenges, he remains active in the Iranian Sociology of Education Association and Iranian Higher Education Association, and he was awarded a PhD scholarship in 2000 through cultural exchange between Iran & India (ICCR).
Email: abbas_arani@yahoo.com

Beatrice Avalos, a Chilean, is currently a Research Associate at the Centre of Advanced Research in Education, University of Chile. She was professor and researcher in universities in Chile, Great Britain (Cardiff University), and Papua New Guinea, and currently heads a study on the trajectory of new teachers from university to work in Chile. She directed the national study on the Teaching Profession (2008-2011), was national coordinator in Chile of the IEA TEDS-M study (2006-2010), and is member of the Joint ILO/UNESCO Committee of Experts on the Application of the Recommendations Concerning Teaching Personnel (CEART).
Email: bavalos@terra.cl

Zehlia Babaci-Wilhite is a PhD Candidate at the University of Oslo, Norway. Her thesis on local language of instruction as a right in education focuses on recent curriculum changes in Zanzibar (Tanzania). Her research interests include language in education, language medium of instruction, language and human rights in education in Africa, curriculum development in Africa, and human dignity in education. She is a member of the Education Team and the Global Research Team for the Human Dignity and Humiliation Studies (Human DHS), and she coordinated a North-South seminar at the University of Oslo, Norway. She has taught various languages as a second language in several countries, including Japan, India and Norway.
Email: z.b.wilhite@admin.uio.no

K.P. Binda is a Full Professor in the Faculty of Education at Brandon University, Brandon, Manitoba, and an Adjunct Professor in the Faculty of Education at the University of Manitoba. He is past-President of the Comparative and International Education Society of Canada and was a member of the National Board of the Canadian Society for the Study of Education. Currently he serves as an External Examiner in Curriculum Studies, Faculty of Education, University of the West

237

Indies, Trinidad. His research interests include Comparative Education (Indigenous and International Education), Curriculum and Educational Administration. He has done graduate studies at the University of Toronto, University of Oregon and the University of Manitoba.
Email: binda@brandonu.ca

Constadina Charalambous is a Lecturer in Language Education & Literacy at the European University Cyprus. She specializes in language education in the contexts of conflict, and her broader research interests include linguistic ethnography, identity, intercultural communication, and peace education.
Email: co.charalambous@euc.ac.cy

Panayiota Charalambous is a Research Associate at the Research Centre of the European University Cyprus. Her research focuses on the manifestations of various ideologies (e.g. nationalism, racism) in educational settings of divided societies.
Email: panayiota.charalambous@gmail.com

Danae de los Ríos, a Chilean, is Director of Undergraduate Programs and Quality Assurance at Diego Portales University (Chile). Previously, she was Director of Undergraduate Programs at Andrés Bello University and professor of Educational Sociology, University of Santiago (Chile). As a researcher at the Centre for Advanced Research in Education, University of Chile, she participated in the national study on the Teaching Profession in Chile. Her work focuses on educational segregation, access and retention to higher education, and teachers' work and identity. De los Rios earned a BA in sociology (Catholic University, Chile), a master in Public Policy (University of Chile) and a PhD in Education (University of Michigan).
Email: danae.delosrios@udp.cl

Renée de Palma received her PhD in 2003 from the University of Delaware (USA), where she helped to establish La Red Mágica, a collaborative project to promote intercultural relationships between university students and urban minority children. She was Senior Researcher on the UK-based No Outsiders action research project to address LGBT equality in primary schools. She is a member of the Faculty of Education Sciences, University of A Coruña, Spain. Her research and teaching focus on equalities and social justice in terms of race, ethnicity, language, sexuality and gender, especially the social construction of marginalization within and beyond schools, success and failure co-construction in institutional settings, and design of counter-hegemonic institutional contexts and classroom practices.
Email: r.depalma@udc.es

Éva Földesi holds a BA in Economics and an MA in Sociology and Anthropology from Central European University. She works for the Roma Education Fund (REF) in Budapest, an international organization specializing in the educational

advancement of Roma. Currently, she is a programme officer for Hungary, responsible for the coordination and management of the country portfolio. She has conducted research in the field of Roma education including a desegregation study for Chance For Children Foundation (2007), and research on the REF Scholarship Program (2008) within a broader study entitled Equalizing Programs in the Higher Education. Her research interests include multiculturalism and integration, good models and dilemmas of desegregation.
Email: eva_foldesi@vipmail.hu

Katalin R. Forray is Emeritus Professor at the University of Pecs, Institute of Education where she established a Chair in Romology and a doctoral program in educational foundations. She holds a teacher university diploma in German linguistics and literature (University of Szeged) and sociology (National Institute of Education, Budapest); Dr. Univ. in sociology of education (University of Szeged, 1976), and CSc (Candidate of the Sciences) and DSc (Doctor of Sciences) (Hungarian Academy of Sciences, 1983 and 2003); and habilitation (University of Debrecen, 1999). Her present interests are twofold: small-size educational institutions and their impacts on their catchment areas; and Roma schooling and formation of a Roma cultural and political elite in Hungary and neighbouring countries.
Email: forrayrk@gmail.com

Lesley Graybeal received her PhD in Social Foundations of Education from the University of Georgia in 2011 and is a faculty member in the English Department at Wake Technical Community College in Raleigh, North Carolina. She also serves as Secretary of the Underrepresented Groups Committee of the Comparative and International Education Society. Her research interests include non-formal education, community and grassroots education, museum rhetoric, and Indigenous Knowledge and methodologies.
Email: lgraybeal@gmail.com

Lida Kakia holds an M.A in Comparative Education and at present works as a teacher counselor at different schools in Tehran. She has written 30 books on different aspects of education and published more than 300 papers at Iranian newspapers. She has been selected two times as a Merit Teacher and was awarded by Iranian Presidents. She has also presented some articles at International and National conferences and seminars.
Email: Lida.kakia@gmail.com

Panayiota Kendeou is an Assistant Professor of Educational Psychology at Neapolis University, Pafos and an Adjunct Faculty at the Open University of Cyprus. She specializes in learning processes and research methodology.
Email: p.kendeou@nup.ac.cy

Tamás Kozma is Emeritus Professor (sociology of education) at the Institute of Educational Sciences, and President of the Center for Higher Education Research and Development, at The University of Debrecen, Hungary. He studied theology, history and education in Budapest, Szeged (Hungary) and Cluj (Romania). He holds a PhD (University of Szeged), C.Sc and D.Sc (Hungarian Academy of the Sciences), and habilitation (Debrecen). He is a scientific adviser at and past-Director of the Hungarian Institute for Educational Research, Budapest (1990-2000). He publishes in Hungarian, English and German and his present research interest focuses on the dissemination of LLL demands and corresponding supplies within Central Europe.
Email: kozmat3@gmail.com

Stephen Lack is a graduate student at the American University in Cairo, Egypt. He is currently pursuing a Master of Arts degree in Migration and Refugee Studies. In 2011, he worked as an intern for Adventist Development and Relief Agency in Yemen. He received his Bachelor of Arts, in International Studies from the University of Southern Mississippi in 2010.
Email: stephenlack@hotmail.com

Mel Lall is Chair of the Department of Community Based Initiatives, and a Professional Associate, Faculty of Education at Brandon University, Brandon, Manitoba. He was an Academic Program and Field Experience Coordinator, Field Services Coordinator and is past-Director of the Brandon University Northern Teacher Education Program, with more than thirty years in administration and teaching in community based teacher preparation programs for Aboriginal, northern and rural communities in Manitoba, Canada. He served as an External Examiner in the Graduate Department of Curriculum Studies, Faculty of Education, University of the West Indies, Trinidad and on the National Executive of the Comparative and International Education Society of Canada. His research interests include community based education, teacher preparation and Aboriginal education.
Email: lall@brandonu.ca

Monde Mbekwa is an Associate Professor at the University of the Western Cape, South Africa. He teaches undergraduate and postgraduate students in mathematics education and at the University of the Western Cape, South Africa. His research interests are on the relevance of school mathematics education, mathematical literacy, the use of technology in mathematics education, mathematics teacher education, and the use of learners' home language in mathematics teaching and learning. He focuses on these issues primarily within the context of South African post-apartheid educational transformation but also in the southern African regional context and relative to global priorities.
Email: mmbekwa@uwc.ac.za

240

Nagwa Megahed is an Associate Professor at Women's College, Ain Shams University, Egypt. She was a Fulbright Scholar, teaching Middle Eastern Studies at the University of Southern Mississippi (2009-2011). Previously, she worked as a Senior Technical Advisor at the USAID-Funded Education Reform Program in Egypt in cooperation with Michigan State University and the Academy for Educational Development. She received her Ph.D. from the University of Pittsburgh, where she also served as a researcher and Assistant to the Director, Institute for International Studies in Education. Her research interests and publications focus on the reform of educational policy and practice, teachers and teacher education, education and Islam, and gender and education in the Middle East.
Email: nagwa_megahed@yahoo.com

Vuyokazi Nomlomo is a Senior Lecturer in the Language Education Department at the University of the Western Cape, South Africa. She specializes in language communication and teaching with a special focus on the teaching of African Languages at primary and secondary school levels. Her research interests are in the following broad areas: language policy and planning, linguistics, teacher education, pedagogical strategies, classroom interaction and gender equality in education, and African languages in teacher education. She focuses primarily on these issues in the context of South African post-apartheid educational transformation but also more broadly in African and global contexts of the issues.
Email: vnomlomo@uwc.ac.za

Amir Sabzevari Qahfarokhi holds an M.A in English language teaching from Isfahan University, Iran. He is currently completing his PhD in English language teaching and learning in the research and science branch in Khorasgan, Isfahan. He is a full-time faculty member at Shahrekord Azad University, Iran. His research interest is in education in general, and language learning and teaching in particular, with specific research interests including comparative education, second language writing, critical discourse analysis, translation and lexicography, and language as a creator of social power and injustice. He has published several articles and presented at conferences. He is currently working on two books, a dictionary of sport terms and glossary and a dictionary of English proverbs and idioms.
Email: Amir.sabzevari@yahoo.com

Cathryn Teasley is an Interim Assistant Professor of Curriculum, Instruction and School Organization at the University of A Coruña, Spain. Her research focuses on the pursuit of cross-cultural justice through ethnography, critical pedagogy, anti-bias teacher education, and peace education, areas that form part of her research on the recent incorporation of Roma/Gypsy students into secondary-level schooling in Spain. In addition, her publications and research focus on transnational perspectives on culture, policy and education, Neoliberal contexts for reform, and critical issues in education across the globe. She is native to the San Francisco Bay Area of California, but has been living in A Coruña (Galiza, Spain) since 1991.
Email: cathryn@udc.es

Nathalie Thomauske is a PhD student in Science Education at the University of Bielefeld and the University Paris. She holds a Master in Intercultural Education (Oldenburg) and a Master in French Linguistics and Literature (Bremen). She is currently writing her PhD dissertation focusing on hidden agendas in language policy in the context of early childhood education in Germany and France. Her research interests include power and discrimination, plurilingualism, Francophonie, postcolonialism and racism in France and Germany, and the relevance of multilingualism for teachers and immigrant parents in early childhood education and care in Germany and France.
Email: nathalie.thomauske@web.de

Michalinos Zembylas is Associate Professor of Education at the Open University of Cyprus. His research focuses on how affective politics intersect with issues of social justice pedagogies, intercultural and peace education, and citizenship education. He is also particularly interested in teacher perceptions and contested narratives in the context of past and present conflict and the prospects for reconciliation in Greek-Cypriot relations in schools and society, and in other contexts.
Email: m.zembylas@ouc.ac.cy

THE EDITORS

Diane Brook Napier is a retired (2012) professor in the College of Education at the University of Georgia, specializing in Comparative and International Education, and she is a member of the UGA Institute of African Studies. She was born and raised in South Africa where she received her undergraduate education. She is a naturalized American citizen, now residing in the United States where she completed her graduate education. Her research and teaching specialties focus on post-colonial educational reform and democratic transformation policies and their implementation in sub-Saharan African states, and in Cuba and the United Arab Emirates. She has conducted field research on these issues extensively in South Africa but also in Namibia, Botswana, Zambia, Zimbabwe, Somalia, Kenya, and DRCongo. Her research focuses specifically on issues of globalization of education, reform policy-practice and implementation, race and deracialisation, ideology, language, justice/injustice, human resources development (in education, health, housing, water supply, labor), also on migrant and refugee issues, environmental issues, and teacher education implications. She has published widely on these topics and she was co-editor of the 2011 Volume in the Sense Series from the 2010 Istanbul World Congress of Comparative Education Societies (Pampanini, G., Adly, F., and Brook Napier, D., co-Eds. *Interculturalism, Society and Education*). She is currently Secretary-General of the World Council of Comparative Education Societies.
Email: dnapier@uga.edu

242

Suzanne Majhanovich is Professor Emerita/Adjunct Research Professor at the Faculty of Education, Western University, Ontario, Canada. She is the Chair of the WCCES Standing Committee for Publications and former editor of the journal *Canadian and International Education*. Her research interests include first and second language acquisition, the teaching of English as a Foreign Language in international contexts, globalization, educational restructuring, decentralization and privatization of education. She is the author of numerous articles and books, and most recently has co-edited with MacLeans A. Geo-JaJa, *Education, Language, and Economics. Growing National and Global Dilemmas,* (Sense, 2010) and with Christine Fox and Fatma Gök, *Bordering, Re-Bordering and New Possibilities in Education and Society* (Springer, 2012).
Email: smajhano@uwo.ca

CPSIA information can be obtained at www.ICGtesting.com
Printed in the USA
BVOW041423030613

322293BV00004B/61/P